Alias
Pegge Parker

Alias
Pegge Parker

By Pegge (Parker) Hlavacek

Hlucky Books

Omaha, Nebraska

Hlucky Books is an imprint of Concierge Publishing, Omaha, Nebraska

Books are available through Baker & Taylor or
www.HluckyBooks.com

Hlucky Books
c/o Concierge Publishing
13518 L. Street
Omaha, NE 68137
(402) 884-5995

ISBN13: 978-0-9819034-3-9
ISBN10: 0-9819034-3-6
Library of Congress Control Number: 2009905855

Printed in the United States of America

10 9 8 7 6 5 4 3 2 1

Contents

Introduction

A freighter called the *SS Marine Lynx* docked at a pier on the Shanghai water-front. The passengers were mostly American missionaries. There were hundreds of them. A few vacancies were allotted to "civilians": a handful of Chinese and one young, American, freelance reporter—Pegge. In the dark, confusion reigned as all waited to clear Customs and disembark.

"I can relive that first fear and dread of stepping ashore, even from the unlovely unhappy decks of the *Marine Lynx,* into the roiling unknown of Shanghai in 1946! I was overcome with my own aloneness. Along with the missionaries I too felt woefully unwelcome, unwanted and worse, *unnecessary!* I was a writer, but no one had sent me to China to write anything."

Afloat in "nothingness" and filled with the "queasies," Pegge received some valuable advice: "Don't panic. Just don't lose your passport. Keep it between your teeth if necessary, but forgodsake, don't let it out of your sight...You'll be okay."

Good advice. That passport, tightly secured, had a "mighty funny line." The passport read "alias Pegge Parker." "*Alias,* that's a fine thing to call a byline!" Pegge observed.

Stepping out on her own was nothing new to Pegge Parker. Traveling on her own since she was 17, she had already logged many story-telling miles before her nighttime arrival in Shanghai. But crossing the big pond, with just enough funds for a one-way ticket, was really stepping out on her own! Off she went anyway, with a Panglossian philosophy. Things would work out. Go after the adventure—the stories would follow. That was Pegge's lifestyle and her way of following her dream.

Pegge Parker started out as a teen reporter for a local Harrisburg newspaper, then moved on to the *Washington Times Herald* (now the *Washington Post*), and then to Arctic reporter for the Fairbanks, Alaska *News Miner.* But now with her brand new passport, alias Pegge Parker went on to China (where she covered the news before newsmen were barred from that country), Pakistan (where she became a Vice Consul at the American Embassy), India, and then Jamaica where for three years she was a Time-Life correspondent. NBC's "Monitor" carried her radio reports from Cuba, just before the missile crisis.

The rich, the famous, and the not so famous—all of them interesting characters—walked across the path, pen, and Smith Corona of this freelance, foreign correspondent, who learned the job the hard way, by doing it. Good ol' on-the-job training.

Her interviews are a virtual Who's Who: the Kennedys, Lyndon Johnson and Lady Bird, Princess Margaret and Lord Snowden, Billy Graham, Clare Booth Luce, Margaret Mitchell, Lillian Hellman, Errol Flynn, Ian Fleming, Oscar Hammerstein, Indira Gandhi, Castro, Batista, Peron, Trujillo, Duvalier, and many more.

Told with charm, sometimes with an edge, but always on point, this work *works*. It's fun.

Pegge met with the Dalai Lama; they walked and talked. But the real interest for Pegge was his mother, whom she called "Mama Lama"!

"Mama Lama was simply marvelous, responding to each new earthy, twentieth-century discovery in New Delhi with cries of delight.... Aggressive and acquisitive, Mama quickly collected a store of goods. But she really lost her head over automobiles. Off on her own one day, she bought a Ford station wagon with whitewalls, radio, and power steering. She must have paid for it with a brick of gold bullion, of which the Dalai had an impressive supply!

"When their state visit was over (Nehru told her alarmed and frightened son to go back to Lhasa and not cause trouble—above all, he was not to rock India's boat of friendship with the Chinese), Mama Lama wanted the station wagon delivered "FAB" (Foot And Back) straight to the capital of Tibet. When her son refused, she had a royal fit. The wagon could not go. It had to remain in Darjeeling with two other sons living there as quiet businessmen in the import-export business. It was at their home one day that I not only learned about the car but had a ride in it with Mount Everest climber Tenzing Norgay at the wheel."

There is a personal side to the Pegge Parker story. In China, Pegge met and married a young scientist from Boston, Doug Mackiernan, then an American Vice Consul stationed at a small consulate in the interior of China. They had twins, Mary and Mike, in 1948.

When China fell to Communist forces and Chairman Mao's regime came to power, Pegge and the kids were forced to leave. Doug Mackiernan stayed behind to close down his station outpost in Tihwa, China. Soon after, he was shot and killed on the Tibetan border while trying to make his escape out of China. The Doug Mackiernan part of this story didn't end there. Fifty years after his death, he was posthumously honored by the CIA. In a ceremony recognizing covert operatives lost in the field, Mackiernan was one of the anonymous stars inscribed in both the CIA's Book of Honor and on their Wall of Honor. His death was in the line of duty.

Pegge later remarried. Her second husband, John Hlavacek, was Bureau Chief for United Press in Delhi, India. Three more children followed, one of whom is writing this introduction. How do you juggle *five* kids and a marriage while chasing stories around the globe and meeting deadlines? Being a career woman and mom was no easier then than it is today.

◆   ◆   ◆

By the way, did Rhett go back to Scarlett? What did Margaret Mitchell tell Pegge Parker? And what did Pegge's hat have to do with the end of the story? Take a trip with Pegge Parker and find out.

Suzanne Hlavacek

1

India

✦

(ca. 1955)

I was talking with Indira Gandhi, daughter of Indian Prime Minister Jawaharlal Nehru. We stood in the Prime Minister's New Delhi garden shading our eyes against the brilliant scene. Indian sun flooded down upon us, and the very air was an Arpege ambrosia of roses, jasmine, and ginger blossoms.

"TITO—" Indira cried suddenly, startling me. "TITO—that *naughty* man! What a practical joke he has just played on Father!"

I hadn't given Tito a thought. Nor did I expect I would ever hear a Nehru refer to Yugoslavia's burly marshal, the neutralist, the first independent socialist and, lately, the Arab's friend, as *naughty.*

Indira began to laugh. "Come along, I'll show you Tito's little joke—a shameless naked lady! Made of stone, but look at *that—*"

Beyond the rose beds, in an obscure corner of the Prime Minister's vast garden, stood an enormous hulk of modern sculpture. Upon closer inspection, Tito's gift to Nehru proved to be a seductive, gigantic female, in black basalt, with bosom and buttocks like small Dalmatian Mountains! Was this just a showpiece of Yugoslav modern art? Or was Tito, the lusty peasant partisan, taking a playful swat at the world's purest moralist?

Indira took the latter view. "He told us when he was here that a state gift would be arriving within a few weeks, but we had no idea it would be a thing like that! We didn't want to put it in a museum or in any public place. Finally we thought the best thing to do was hide it out here and plant fast-growing trees and shrubs all about to screen it from view."

My visit to the Prime Minister's garden had begun with Indira's invitation to my young twins, son Mike and daughter "Ike" (Mary's nickname), to see Nehru's pet pandas before they were shipped off (by special plane) to the cool hill station of Naini Tal for the summer. The pandas—the world's most pampered "people pandas"—were lovingly cared for by Nehru himself. All the Nehrus are animal lovers, and the spacious garden held a small private zoo with an amazing rotation of pets from India's jungles and mountains or from visiting heads of state.

No touring houseguest of the Nehrus had caused quite the stir, and often awkward embarrassment, of Marshal Tito, an important ally of the Indian premier in the neutralist bloc which included that other odd friend in need, Gammal Nasser of Egypt. Tito may or may not have enjoyed the mystic East as he saw it in India, but he came forewarned, and in style, like visiting royalty, aboard a dazzling white yacht. He came to India on his own terms, too: to enjoy himself. Knowing all about India's cheerless law of prohibition, Tito brought along his own robust stock of beverages. Enough Yugoslav wines, fiery *slivava*, (a perilous plum brandy the Slavs are infamous for) and scotch and beer came off the dictator's yacht to set dry Bombay afloat. Morarji Desai, Bombay's most passionate prohibitionist and then its state governor, could say nothing. An extremist, a fanatical Hindu who is against everything including sex, Morarji and all his city officials spluttered but signed the orders waiving alcoholic regulations, and the enviable wine cellar was unloaded.

As he traveled about in an air-conditioned luxury train, no doubt Communist Tito found Democratic Nehru's "free" India, with its primitive backwardness, its free but half-starved, half-naked, illiterate people, both oppressive and ironic. In Yugoslavia, people were not free, but they at least lived like human beings. They did not sleep on pavements or worship diseased, emaciated cows. Slavs, even under socialism, knew how to live.

Millions of Indians barely had a chance to think beyond each day's survival.

Tito thought his own thoughts, drew his own conclusions on India, and eventually sent Nehru his compliments with the winsome nude.

Nude, indeed *lewd*, sculpture abounds throughout religion-obsessed India. Many a scandalized school-teacher on a cultural pilgrimage is shocked out of her Keds to realize the large bronze, flower-bedecked pillar she has been leaning on, sitting on, or where she changed film in her camera, is actually a stark replica of the vital male organ!

Many old Hindu temples are covered with pornographic and shocking tableaux! Really gasping, eye-watering, deliciously sensuous carvings surround whole temple walls, and show gawking, straining tourists very, very naked and *fantastic* lovemaking positions! Indian temples with the "best" sculpture are known to every American! No matter how far distant, inconvenient, without water, rest houses or privies, reached only by chartered plane it may be, India's savory temple art does not blush unseen. For years, it has all been *minutely* inspected and photographed. There's no culture like erotic culture, Mable.

Tito's visit came during what might be called India's golden age, when Pandit Jawaharlal Nehru rode proudly, and with princely grace, at the helm of India's shining independent democracy. It was his time, his hour. The world believed in India then, its destiny and future looked "possible" if not promising, and people talked about India as the only hope for Southeast Asia. As India goes, we said, so goes the overwhelming land and population mass of all Asia! India, we firmly believed, was the test case for the world. If democracy could work here, if people could be free and not falter altogether on the long road to education and identification with the twentieth century, it would be a tremendous triumph. Peace and progress were the elusive jewels seemingly held securely in the graceful, slim-fingered, aristocratic hand of this handsome, brilliant, and exasperating man, Nehru.

My family and I had for some five years been caught up in the whole unrealistic, high-minded glittering show of New Delhi in Nehru's day. We lived there. India was home to us, deep-rooted and familiar, and we loved it. Especially since we, by profession, shared the privileged close-up views of the people who ruled the world and who came in an unending stream, with full entourage, to visit the sun king in New Delhi. If India was a "poor" country, you would never have guessed it from the splendor of Nehru's hospitality. It was a great show while it lasted; those days will not be seen again. India has been slipping into decline, division and appalling disintegration ever since. No, it's not going communist. I doubt if the communists can afford the Arabs *and the Indians*. The country's trouble seems more profound.

Today, people often say to me, "My dear, India must be fabulous! I would love to see it all someday: the Taj—the houseboats in Kashmir, Nepal, the Shangri-la with good hotels and good food, Gandhi's tomb (there is none; he was cremated, and a marble slab marks the spot), the jewelry shops, Benares, the place where you get saris handspun from pure golden thread." Even in an age of jets and quite neatly priced packaged tours, "someday" to India is an illusion and a lie. Even dauntless tourists don't really want to go to India, not even someday. At least not until they have been everywhere else first, even to Africa. Life in darkest Africa is colorful and picturesque; in India it's simply unbearable.

Who can blame travelers for shunning India? This fascinating but tragic land is not for casual and retired or fun-loving visitors and never will be.

India is culturally exciting, yes, and other-world adventurous, different, stunning the eye and senses with color, sound, taste, and a way of life found nowhere else. But the shocking spectacle of the cruel, creature existence of human beings, mostly women, and India's large-eyed urchin children reduced to less than India's worshipped animals, is disturbing and haunting to Americans. The sight of wrapped forms sleeping on Bombay or Calcutta sidewalks, or back-turned public urinating or filthy beggars running after foreigners is just too much. Then there is the heat. You can't live in an air-conditioned cave all the time. You must go out on streets hot enough to flip pancakes, and in India they have the pancakes but they call them *chapatis!*

Once, while basking in the sun on the top deck of our houseboat in Kashmir, I saw a row of boys staring at us from the riverbank. They were dressed in what looked like old burlap bags. As our houseboy brought us a tray of Danish Tuborg beer, I stared back at the children. The money should have been spent on *them* instead of for the Tuborg, I thought guiltily.

I discussed this awful disparity with an Indian friend one day. She is a doctor and sees a lot of Indian life. "What we spend on clothes," I lamented, "on knick-knacks, trifles and baubles in the bazaar, on a sari we'll never wear but couldn't resist because the colors were divine, the money we spend on endless dinner parties or for country club dues would buy food and medicine for a whole village of women and babies, or would keep a whole family going for months, or teach a street boy to read and write. How do you live with all this depressing, hopeless imbalance?"

She shook her head. "You mustn't feel that way. You do what you can, and you can't worry about it. Indians themselves do not see their struggle and poverty as critically as you do."

"Piloo, dear," I interrupted, "forgive me, but what about wealthy Indians, why don't *they* help their own people?" My doctor friend, a lovely, Westernized, highly skilled pediatrician who studied in England and at Boston's Children's Hospital, and who has cared for many Nehru family offspring, comes from a wealthy Parsi background. Her husband is also a doctor. They have three sons, live in a large Bombay apartment, have three cars and many servants, but for these doctors, their children and their work are all that they live for. Piloo's only jewelry is her wristwatch. If she has any dowry treasure, she never wears it. If she has any worldly ambition, it is that her two elder sons, both of whom quite naturally want to be doctors, can finish their education in "your wonderful America."

The role of wealthy, powerful Indians, in government and industry, in uplifting or benefiting the social condition is meager and vague. There is no Eastern tradition of community services; there is instead a passionate, centuries-old struggle to preserve land, wealth, and power for the individual, the family. As Piloo pointed out, "in a country where millions never get enough to eat, consider what New Delhi spends on one state banquet, or on a new airplane, or for the army, or for some hopelessly wasteful, inefficient government-run project! If you are going to live in India for some time, you must get your sense of proportion or perspective properly oriented. You are an American. Your country does a lot more for India than India does for its own people. Americans not only *care* and see 'needs' Indians ignore, they do something about it when they can. Our own government spends laks of rupees (thousands) on all sorts of foolish things, and the people, well, they're always there, like the water in the sea. Things are improving—year by year I see it—but slowly."

It has recently become something of a fad in India to find an escape world, or at least a *guru* or spiritual guide, like a golf pro, who leads the "way." Those who insist upon seeking spiritual shelter in India will find it, because they bring the image along with them and hold it up against the scenery. If the soul needs mountains, India has the most spectacular mountains in all the world. But India, alas, has found no answers or mystic wisdom to impart to foreign pilgrims. It has yet to find its own soul in the mirror of reality.

I once wrote a long story about a foreign correspondent's family life in India. I called it *Diapers on a Dateline.* The younger members of our family numbered five, and they provided me with abundant material and stories.

Our family lived with our dateline, that little line of print usually skimmed over when you read the first line of a story in the newspaper. A dateline is the story's where and when: Washington, January 10 (UPI)—or Bombay, August 6 (UPI)—.

For many years our dateline read "New Delhi, India (UPI)" when my husband, John Hlavacek, was the United Press International bureau man for India and Pakistan. Our name takes some practice to pronounce. It is Lav-a-check. As in Higgins, the "H" is silent. The name is Czech and not too difficult on the second try (as any Bohemian around Chicago will tell you).

John had been in India nearly twelve years, all told. He was recognizable—standing six feet tall, usually wearing a red baseball cap, flap up—and so well known that he was a big, friendly fixture all over the country. If, upon occasion, he came upon a new man in the cable office and had to spell out Hlavacek in full, it went something like this: "H for Hyderabad, L for Lucknow, A for Allahabad, V for Vishnu...." This could take a little time and give the "AP" man time to jump your story! Some years later, when John was with NBC in the Caribbean, the names of the network's newsmen read like the "fighting Irish" of Notre Dame: Robert Gerowski, Martin Agronsky, and John Hlavacek.

John always said he had more legends than hot-exclusives to his credit. One of his legends had to do with being arrested in Nepal, thrown in the royal jail, and having all his clothes impounded. He had company! Rawle Knox of the *London Observer* was with him. This was during some touchy little uprising which always makes despots nervous as they reach for their crown to make sure it's still there. When the touchy little uprising was brought under control, the king thought it a bit awkward to have two foreign guests in his jail, one British and one American. He thought the whole matter could best be smoothed over if he treated the guests royally and quickly got rid of them. Having taken away his visitors' clothes, the King sent his compliments and his tailor to the jail. The warmth of the King's apologies was more than matched by the warmth and quality of the British worsted fabrics from which the two guests were to choose and from which fine custom-made suits were to be fashioned. John chose a charcoal-grey pinstripe which, on a 6-foot, 200-pound frame, was a lot of jazz, but the king's new clothes and the king's hasty exit permit did help take the edge off the memory of dark days spent in the Katmandu jail. Both correspondents had good stories to file in, as they had been reported missing for days and finally, ominously, were even "feared lost"!

Working over a vast area on a scrooge-tight UPI budget kept John constantly on the move. If he hadn't, he'd never have been able to cover all his territory. Although New Delhi was John's main responsibility, UP was always generous with its geography and sparing with its correspondents. John's territory actually included East and West Pakistan, of course, as well as Afghanistan, Ceylon, and Burma, and at times he went as far away as Singapore. While he was gone, which was often, I covered the mail, took the office calls, answered and sent cables, went to press conferences, clipped the Indian newspapers, and generally coped.

People always asked me what newspaper John worked for. My answer always left them in awe: we worked for every newspaper in the world. Nearly every newspaper bought the UPI news service and their pictures, too. Today, of course, UPI clients include every radio and television station, news magazine, and an increasing number of private businesses and news-related government offices. All that is required is the need and the down payment for installation of a Teletype machine. A daily news service piped into an office is not only a great status symbol these days, but also a handy expedient. It pays to be informed, and almost immediately, on what is happening everywhere. Being rapidly informed can at times be a matter of life or death. I was fascinated to learn that all during the Bay of Pigs fiasco and the follow-up tension of the missile crisis, Fidel Castro bought and paid for an American wire service to keep informed from a news source independent of Moscow. Fidel isn't a very good dictator or even a good baseball player, but he knows it pays to watch all bases, especially when they're loaded.

One Saturday morning in Washington a friend who was then on Dean Rusk's staff took me into his office. Heavily badged, three times Signed In, and under personal escort, I was permitted to step inside the State Department's Flap Deck, as its communications news room is called, just a step from Rusk's private suite.

The communications center, humming and buzzing with several wire services, is staffed around the clock. The secretary gets all the bad news almost instantaneously before it goes on the air or into the newspapers.

Looking back now over the years on those young exciting days in India, I find I am still sentimentally attached to that strange land. Every time I pass in and out of New York, I think, "Ah, well, India is not really so far away." There is a vivid reminder right in New York harbor.

Once, I stood at the ship's railing of a Cunard liner, surrounded by the children, all of us going back to India after a long visit at home, seeing editors and grandmas and shopping from Sears to Saks. John had flown back to Bombay weeks earlier, leaving me to trundle along at my own speed with kiddies and baggage. I was not abandoned to struggle with everything alone. For one thing, there were then only four kiddies, and for another, I had taken with me an Indian nanny called Tai Bhai (pronounced "Tie Bye"). She was an amazing woman. In India she was, strictly speaking, an Untouchable, from the lowest Hindu caste. She was totally illiterate in every language including Hindi, which was not her mother tongue. She was from South India and spoke Maharashti. Unschooled but not untrained, she was a precious jewel to the mother of four all under the age of six!

A truly close member of the family, she lived with us, slept in the children's room, went where we went, and ate our food (even hamburgers, until she discovered they weren't made from ham). Tai Bhai was little and round and very dark. Her gentle peasant face was tattooed with flowers across her forehead. An itinerant tattoo artist had wandered into Tai Bhai's village during her youth, and all the women had been entranced with the idea of permanent cosmetic glamour tattooed to their faces for a few rupees. Tai Bhai's skin was so South-Indian dark you could scarcely see the tattooed daisy chain of flowers across her eyebrows and down her cheeks.

As a child, Tai Bhai had earned her curry rice by cracking rocks for roadbeds between Poona and Bombay. Later she got a job as an *aiha* (baby nurse) in a British nursing home, and it was there she learned, with tenderness, natural instinct, and an innate native rhythm, how to bathe, massage, handle, and care for small infants. She had the touch. The most squalling baby could be shushed to a whimper when she picked him up.

Tai Bhai wore white cotton aiha saris and sandals most of the time. When we traveled in the United States or went visiting, I encouraged her to dress up and usually gave her my own saris to wear. On these special occasions, Tai Bhai went even one step further and wore her dowry jewelry, an Indian woman's social security or bank account against calamity. Tai Bhai's dowry happened to be a solid gold flower, which she wore on her nostril like an earring. She screwed it gingerly into place through a pierced nostril! This gold flower naturally fascinated the children. The twins had to "see" how Tai got her "earring up her nose"! Baby hands would try to pluck it from her nostril. So Tai took it off, "put it by" for safekeeping and, alas, lost it! We opened a savings account for her in a local bank as a replacement.

Tai Bhai's knowledge of the world and things was entirely visual. What she could *see*, like the gold flower for her nose, she believed in and understood. When we took her to the bank and she saw money handed to the man behind bars and she was given a little booklet after signing papers with an "X", she was miserable and confused and full of doubts. When I showed her that I too had a little book, and sahib also, she was somewhat reassured.

Preparing her for the long trip to America took patient preparation. I got out maps and *Life* magazine and books with pictures. But a picture of New York wasn't proof of a city; it was only a picture. We tried slowly, and with much encouragement, to teach her to sign her own name and to read, just enough for her self-protection, so she could handle money and her savings account when we would not be there. I never before understood the tedious problem of adult illiteracy. I found it very difficult to curl Tai Bhai's coffee-brown, unaccustomed fingers around a pencil, where at the same table, the children so quickly and naturally grasped a pencil or crayon without any instruction. After a long daily struggle, she learned to write a little, including her name Tai Bhai. One day she came to me wreathed in triumphant smiles. In the kitchen, on her own, on the back of a brown grocery bag, she had copied the label from a can: "Campdells Tomato Souq." I hugged her!

When we decided to make the supreme effort and take her with us for three months to the United States, I explained what ship travel would entail, but assured her she would not be off in some servants' quarters but with *me* and the children all the way, right in our stateroom all the time. She would eat with us at the same table in the ship's dining room, and on an Italian liner the food would be wonderful. We were going from India here, to Italy there, and then on to New

York over here. "Yes, yes, memsahib," she murmured. "Very nice." But it was all mysterious. She had no idea what the world beyond India could be like.

Her reaction to Italy was lukewarm. It was a place with bathrooms down the hall and no place to do diapers and no hot water to heat babies' bottles and "Italy people so loud talking all the time!" but New York City! Oh, Memsahib!

A few days after arriving, I had insisted on giving her a breather and taking her for a sightseeing whirl. Leaving the children with Daddy in the hotel, I sped with Tai Bhai, magnificent in a red silk Bangalore sari of tie silk, down Fifth Avenue. How festive and gorgeous New York City is in the spring! We hurried through Radio City, oh'ing and ah'ing at the gushing fountain in the plaza, the sun-drenched terrace filled with blossoming trees and spring flowers. There were flags everywhere, even down Fifth Avenue for some reason, so there was a flutter of color everywhere. People passing by and observing us were not the least bit blasé; they smiled and spoke to Tai Bhai, asked what country she had come from. Then, holding hands securely in Fifth Avenue traffic, we dashed across the street to have a look at Saks Fifth Avenue's windows: they were jewel boxes in a row filled with summer cocktail dresses, short-skirted, sequined, sparkling, and swirly.

"Oh, memsahib," gasped Tai Bhai over and over. "Oh, Memsahib—just see. How clean! Everything so nice and *clean!*"

Later on, she got to Macy's (as does every Indian in America—I swear there are more Indians in Macy's any day of the week than at the UN!). Here the word wasn't clean, but *cheap!* It wasn't merely smart to be thrifty, it was heaven sent! In her sari and sandals, Tai Bhai created a great bugging stare. With so many Indians in and out every day, I had thought she would pass unnoticed. But curious housewives, hesitating slightly, would approach me with questions: "That's a sari she's got on?" "What's she doing in this country?" "Is she Indian or what?" "God love her—such a kind face." "She speaks English? How'd she learn English?" "Why doesn't she wear one of those red dots—whatever-you-call-'em—on her forehead?"

Another time we sailed into Bergdorf Goodman's, where an end-of-season clearance sale was underway. As we paused by the elevators an elegant floor manager approached Tai Bhai, wreathed in smiles. In a voice of imported suede, he inquired if he might assist Madame.

"No, thank you, Sahib," Tai Bhai replied without hesitation. "I just go looking with Memsahib," and she stepped into the elevator as though bargain hunting at Bergdorf's were all part of the routine.

Her favorite Sahib in all the United States, however, she discovered on television. His name, as she pronounced it, was Jock Paar. She would sit on the floor

Indian-style night after night watching Jock. What did our little, unlettered Harijan Hindu aiha "get" from the old Tonight show? We'll never know, but nothing would budge her, even though the first baby would scream for a bottle at six the next morning.

When the long, exhausting mixed-delight of a family-and-relatives-and-four-kiddies holiday was finally over and we were going home, the Cunard Liner was a haven, a lifesaver, a blessed white swan which would sail us effortlessly halfway home, as far as England. So we stood wordless but with happy anticipation of "home" and Daddy waiting in Bombay as the New York harbor scene moved about us. Tugs hooted, and our ship out-hooted them all. The water looked grey and bilgey; a cold, raw wind blew strange odors over us. The distance widened between us and the pier. We moved slowly out to sea, and through the late afternoon grey and pink and blue haze we caught the rising skyline, a sight which almost always moves me to tears. Suddenly we came upon the Statue of Liberty, so massive yet so graceful, so impassive yet so moving in her "message," holding high her torch. Tai Bhai clutched my arm: "Memsahib, look—look." She pointed to the Statue of Liberty, which she was seeing for the first time without any idea of its meaning or history. "Who is the lady in the sari?"

Had anyone before mistaken the classic Grecian drapery on the Statue of Liberty for an Indian sari? Historically, of course, my little Tai Bhai was on very good ground. In all probability the Greeks took their togas to India with the armies of Alexander the Great. India had simply lengthened the skirt and years later added the *choli* blouse.

Thanks to Tai Bhai, I love to recall that a touch of India, a lady in a sari, is no farther away than the Statue of Liberty.

When the granddaughter of Mahatma Gandhi was getting married in New Delhi we received a brilliant red wedding invitation, so dazzling I saved it to have it framed. Indian wedding invitations are sometimes works of art: lavish scrolls with silken tassels, delivered by hand by the family's "boy," or bearer, on his British bearer's bike.

But this invitation, which announced all the details of time and place of the ceremony in curly Hindi script on one side and in English on the other, was a keepsake. The wedding was a love match, shattering tradition and caste. That the bride was a Gandhi added much significance to the memorable occasion. In the manner of the most modern love match, she had chosen him. He was madly in love with her. Her caste was higher than his. No matter. Theirs was a college campus romance at Santi-Niketan, which blossomed to marriage and had finally won over the couples' parents. The two had met in the West Bengal coeducational school established by India's Nobel Prize poet, Tagore. Indira Gandhi, the Prime Minister, had also studied there. The bride—slim, animated Tara Gandhi—was radiant in her wedding sari laden with family jewelry and flowers. She was the daughter of Devadas Gandhi, a newspaper editor of the English-language daily, the influential *Hindustan Times*. Devadas, now dead, had been a friend of John's for many years, so although we were only two among hundreds of guests, I felt the invitation had been personal.

The Gandhi wedding reception at 1 York Place, New Delhi, was typical of all Indian weddings in well-to-do families. The guests included nearly every man, woman, child, and servant from Delhi to the Punjab border. One invitation to a family literally brought out everybody.

The gods were not disposed to smile upon those who defy the old ways, I suppose. For that afternoon, from 5 to 7 p.m., the heavens opened. Although it was not the monsoon season, we had a monsoon downpour that day. The Gandhis, lamenting that 1 York Place wasn't Palam air terminal, which the invited guests could have filled while staying dry, had no choice but to proceed with their "garden reception." Among the hundreds of guests expected was Pandit Nehru!

An enormous, State-Fair-sized canvas tent was hastily ordered and set up, and over the sopping sea of mud and lawn was spread another heavy canvas on which the reception guests stood. The wedding proceeded. Guests poured in. No one minded an occasional splash or spray. I stood for an hour rooted to one spot because my high heels had pierced the canvas and I was into mud up to my arches, but I was enthralled with the obvious happiness and romance of this young marriage, which I hoped would encourage others.

While I was talking with the bride about college dating in modern India and about her school, the name of Tagore came up repeatedly. His poetry, just two lines, read like a passionate caress. I had read some of his things, but I didn't know enough about him. When I finally got home that night, having walked barefoot to the car toting my shoes which looked as though they had been dropped in a pan of fudge, I looked up Tagore. Entranced, and with the mood of the wedding full upon me, I read and read. I got out a little notebook and copied down some of the refrains. Tagore could make an epic out of a few lines. Two I remember, even to this day:

> He who comes to do good, knocks at the gate.
> He who loves finds the door open...

Newly married, I had gone to India to live, to see, to observe from the sidelines, to help where I could, but to live in sympathy with what I could not change, and perhaps eventually to write down what India was like.

I was young. I had small infants and twins and their hour-by-hour routine to absorb me. There were also the cables and news reports and the whole "home office" churn to keep me going, so the years flew by. I was not aware of Tagore's gate, or even of knocking at it. It was my innocent, quite merited reward, some years later, to find India's gate so wide open....

No, Tagore, not every American comes to India to do Organized Good, or even to revolutionize the intolerable condition. I rarely insisted upon American ideas outside my own home, mostly because I was too busy. India is too vast, too old, too overwhelming. India even defies Indians. An umbrella is helpless in a monsoon: the elements overpower and drown!

There are inspiring and dedicated mountain-movers, brave reformers, among the Indian people. But they are too few. The bravest Indian I ever met was a teacher, headmistress of a large school for girls. This little brown wren of a woman stood up one day before an impressive UN delegation of international educators attending a well-publicized conference on Indian education. She stood there before everyone, and in a voice like a note gone too high and wild on a child's clarinet, shrieked, "We are all talking nonsense here today. Words...words...words! I tell you, this country can make no progress in education until we wipe out India's accursed Hindu religion. Hinduism is India's enemy, India's disease: it corrodes everything. The Hindu religion is evil, medieval, India's nightmare, a terrible tyrant ruling our people, our habits, our customs, even the food we eat! Until we can openly fight the menace of this dreadful, cruel religion, we shall struggle and talk and give lip service to modern education and not advance or progress one iota! We all know what I am saying is true, but no one will admit it or go against the fanatics, the priests and the *sadhus* and the temples...."

Ah, but there was one man who agreed with the little schoolmistress and who repeatedly raised his voice in scorn and abomination of the hold of a corrupt priesthood upon the ignorant and superstitious. And that man was Prime Minister Nehru himself.

He is often quoted as having said, "That which passes for organized religion fills me with abhorrence!" Whether he ever said those exact words (he covered a lot of ground with the words "organized religion") I do not know, but certainly he did abhor what Hinduism did to the social order of his struggling people.

It is also extraordinary that in a country saturated with religion to a depraved, shocking degree, not even the admonitions of a beloved leader and prime minister who had a tremendously strong emotional tie to his Indian people could faze them in the least when it came to religion.

Another time in Parliament, Nehru spoke out against the worship of diseased cows who prey upon starving villagers. "In countries which do not worship the cow," Nehru cried angrily, "they take care of them, they are clean, healthy and well looked after!" Hindus in the Lok Sahba (Parliament) leapt screaming to their feet. A scene of pandemonium ensued and Nehru, furious but prudent, hastily left the house and went home. It was just the hysterical sort of mob scene that triggers violence or assassination! And this alarming, undisciplined outburst over *cows* sprang from educated or semi-educated members of the Parliament, elected to office by India's faceless multitude.

All of this happened several years ago. Today, it would seem the leprous claw of Hinduism is weakening its hold on the country. On my most recent trip to India, I was assured "things are changing, liberalizing," especially among the young. Even a little change is a big step in a wholesome direction, but inch-by-inch social change is almost meaningless in the total effort India must make in this modern world to survive and sustain itself.

Indira Gandhi, like her father, sees the impediment of Hinduism clearly. She was recently quoted as saying, "Religion, as understood by most people, is a crutch. I don't need that kind of crutch." Reconsidering after a moment, though, she reframed her statement: "And yet I have faith. In the Bhagavad Gita (India's literary equivalent to a Bible), Lord Krishna says, 'I am the beauty in beautiful things. I am the evil in sin.' That is what I believe—that each person has God within him."

No organized religion could find fault with that statement, or with Indira for voicing it.

2

Washington, DC

✦

(1941–43)

A long, many-storied road had originally brought me to this part of the world, to meeting John and eventually marrying him in a Catholic Jesuit chapel in Bombay. I had been led down the aisle by a venerable Foreign Service careerman, then the American consul general: the very amiable Prescott Childs. Childs, resplendent in white linen, told me afterward at our champagne breakfast that I had kept muttering to him all the way to the altar: "I'll never do *this* again as long as I live! Never, never, never!"

So far, I haven't.

Dauphin County, Pennsylvania—rich in agriculture and industry with the added bonus of Irish, German, and Dutch tradition, speech, and cooking—was the place of my birth. Small-town Pennsylvania origins equipped me well, if unintentionally, for the wholly unforeseen career which lay ahead in remote Southeast Asia.

In very special ways, Pennsylvania was a fortunate state in which to be born. First, for its true Americana, deeply rooted in productive enterprise and rich agriculture. True, there's Pittsburgh, and a vital network of railroad, and heavy industry and lots of steel and smoke. But the memory of my native state I love best when I return is of bustling Saturday markets pungent with the smell of Lebanon baloney, sausages, head cheese, pickle relish. and home-baked bread. In summer, I loved to drive past cherry, pear, and apple orchards, rolling green hills, red barns, fields of corn, and miles of neat fences enclosing prime fat cattle.

In winter, the areas I knew best, between Harrisburg and Philadelphia and New York, all looked like "New England" Christmas cards straight out of the American artists' catalogs. I remembered them that way in India. They were still there when I returned.

Progress has taken its toll of the towns, but the Pennsylvania Dutch country-side and the henna-red barns with their round good-luck hex signs remain.

And here and there around Lancaster and York and Harrisburg, especially on market days, one still sees white-capped Amish women, so cheerful and shining, clutching by the hand equally shining, cherry-cheeked youngsters in awkward, old-fashioned clothes and high-topped shoes.

During my student days, I would have scorned the idea that the abundant agriculture surrounding me every day offered more practical instruction and insight into the problems and eternal struggle for existence among the world's farmers than all the Asian "culture" imbibed in lecture halls and in books. Agri-culture—the science of the world's food supply, the balance of life and death for millions—far, far outranks in importance all the cultural emphasis on Asian reli-gions, politics, and conquering armies of the past. Ten minutes' drive outside the capital of any Asian country is another world of the toiling people, and that world is almost entirely rooted in the soil. I do not wish to say that future Asian stu-dents should go out and plant corn or try to grow rice, but without some under-standing, some practical appreciation of what it means to have an entire family's survival depend upon the "supermarket" of a few acres of land, the purely cultural approach to Asia is pedantic and fatuous.

But my family were city folk. Farm contact escaped me. I knew no one who lived on any of those prosperous, picturesque farms. I petted no baby calves, climbed no apple trees, slid down no haylofts, never figured out where the hen's eggs came from! Yet the day was to come when I would proudly identify my homeland in America as rich farm country "like the Punjab," and I scarcely men-tioned all the iron and steel!

I can claim no credit for sharing my state with two great writers who have devoted their enormous talents to the humanizing of Asians so that they are no longer too distant and too different to be understood and loved: Pearl Buck and James Michener. And I must glow with pride, too, that the greatest *humanist* painter of our times—Andrew Wyeth—has immortalized the homey Pennsylva-nia scene on canvas.

Beginning a newspaper career in my town was no easier then than now. Atti-tudes toward women journalists were blunt: "We're agin' 'em! They belong on the society page, period!"

My hometown paper in Harrisburg, where I mined and tunneled my way into a beginner's job, is now only a historic name. The *Telegraph* was swallowed up years ago in a Newhouse combination, leaving the town with only one morning paper. But the old *Telegraph* building is still there near the Capitol in downtown

Harrisburg, a city which has become sophisticated, affluent, and increasingly influential on the national political scene.

I began writing blurbs for a big advertising supplement promoting furniture. No one cared what I wrote, as long as I wrote fast, clean copy, reasonably well spelled. But *I* cared.

Furniture was not quite the holy grail of my soaring ambition. I barely knew a picnic table leg from Sears from a tip-top table by Hepplewhite, or a Chippendale from a Phyfe, but I really plunged into furniture as though a Ph.D. depended on it. It really was a thesis. I have never recovered from the furious thoroughness of that first furniture assignment. I have, in fact, continued my furniture research to this day.

I never pass through a city where a devoted and caring historical society has a restored house without paying a visit. Hostesses, at my entreaty, have moved authorities and turned keys on closed days, and I have seen nearly all of the most famous historical homes in America. What treasure, what mementos of another America always peopled my mind's eye as I walked from room to room. (I even sometimes looked for a potty or wonder how they managed a bathroom for a large family.)

My years in Asia sharpened my vision and intensified my appreciation and love of my own country. I learned to take nothing American for granted. I never ceased to marvel at those tough ancestors of ours who built this country by hand and by heart and wrote its laws. At the Hermitage in Tennessee I felt my eyes rim with tears as I gazed at Rachel Jackson's guitar in the parlor and recalled the villainous cruelty heaped upon her in her lifetime and how grateful she must have been that death saved her from the ordeal of entering the White House.

A friend drove me twenty miles to Appomattox on a day when the national park site was closed, but hasty phone calls had found a guard with a key, so we stood in that Welsh home and looked into the little old-fashioned parlor where Grant and Lee met to end the Civil War. "Look—even the doll of one of the Welsh children remains on the old horsehair sofa," my friend whispered. And there was a well-used little girl's china doll, as it might have been on that day of triumph for Grant and anguish for Lee. I could not help observing with pride that the brief "terms" put in writing that historic day were written by General Grant's aide, whose name was *Parker!*

Thomas Jefferson's fantastic and ridiculous cannonball "calendar" desecrating Monticello's elegant front entrance rouses consternation. Now, really—how could his wife have allowed him to chop up their white woodwork with those silly balls, science or no science? History does not record her words, but I'm sure there were plenty.

One of the truly great sights of America on a summer's day in good company is the drive along State Highway 5, the John Tyler Memorial highway, from Richmond to Williamsburg, past such restored and still-lived-in houses as Belle Air, Westover, Shirley, and Berkeley. There are many of them where you can pause and have a charming visit, but Berkeley is our favorite. My children and I were unexpectedly invited to spend the night. (I had visions of sleeping in the room used by Abraham Lincoln, but it was not to be—modern living is done in a separate building, very elegantly.)

After viewing the houses along the James River on Route 5, we found Williamsburg is an almost too-splendid spectacle. I am inclined to enjoy *one* house with a warmly lived-in look and smell, set apart and alone upon a green knoll with a flash of the river caught through the trees. I love the authentic gardens edged with boxwood and the rose beds filled with fluffy mauve or pale peachy old tea roses, strongly scented.

The ultimate restored house, the White House, recently left me with mixed emotions. I made a hurried but special effort to get there on a Saturday before it closed to the public. It was the same day I had spent looking over Dean Rusk's office. I feared I would be turned away, but they allowed me to enter through the closed visitor's gate. I purchased my guidebook for $1.00 and was told by the attractive young lady at the desk that I must not miss "Mrs. Kennedy's gold drapes in the East Room. They were hand woven in France, you know, and did not cost the American taxpayers one cent. The money for the drapes came entirely from the sale of these little guidebooks."

Thanking her, I hurried to see the gold drapes. I was the only visitor in the room. A guard stood at the far end of the room. The drapes are so magnificent that all criticism of their being woven in *France* instead of the United States vanishes to insignificance. Mrs. Kennedy's flawless taste and correct selection wins complete approval at a glance. Bravo! They are superb!

But as I turned to move to the other rooms, my eyes suddenly fell to the crème-beige carpet covering the ballroom floor. I was aghast! Horrified! Great brown blobs, huge stains and splotches appeared on large sections of the rug. I stared in outrage and amazement. The guard strolled up: "Is something wrong, lady?" I pointed to the carpet. "What," I gasped, "happened here?" "Oh, that," the guard shrugged, "President had a buncha senators in here the other day and, well, they just slopped a helluva lotta coffee. The White House isn't a museum, you know. People live here. Senators smoke a lotta cigars and cigarettes, too. You oughta see what a beating this place takes!"

I shuddered and hurried out of the room. As I left the White House, I think I could have forgiven Lady Bird and her task force of tax-paid housekeepers had I seen one, *just one*, flower in a vase. Or had our first lady of beautification placed just one green plant, one small fern or trailing ivy, one lovely, living touch of green somewhere in all those rooms!

A friend of mine, who is an architect with cultural ties to the White House, was a member of one of those special committees that look into everything from pollution to Appalachia. He told me about a stag luncheon at the White House for the nation's top architects, builders, and designers. He was standing in a group that included Edward Durell Stone, the New York architect whose modern Taj Mahals dot the globe. As LBJ entered the room, Stone, anticipating an imminent handshake, calmly dropped his cigarette on the White House carpet and ground it out with his heel!

If architects can get away with that, why not senators? Only housewives, mindful of taxes and what a little bottle of blue liquid Glamorene can do, might call such behavior *outrageous*.

You see how thoroughly I was carried away with my very first newspaper assignment on furniture. After that, my editor gave me an even more honorable job: the obituary page. It is a perfectly respectable slot for a beginner. But the war was on, and the obituary page was the saddest assignment on the paper, especially for a tender-hearted innocent. So many times I had to telephone a stunned family for all the details, and to ask them for a last photograph of perhaps an only son, dead at nineteen! I wrote those obits lovingly, swallowing hard, often with swimming eyes (which did not improve my spelling much).

After that, the paper launched a new subscription drive, and I saw my opportunity. Now was the time for something new, something like a sparkling new teenagers' column to attract young student readers. My idea was not greeted with the slightest ripple, but I beat on every door until finally I thought, well, why not try the real boss, the publisher and owner? He was mildly intrigued, and he thought my girlish eagerness should be given a chance. Thus was launched "Teen Topics" by Pegge Parker. At the head of the column went a dazzling, syrupy picture of me and a tag line: "Send Miss Parker Your Problem."

FRIDAY EVENING

'Teen Topics

By Pegge Parker

——— Send Miss Parker Your Problem ———

Are you the girl tonight we ask,
And cross-examining is our task—

Are you the girl—who bends her knees and swishes awkwardly before sitting down? Of course the idea is to spread your skirt and not muss the back of your dress, but these graceful intentions go astray in the slouch-slump "sit." We noticed several of you 'teenettes doing this on the stage in your class plays recently. Which won't do at all, so—

Practice walking across the room and sitting down with mind more on grace than dress. Once charmingly squatted smooth out your dress and there you'll be—sitting pretty!

Are you the girl—who has a habit of telling the same thing two or three times to the same people? Suggested cure: preface all kabitzing with, "Did I tell you about—" or "Stop me if you've heard this before."

Are you the girl—who wears her date dresses to school? There are two loops in this straight, strict bow: if you are piece-speaking in assembly or there's to be a tea dance in the gym after school.

Are you the girl—who never thought how "different" 'twould be to wear the sleeves of her sweater down to the wrist instead of shoved up in a wrinkled wad at the elbow?

Are you the girl—who takes her woes out on the family? The telephone doesn't ring for days, the mailman doesn't bring THAT letter—and immediately Mother's been moving your things so you can't find them, or she never has anything for dinner you like. The teacher catches you talking and keeps you after school—and you come home and call Dad an "old grouch." It's hard to be pleasant and smiling when you feel droopy and grumpie, but you only get in deeper when you go around asking for a scolding or canceled allowance.

Are you the girl—who is still wearing anklets to school? Then you are the girl with the three-alarm legs: fire red! Soothe with cream and lotion at night.

Are you the girl—who lets nature take its uncertain course in making introductions? We've told this before but it wants telling again; Say the girl's name FIRST and blunders will go un-blundered. Suzy Sweet, Tommy Tall. Mary Muddle, 'n Flossie Fat, this is Sammy Smooth.

Are you the girl—who is super-sensitive, or more accurately, self-cuddling and self-centered—if you'll pardon our ouch?

Are you the girl — who helps herself to perfume, powder or combs on the bureau of a sorority sister's bedroom-turned-cloakroom for a club meetin'?

Are you the girl—who eats between meals? It's as much a habit as the hips you have!

Are you the girl—who doesn't read? Conversationally you're as interesting as a tube of last summer's white shoe polish.

Are you the girl—who is too much of a good thing? You visit too often and stay too late. Switch to: Come less, be welcomed more.

Are you the girl—who bores everyone with continual references to some adored member of the family: "My Dad, Brother, or Cousin says, thinks, does, feels, told me, went, did, might, explained, helped, was invited," and a very long etc.! Keep your gush and you'll keep your friends.

This "Teen Topics" column appeared in the January 9, 1942 issue of the *Harrisburg Telegraph.*

In a capital city with many high schools and junior colleges, "Teen Topics" was so successful I was relieved of other assignments and put on the column full time. Until the mail began to gather its own momentum, my mother, sister and I had spent many an evening writing "fan mail" on dime store stationery so the city room diehards would see that the new column was really "pulling in new readers." Soon there was no need to fudge, as the letters came in volume!

Eventually, when the time came to move on, and I landed a reporter's job on the night staff of the *Washington Times Herald* (since absorbed by the *Post*), my column had become such a fixture that the editor said, sure, I could go but the column stayed. They would simply hire someone else to be Pegge Parker and continue the feature. I felt immensely flattered.

I got my job on the *Times Herald* because I walked in at the right time, about midway during World War II. Timid and small-town, carrying a clipping book loaded with "Teen Topics" under my arm, I was given a probation trail because I was female. I would not be called to the Army. Veteran ranks were thinning every week. Newspapers had only us Girls to depend on and more senior males. I was put on the 4:00 to midnight shift and went home in a taxi every night by order of the night city editor. He gruffly insisted he didn't worry about me out on stories late at night and getting home at all hours (I worked well past midnight), but he did. He was the most critical, cussingest, roughest editor—when he wanted a new lead, he *wanted* it; when he said clean up the copy, you scrubbed it; when he said see that clock, boil this goddamncrap to two paragraphs, you *boiled!*

Although Cissi Patterson led the Washington press competition because she kept the *Times Herald* in a constant state of rawhide attack and sensation, I have seen my tough night editor, Wayne Randall, bless him, linger over a story, considering "What will this do to the family? How can they live with this?" If he decided the issue was not important enough to the general public for the private shame and grief publication would cause, the story went in the wastebasket. This happened a number of times to my own stories, and it taught me a lot. I worshipped Wayne Randall, but he never spared me.

Once, very close to deadline, as I struggled with a lead, he got up and came to see what was holding up my copy. Suddenly, with an oath, he ripped my paper from the typewriter. Rushing to his own desk, he began writing my story himself, snapping at me to fill him in on details from my notes. When his rewrite of my story went running to composing, he turned to me with terse instructions about writing leads. The lecture went through me like a buzz saw, destroying all my confidence. I was no longer a "budding journalist," but just some "kid from the sticks" who couldn't write a respectable lead! I fled to the little girls' room and had hysterics, weeping into horrible wartime brown paper towels.

I was discovered in one of these blubbering states by a casual outsider. Mortified to be caught in such disarray, I barely recognized the tall, tanned blondish girl who tried to console me as the young woman who worked alone at a somewhat isolated desk by the far windows. She was, I recalled, totally apart from the rest of the staff. She would come and go, put her copy on Randall's desk without a word, and disappear. He never—or seldom—fussed about *her* leads. An Untouchable! I never guessed why until later. I assumed she was a big byline writer since the paper ran her picture and gave her a boxed column all to herself. Yet, here she was, coolly taking me in hand, defending me from Randall's blast. She offered to take me home in her car, and on the way we stopped for coffee. Discovering I knew "no one" in Washington, she suggested I might enjoy a Chevy Chase weekend. She arranged a double date, and I gazed through another window of the Washington world. We were friends, touch and go, from then on. One day she suddenly quit the paper.

But she first came and smoked a last, thinking-out-loud cigarette on the end of my desk. The sudden decision to leave seemed to have unkeeled her cool balance. She was disturbed and anxious about something very personal but not quite clear to me. Her Boston accent was strongest when she was upset.

"I'm going off to England. I went today and signed up and took all those tests so I'll be a hostess for the Red Cross in London soon, if I'm lucky. Why don't you think about it? Should be terribly exciting, and I hope I can make myself useful as well. I want it all to be really worthwhile, not just a lark. Family's not too keen. If I go, I'll be right in the blitz and I'll love it, even with things popping!"

We shook hands warmly, and she left. I never saw her again. She did indeed go to London and to a popping whirlwind life there. She eventually married the Marquis of Hartington, a cousin of Lord David Ormsby-Gore. The marriage had been a romantic, if star-crossed, event because there were religious difficulties and other complications. And then the fairy tale of her life ran out. The Marquis was killed, and not long afterward Kathleen herself died in a private plane crash. My friend was Kathleen Kennedy.

By odd coincidence, one of Kathleen's future in-laws worked on my newspaper after I had left, and I did not meet her until years later when her name was Jacqueline Bouvier Kennedy.

Another amazing woman dominated the Washington scene in those days and was responsible, in a way, for my boost from the 4:00 to midnight hitch to becoming Woman's Page editor. The very brilliant and glamorous Congresswoman from Connecticut, Clare Boothe Luce, had her day with the press, and it had been a feather-flying hen fight. Lady Clare, in those days, suffered criticism or opposition with scant grace, and a sharp tongue matched her sharper wit. Women in Congress were no novelty, but a sensational woman, a Vogue-ish, stunning *female*, with great legs and ribbons-on-combs fluttering in her blond hair—well, all this was unforgivable. No one woman should be allowed to Have It All! Ladies of the press wrote stories on Clare Luce with bared teeth. Clare repaid their compliments in kind. She had not written her famous play *The Women* without intimate, surgical knowledge of her subject!

I wrote a frothy little piece about all this cat howling over Clare, and my article caught the eye of the paper's publisher, the famous cyclone lady: Cissie Patterson.

To be noticed by Cissie usually spelled doom. She adored you one day, fired you the next. I managed to ride the waves, just inches ahead of disaster, for about two years.

Meanwhile, because of the Luce piece, she moved me from night assignments to running her Woman's Page. Here she could keep an eye on me and prod me with her little pet ideas. I would often receive calls at odd hours from the Patterson mansion on DuPont Circle. I would rush up for "consultation," then taxi off to the house of a friend who had "some new ideas going" on knitting or tablecloths or how to make earrings to some yuk stirred up in the kitchen! With a photographer, I trailed all the way out to Virginia, to do stories on her friends' farms and horses. We did recipes from all the embassies, and visiting actresses in hats from Garfinkels. This egg-walking spot as Cissie's "favorite" had its price and rewards. I went everywhere in Washington in those days, saw and heard more than I cared to hear or could write or publish. I became saturated with Washington.

I wanted out. I had had enough—too much.

Unexpectedly one day I received a phone call from New York, from the William Esty advertising agency. Would I pose for a Camel cigarette ad? I was a small-town Harrisburg girl who had never learned to smoke. Not with an air, looking like Lauren Bacall, that is. So I told the ad lady, "I'd love to, but I don't smoke!" As though *that* had anything to do with posing for a cigarette ad! "You could try, dear," she responded crisply. "We'll put you up at the Plaza and supply your wardrobe. Should take only one day of shooting, okay?"

Times Herald
WASHINGTON, D.C.

ELEANOR PATTERSON   May 21, 1943

Dear Pegge:

   That was a swell job you did in and out
of Annapolis. Please let me congratulate you--
and I am kind of pleased with myself, too, because
it was I who suggested your going.

                   E.P.

                Eleanor Patterson

Miss Pegge Parker,
Washington Times-Herald.

P. S. I just heard you are going to get an exclusive
      interview with Mrs. Randle, and that makes it
      all the better. I am sure you will get an A-1
      story.   E.P.

Pegge saved this note from Cissie Patterson.

And so I became a *back cover* girl, earning a dishonest dollar advertising cigarettes I have never smoked! The windfall of the ad gave me not only unexpected
mad money, but a terribly restless urge to buy a ticket to *somewhere*—somewhere
far from the too-muchness of Washington. I was very impatient to be on my way
to where the real world was, where really important things were going on.

GIVE HER A TYPEWRITER...
A PACK OF CAMELS...AND LET THOSE PRESSES ROLL!

PEGGE PARKER, ace war reporter, is an expert on G. I.'s, camps, and Camels

By PEGGE PARKER

I AM writing this on a G. I. soap box after a day in a Tiger Division tank under simulated battle conditions that seemed awfully real to me.

I've also been up with the paratroopers, finding out what 1500-foot jumps are like ... I've spent a week aboard a Liberty Ship, covering the Merchant Marine ... I've flown on stunt maneuvers in a glider ... run an obstacle course with tracer bullets practically grazing my head. It's all been plenty rugged and, take my word for it, that Camel tastes good when you get a minute out for a smoke. And the G. I.'s I've seen certainly seem to agree. Camel's their favorite*—and mine!

Little did I dream back in my girlish, organdy, pre-war days that I'd be riding as gunner in a tank.

Those paratroopers are wonderful! ... They jump with only 1500 feet between them and the ground, non-chalantly as you'd light a Camel.

You give up the comforts of home on a job like mine ... but one of them always goes along with us.

● Camel would like very muc[h] a date with your T-Zone—th[e] Throat and T for Taste. It wou[ld] demonstrate the mildness and c[...] its magnificent blend of costlie[r ...] —to your own throat. And the[...] flavor to your own taste. Bec[...] throat and your taste are surel[y] judges of which cigarette is be[...]

Every story that took me out of the office, and out of Washington, was eagerly pursued. And then came the story that led to my spending an unforgettable day with Margaret Mitchell in Atlanta.

One day, my ear funnel picked up the hint of a rich prize: Margaret Mitchell, the elusive little Southern matron who took almost a lifetime, considering she began to gather material from stories told to her in childhood, to write one book: *Gone With the Wind.* Well, my source reported, Margaret Mitchell was in Richmond, Virginia, hard at work on "something." My informant declared she was going through old records, taking voluminous notes, by hand, in a notebook. There was no mistaking who she was, my friend insisted. She signed "Marsh" (in private life she was Mrs. John Marsh) on all the reference room slips.

I went to Cissie with my tip. We both hoped it was either the sequel to *Gone* or a new book and that I would somehow be able to beguile out of her an exclusive interview telling me all about it! "Take a plane to Atlanta tomorrow," Cissie ordered. "I'll give you a personal note to Ralph Magill at the *Constitution.*"

Magill was a personal friend of Peggy Mitchell who had worked on the competing *Atlanta Journal* in earlier newspaper reporting days. I never doubted for a second that Magill would help me, nor did Cissie Patterson.

What gall, what Washington arrogance! On Peach Tree Street, in Margaret Mitchell's day, no one conquered in a day, not even with a note to Ralph Magill!

"I'm sorry you didn't consult me before you came all the way down here, young lady," was the cool reception I received at the *Constitution.* "Peggy Marsh gives *no* interviews to anyone anymore, and I wouldn't think of disturbing her. The Hollywood ballyhoo over her book was a nightmare for someone like Peggy. You have no idea what it did to her physically and mentally. Things have quieted down now, and that's just the way we intend to keep it."

Utterly crushed and sensing I was having my Washington wings clipped back to size, I got up without a word to leave. The Southern gallantry in this remarkable man got the better of him. He could not help himself, so he broke down and "helped" me.

"Look here, Miss Parker, I suppose I might as well tell you where you can at least *see* Margaret Mitchell. Remember, I am not sending you there, but she is selling war bonds in a bank to raise money to buy a replacement for the *SS Atlanta* aircraft carrier, which was destroyed. You can go over and buy a war bond from her, I guess, same as anybody else."

"How will I know which one at the booth is Margaret Mitchell?" I asked. "The one wearing black stockings, very short, has a round face and wears rimless glasses. She'll probably speak to you first, especially if you wear that hat."

Upon "that hat" hangs my tale of Margaret Mitchell.

I have always loved hats, and in those days I made a lot of my own. I even did a series of picture articles for the Woman's Page on how to make your own hats without sewing a stitch! I *pinned* all my hats together with long corsage pins. Pink was my favorite color, and I had with me in Atlanta a new spring coat. To go with it I had pinned onto a plain felt (costing $2.00) a wrap-around swash of pink maline (59¢ and no tax), and over one eye I had added a beautiful pink silk rose from Garfinkel's (about $5.00 in those days).

This creation was "that hat" to Mr. Magill. I prayed it would also draw the eye and spontaneous friendship of the famous lady in the black stockings. There were no other bond buyers when I entered the bank, so all the ladies at the booth chorused as I nervously approached: *"Wherever did you get that hat?"*

Behind the booth I could not see the ladies' legs. Absolutely no one looked anything like the book jacket picture of America's most celebrated woman novelist. I began to buy bonds, slowly, extending the conversation, trying to elicit some clue. "You're from out of town," one woman said in a velvety Southern accent. "Where did you come from? Washington? *What brings you to Atlanta?*"

This was Margaret Mitchell. I sensed it so strongly, I gave her all the money I felt I could afford for bonds and moved in closer to her. She kept her eye on the pink hat. "It's all pinned together," I murmured. "Ah don't believe it—show me!" she gasped. I took it off and showed her. She studied it carefully to see how I did it without the pins "stickin'." "Ah love hats, but ah can nevah find one ah can wear. Ah'll have to have a hat to wear to the launchin' ceremonies of our new *SS Atlanta.*"

By this time I felt brave enough to admit who I was and why I had come to Atlanta!

She was very upset. "Ah *am* so sorry to say no to you. Ah just can't bear any more commotion. Ah am so sorry you came all the way down here to see me and ah can't help you! Can't ah do somethin' *else* for you, though? Ah know—will you be my guest at the Writers' Club this evenin'? It's a little group of professional women writers. You'll love them! We just meet for a little fun and get together once a month, and ah'm sure you would enjoy the other lady writers. Some of the best murder-mystery writers are women who live right in this town. They'll be comin' to our tea (though we don't really drink much tea!). Ah'll pick you up at your hotel about four in my car and, oh please, Miss Parker, wear that hat!"

I still had no story, had not even asked her about her appearance in Richmond, but that would all come later. In her huge black car—I believe it was a Cadillac—which she complained was "jes' too big" for her short legs (in the black hose), we set off to the ladies' literary circle. Linking her arm through mine, Margaret Mitchell *introduced my hat* to her friends, telling them all about the pins underneath, then vaguely mentioned I was Miss Parker from Washington. It was a gay, babbling afternoon. I was so enthralled with the murder story writers I almost forgot to sound them out on Margaret Mitchell. "Will she ever write another book?" I asked several of them. "Oh-god-no!" was their answer. "This one nearly killed her. She's not strong, you know. Fame and excitement and public intrusions are not for our Peggy. Others might take it in stride, but not her."

"Would anything important have taken her to Richmond?" I asked them. "Does she have relatives she might have been visiting? She spends lots of time in libraries as a regular thing?" No one raised an eyebrow. Richmond cued no one to any information whatsoever. Peggy M. moved back and forth about the room, animated and gaily laughing. (Did I imagine flashes of her Scarlett as she told some amusing story?)

When the literary tea broke up, Margaret Mitchell led me to her car and we drove back to my hotel. Now or never, I told myself. I asked her about another book. "Never!" she gasped. "At least, no more Scarlett and Rhett." What about the visits to Richmond's Archives? "I have spent half my life in public libraries checking research. I wanted my book to be historically accurate. I wanted it to stand up to every test in the future—every date, every detail as exactly correct as it could be. Whenever I got a letter from someone seriously questioning my historical accuracy, I checked it out. Long after the book was published, I was still checking my research. Had I made an error, I would correct it in the next edition of the book. I don't think you can take liberties with history. Move your plot around the history, but never make your history fit the plot." This was Margaret Mitchell, the Pulitzer Prize professional!

We reached the hotel driveway at nearly 6:00. Traffic was heavy, taxis came in and out, but Margaret Mitchell drove her big car gingerly up to the front entrance, switched off the motor, and settled down to finish our chat. A doorman yelled, a taxi horn blasted. "Hey lady, ya can't park here! You're blocking traffic! Keep moving!" With cool aplomb, this mite of a woman leaned out the window. "Now you just hush up!" she commanded. "Ah'm talkin' to my friend for just a few minutes, then ah'll move."

She had one real beauty, I discovered, studying her face intently. She had wonderfully intelligent, very expressive eyes. You didn't notice them at first because of the rimless glasses she wore. In her youth she must have been extremely pretty, in a bows-and-ruffles Southern way. But she was sophisticated too and, I sensed, could be daring, full of Irish spirit, and very gay in her very private world, among her very, very private circle of friends.

"Ah want to ask you a favor, Pegge Parker," she said quietly. "Please say no if you don't want to. But *will you make me a hat to wear for the launchin' ceremonies?* They've asked me to come and break the champagne, and ah'm thrilled to death, but ah must have something pretty to wear on my head, and hats look awful on me. Ah'm so little, and with my hair fixed this way—well, ah'm certain you could make me just what ah need. They'll be taking lots of pictures of me, too, and this hat has to be just right!"

She took a piece of paper and began to make a rough drawing of a small hat to be "trimmed in little forget-me-nots and matching blue ribbons to bring out my eyes."

I assured her I could manage a pretty hat covered with forget-me-nots. I would whip something together, I thought (or have a New York milliner do it by my direction) and send a trial hat down to her as a sample. She patted my arm, gratefully thanking me.

"Now, then," I begged, "give me your *final* word, very honestly—do you plan ever to do a follow-up book to *Gone With the Wind?* Or even another book?"

She shook her head with a slow finality which convinced me at least that no new book was being written or drafted at that time.

"All right, now *I* must know, and only you can tell me, did Rhett ever go back to Scarlett? You left him banging the door and rushing out. Surely he came back to poor Scarlett in the end?"

Margaret Mitchell shook her head with finality. Thousands had demanded the same final answer from the author. "Mah dear, when ah finished the last word on the last page of that book, ah didn't have any more words left! Ah just came to the end, and there wasn't any more. Ah really don't know!"

"Oh no, you can't leave me dangling!" I cried in mock horror. We were talking about real people whose very real story had somehow been left inconclusively unfinished.

"Wouldn't Rhett be miserable without Scarlett, and didn't he really pity her as a pathetic child?" Margaret Mitchell smiled. "Ah suppose so, yes, ah suppose Rhett would be lonely without Scarlett, but ah have no idea—the end of the book was the *end* of all ah ever knew about them! The very, very last word!"

We clasped hands warmly, and I left her. We corresponded about the hat, but the letters came from a secretary. Margaret Mitchell was in Johns Hopkins Hospital and could not, it seemed, possibly launch the ship. A close relative wrote me a polite note, explaining just this.

So my story of Margaret Mitchell is as unfinished as Rhett and Scarlett's, and I am sorry now that I didn't go ahead anyway and make her the pretty hat with forget-me-nots and blue ribbons even if she never wore it.

Pegge in the process of creating a new hat.

3

Alaska

◆

(1943–46)

The turning point of the war was rapidly approaching. I thought restlessly about joining the Red Cross and getting overseas as Kathleen had done. But the minimum age for recruits was twenty-five, and I was too young (to think *that* could be a problem!).

Eventually I chose one of the few places where there was no war going on: Alaska.

I went to Fairbanks, direct from the *Times Herald*, to a city staff of *exactly two*, on the *Daily News Miner*. The paper's banner read "America's Farthest North Daily Newspaper." At least the Newhouse chain hasn't reached out this far for one more. The *News-Miner* is still going strong, is still independently owned, occasionally does a spiffy color-printing job, has the AP, Ann Landers, runs to 12 pages, and sells for fifteen cents. In my day we got out four pages, Monday through Saturday, and the paper sold for a dime. Our only competition was a very respectable, very spirited, very well put together weekly, *Jessen's*.

At the prospect of Alaska, my parents in Harrisburg were less than pleased. "A young girl all alone up there? Heaven's child—how will you live? How will you get up there?" My father fumed over the risks and perils of a job thousands of miles distant merely "promised" by mail. "Why," he stormed, "you don't know anything about those people up there. You have no contract. That's a long way to go, girl, on just a nice letter saying come when you can!" No, there was more: in a later letter, a check to cover my transportation, one way.

What the folks and I did not know was the way Alaskans did things. We couldn't have understood how strong frontier standards still were in the North in those days. Verbal agreements followed by a handshake and a drink moved mountains, launched deals, opened a business, loaned cash, built houses, and kept a job open when a letter said, "Come." In Alaska, you knew your man. What kind of commitment you made depended upon your man. The pledged word was final as Judgment Day and twice as compelling as any airtight written contract.

Progress and modern times have changed the handshake system. America's largest state now has many lawyers, unions, formal contracts, and other civilized benefits. But Alaskans were a lot prouder of the old honor system which, though far from perfect, was nonetheless their way of doing things.

I flew to Seattle, took an Alaska Steamship boat for the famous 800-mile Inside Passage route through Juneau and on to Seward.

Fellow passengers were wartime cannery workers: a rummy, red-eyed, beer-swilling lot, and there were a number of ladies, fast-buck hefties who told me they go north every season to work the canneries. "We work the stinkin' god-damn fish like hell for the season's run," a strapping girl who was my cabin mate told me. "We make a lotta money, an' its all clear, a good wad, baby, then we get the hell out. It ain't no vacation, but it ain't too bad. Say, hon, if I snore, punch me."

From the doubtful, forbidding, mud-soft streets of Seward I went on to Anchorage by train, thinking my thoughts, and putting down dread misgivings.

Then came the crushing, shocking ugliness of wartime Anchorage! I walked its dismal streets in disbelief. Everywhere I looked were cheap bars, junk shops and crude shacks passing for housing. If Anchorage looked this bad, I began to worry, what could Fairbanks so much farther north be like? What appalled me at first glimpse of this tremendous territory was that everything God made was wildly beautiful; everything manmade—or *nearly* everything manmade—was ram-shackle, cheap, and ugly. The new frontier boom I had read about turned out to be shanty towns on mud roads. Oh, here and there an isolated house or building was made of startling white concrete and of attractive modern design, but these were few. Alaska's long winter shroud of snow was a great mercy, obliterating the towns, leaving only outlines visible. At no cost to anyone, the gentle whiteness mercifully and magically blanketed out all that was hideous!

Fairbanks, which I reached eventually in early summer, was no picture post-card, but where I lived and worked I found astonishingly plushy luxury and comfort. The people I "knew nothing about" at the Lathrop Company lived in the company's small but elegant apartment building. Because I was to work on the Lathrop newspaper, I was entitled to Lathrop "housing."

The Lathrop establishment was vast and varied, but cozy-friendly—the kinds of folks who welcomed you with a pan of homemade brownies and took you home to dinner and loaned you an ironing board. It was more like an adoption than a welcome.

The man who built the Lathrop empire was a corrugated character named Cap, or in full, Austine E. Lathrop, one of the most remarkable men I was ever to meet. Self-educated to a large degree, a born innovator, a do-it-*now* man, Cap was then Alaska's only millionaire. "An' I never made a goddamned nickel outta gold, girl! Started with the boats, then a bakery, an' a movie house, then a bank an' radio station and coal mine and good lord, I was into everything! Then I came up here to Anchorage and Fairbanks. That's how ya make money in Alaska, girl. Buildin' things, and buildin' only the best, buildin' to last. Nobody's made it in gold, big, an' kept it."

In our town alone, Cap owned the banks, two theaters as well equipped and carpeted as any in Seattle, the radio station (now a TV station as well), my newspaper, the *News-Miner,* and my splendid apartment building. Radio station KFAB was on the top floor, the newspaper on the street floor, and our quarters were well layered in between. The town's bachelor doctor and a favored few were allowed to have an apartment when a rare one was available.

When I thought of my newspaper office in Washington, it paled in comparison to my glamorous mahogany desk in Fairbanks, my pretty pale green typewriter and leather swivel chair! I used to sit there inwardly thrilled, telling myself: think where you *are!* Fairbanks, Alaska, 130 miles from the Arctic Circle!

It took a few years for me really to appreciate the standard and the achievements of that incredible man, Cap Lathrop. He was no absentee capitalist. He may have run a benevolent monopoly, but Cap's fortune stayed where he made it, in Alaska. How many others pontificated on how they "loved Alaska"—and took profits and cash *out* of the territory, far, far away from their grubstakes in the North. Cap's whole life—he had no family, wife, or sons—became what he built. That's why everything with his name on it was the best.

I never chopped wood to keep warm when the dread winter came. I merely tiptoed over thick carpeting to a little thermostat on the wall and set a dial. I had a smart, pastel apartment-sized kitchen with everything built in. The bathroom/dressing room combination, though compact, could have come from the pages of *Ladies Home Journal.* My room was shared with another girl, and our only complaint, when yawny and dead tired, was the struggle to pull down a Murphy bed to sleep on. But then ours was a very special bed. Ingrid Bergman had slept in it before we took over the place. The lovely Ingrid had been part of the Hollywood troupe that came to Ladd Field to entertain servicemen. Someone had offered her the empty flat in town, with its own kitchen, and she had gratefully accepted.

Within a short time of my arrival another "entertainer" came to Ladd Field and also stopped by to visit the apartment briefly en route to an interview upstairs at KFAB: prizefighter Joe Louis.

At the very peak of his fighting career, this modest, panther-handsome young Negro had asked if he might see "how you folks live up here in the cold." He came and looked around with surprise: "It's real Stateside!" He pointed to, and identified, a Karsh photograph of Clare Boothe Luce, then he saw my collection of Eskimo handicraft.

With murmurs of "jes' wonnerful, jes' wonnerful," he studied them with appreciation. "Tell me about the Eskimos. How do they live? Do they get jobs in town?" He was very curious.

Asked about fighting, he waved a powerful hand. "Aw, I don' wanna talk about fightin'," he protested. "I only wish I could do somethin' else. I hate fightin'."

On what I coyly came to call my Fairbanks "snow job," I covered the town every morning. My deadline was noon, so I had to have my stories well launched and written early in the day. I covered every office and coffee shop on Second Avenue, trekked over the Chena River to St. Joseph's Hospital hoping to find something going on to make page one exciting. I could have phoned, but when I went in person I met six people, heard more, saw more, and trebled the items that went down in my notebook. Then on to City Hall and the Post Office and to the biggest department store, the Northern Commercial Co., where George Preston, the manager, might be reading the air edition of the *London Times*.

Then I would slush on down the street to finish up at the airline offices, Wein and PanAm, where I copied down the entire passenger list, incoming and outgoing. I also tried to learn more about who was coming in and going out, and why.

At the leading hotel, our venerable, still thriving Nordale, I dutifully listed every name in the registration book and looked for somebody interesting or important in business or politics for a nice long interview. I had lots of space to fill, especially in winter.

When I was desperate, on a slack, gloomy winter's day, I would call a lot of people on the phone and ask them if they'd had any interesting mail lately. This was fishing for an item or two about well-known Alaskans "outside" for the cold season. Many obligingly offered to read out to me their monthly bills or their bank statements.

I got my biggest boost on space-hungry days from certain well-informed ladies of the town. "Well, Pegge, don't say you heard it from *me*, but I hear Mable Twohead is finally leaving that old walrus Bill Scotch-n-soda! Check PanAm. She was supposed to get her ticket today, and she's telling everyone she's going out for a checkup at Mayo, but she's really headed for Nevada. I'll bet she takes the old buzzard for everything he's got, won't leave him the socks he's standin' in, an' serves him right!"

Items like this I got all the time, but couldn't use. Marriages should have been banded in iron in the North, considering the isolation and the human instinct to survive and stick together. Not so. The divorce rate was high, as was the giddy number of marriages, *re*-marriages, and Arrangements.

One of the best stories which of course was doubly relished on a dreary winter's day, was another which never made my scant news column in the *News-Miner*. This one was about the fashionable matron who sent away for some home exercise records. She wished to take off winter inertia and dismaying pounds encircling her waist. In the privacy of her bedroom one night, when her husband was out and she was alone, she put on the exercise records. In her nightgown she began an ambitious workout following the peppy directions of the gymnast on the record. When it came to a vigorous bicycle churn, lying on the carpet, her nightie got in the way so she stripped it off. One-two-three, *higher,* faster, one-two!

Someone knocked at the door. Mrs. X hastily shut off the record, slipped into a dressing gown and went to the door. It was unlocked. Two ladies dropping in on some trifling excuse—like a nightcap—noted all: exercises in the nude, at *that* hour, husband out, and the door unlocked! The story swept the Arctic Circle, with many additions and embellishments.

No harm whatsoever came to Mrs. X, who had what few other women in the far north would ever have: great style, great legs, and a British accent. And money! When she heard the tale of her midnight exercises had "gone all over" she was amused. For Christmas, her best friend gave her a pair of red long johns so she could exercise in the future with the door wide open and never take a chill!

In winter, what Big Business we had in Fairbanks was almost totally shut down. Miners went south. Seattle-based business agents were gone by October. Offices closed. Most Alaskans who could afford it—and those whose business was literally "frozen" for the season—flew outside to bask the winter months away in California. Before Thanksgiving we were well dug in. We stoically took stock of who was left and prepared to enjoy and make the most of the long, dark days ahead.

Despite the darkness and the cold and the slow-grinding pace, Alaskans boasted the winter season was really the goddamnedest best time of all. On their terms, on what they did for fun, blood circulatin', hellraisin' and social whirlin', curling and sourdough dancin'—they were absolutely right! Things moved and things happened, even at 60 below!

Temperatures of 40 and 60 below zero did not come every day. When they did, Fairbanks really didn't feel one bit colder than at a middlin' 20 below. We wore the same heavy coats, parkas or ski jackets, the same boots, mitts, and two layers of stockings or wool slacks. In the darkness-at-noon climate, we were conditioned to the elements. We obeyed them with automatic response, not aware of special strain or botheration.

At 60 below, no one moved very fast outdoors; no one hurried or ran even a short block. Rapid breathing and deep draughts of air that cold could be painful and harmful. All transportation, including incoming planes from Seattle, was thoroughly cold-conditioned. Every parked automobile had its motor running. Cars purred in the cold, exhaling thick billows of frosty white vapory smog. The problem was to keep the engine, oil, and water from freezing, and to keep the tires from freezing solid on the road. I never had a car the whole time I was in Fairbanks. It was easier to take a taxi or drive with friends on long hauls, or to our little airport. The rest of the time, all year round, I walked.

The extreme cold never closed the schools, except on unusually bad days, nor did it keep the children indoors. Mamas bundled the kids up to the eyeballs, quite literally. They tied woolly scarves over cold, apple-red faces, bandit style, allowing only bright eyes to peer out. Mothers were also extra-careful to attach gloves to snowsuits with long cords or metal clips. Kittens who lost their mittens might suffer tragic consequences.

The terrible cold of winter really locked us in at night with awesome silence and no wind. If there had been any wind along with those temperatures, there wouldn't have been any town. If you ventured to the Post Office to mail an urgent letter at 10:00 at night, you fancied you could hear a wolf howl or a polar bear roar all the way to Barrow 500 icy miles away in that black, deadly vacuum of silence!

Northern lights from time to time flickered in the sky like green electricity—nervous, witchy, like a pulse or spasm of the unnatural. I never thought them beautiful. And I particularly disliked the unspellable, twister-upper name they were given: *aurora borealis*. Even as far north as Fairbanks, they did not appear so often as tourists imagined. When they were particularly vivid, leaping greenly in weird display in the cold heavens, Alaskans ran out of their houses and stood briefly shivering and watching.

Fairbanks surprised me for its added enrichment of a wide range of nationalities. *Gold* has the same attraction in every language, and when the discovery was made in 1901 and 1902 the news raced over the world and people came from Japan and Yugoslavia, from Canada Norway, Switzerland and Germany, from Ireland, England, Denmark...everywhere. This international treasure did wonders for the town's accents, celebrations, flavor, character and cooking. Or should I say the town's *home* cooking, there being no restaurant worthy of the price in Fairbanks in those days. At Christmas what an import-shop bevy of goodies circulated, what ambrosia of homemade breads in six languages hung in an eye-watering cloud over our flour-and-yeast-white village, what nut twists, sticky buns, spiced pickles, rum and brandy soused loaves, squares and balls nestled in wax paper, what cookies with strange names in italics, dusky fruit cakes, steamed puddings oozing brandy, conserves, jellies, and sparkling jams laced with lemon peel and almonds.

I would open my apartment door on Christmas morning and find a surprise assortment of bundles, sometimes huge-bowed, sometimes in brown grocery bags. Not much of a cook myself, this was real Alaskan gold.

"Now, really, child, it was nothin'," my Alaskan benefactors would protest at my ardent gush of thanks. "Just wanted you to have a little tasty bite to go with a cup of coffee. Now don't go on, it was nothing. Just a remembrance."

Nowhere on earth, nowhere from Jerusalem to my Pennsylvania hometown, have I ever known a town where people "remembered" so hard at Christmas. Remembered everyone else, since families were so far away, or ties had been lost over the years. The town—all of Fairbanks—became Family instead.

Next to the Old World marvels on which we sublimely snacked, the imported talent I appreciated most was our local and authentic Finnish bath. An old Finnish woman ran a public steam bath, clean as a surgical ward, at her home. You booked a reservation there as you would make an appointment to get your hair done. To the Finnish bath on a Friday night would I trot along with the Lathrop Girls.

Of all the people who came north under storied circumstances, one was in a class by herself: Alaska's most hilarious celebrity, Eva McGown, first lady of fun. On a refrigerated night at 60 below when you could hear polar bears bellow, on such a night if you turned an ear toward Fairbanks, you could hear shrieks and hollers, and you'd know Eva was holding court somewhere. Anywhere north of Juneau you would hear about Eva, but you would never hear anything like the original.

Newspaperwoman Pegge poses with the latest issue of the Fairbanks Daily
News-Miner.

Eva McGown's career, her formal working career, was scarcely worthy of her scope and powers. For years she was in charge of housing, finding roof and body shelter for anxious newcomers or weary tourists without reservations. During the season Eva had her desk in the Nordale Hotel lobby. She knew every home and every bed in town (and usually who was in or out of them), she also knew those who never took in boarders but would soften like buttered noodles when she got them on the phone and begged for shelter for the poor wee darlin's.

Darlin' was Irish-born Eva's favorite punctuation, and it came at you early and often with a trill at high C followed by anything else she had to say in a torrent of brogue sprinkled with *aye* and *wee* and *gawdluvya, Darlin'*.

At the turn of the century, Eva McGown came straight from Ireland to the early settlement in the gold-struck northland. A Trans-Atlantic correspondence preceded her arrival. An arrangement lured her thence with an "understanding" that she might find romance or a career as a music teacher in roiling new Fairbanks. She had not laid eyes on Arthur McGown, the man she married, until she had made the long adventurous journey from Ireland to America, to the West coast, then up the Inside Passage by boat to Skagway and overland to Fairbanks. McGown was, one gathers, no Prince Charming. His passing was Eva's beginning; her delayed flowering made him a legend.

The town was booming and moving, and Eva was the prime mover, meeting everyone, greeting everyone, selling them on Fairbanks. As the years enhanced her swath she was greatly sought after by every writer and reporter who came to town. She went on TV in Fairbanks, and in California, once for a startling version of "This Is Your Life" (which gave Eva a mixed thrill). She has been in *Reader's Digest* as an Unforgettable Character, and she is in nearly every book ever written on Fairbanks, including the very latest *Time-Life* world series edition on Alaska and Hawaii—and lo, here she is in this very book as well.

I spent a Christmas with her once in Belfast among her assorted Irish kin. Then after a long spin of years and events we met again recently in San Francisco by the Bay, where no hearts were left with little cable cars. We had both left ours years ago up north a bit. But was she vibrant! Her pipey voice shrieked and trilled; darlin's flew all over. I lit candles and poured champagne and had to shush her to get a word in to thank her for the roses she had brought.

"Darlin', is this really the two of us here in San Francisco after all these years?" she cried. "Darlin', I'm an old lady now. Gawdluvus, I'm nearly *eighty!* Aye. What times we live in. Here I am with you darlin', drinkin' me champagne, tomorrow back in Seattle, and day after, back in my wee room at the Nordale in Fairbanks. What a life it has been, aye, the people I've seen come and go! That's the shock of it, darlin', they're all goin' and I'm still here. (Deep sigh matched with a deep sip of California's best champagne.) Been the world over, child. I've seen it all—Hong Kong, India, and the Taj at Agra (dear me, I thought the *monkeys* would run off with me. I've never seen so many runnin' loose!). I've been to Paris! What a kick that was—I've seen it all, and darlin'. give me my Alahska! It really *is* the only place on earth, the greatest of them all. Aye."

Her hair a white cloud, her figure slim, darting, quick with nervous energy, her skin a treasure she was born with, rosy and nearly lineless ("that's the juice of good livin', darlin'), Eva McGown should go roaring on to ninety. Life has dealt her full measure, indeed, but not without blows and grief, which left only secret scars, and intensified her compulsive sympathy, her instinct for reaching out and giving out to all wee darlin's who ever crossed her path.

Eva's latest letter came to me rolled up inside an air-mailed copy of my old paper, the *Daily News-Miner,* which told me Eva was selling tickets for the Ice

Pool. And this summer when the days are aglow with 24 hours of light, she'll be a greeter at a showcase pioneer cabin for tourists. Anytime you're traveling north, just ask for Eva, and you'll know how much I *under*-exaggerated her.

Fighting a fire in winter at 40 below was both a nightmare and a Keystone cop comedy. If no one got killed or went bankrupt from the damage and loss, it was all very funny afterward. But we all trembled when we heard the fire engine in the distance. Fires were always at their dreadful peak in winter when overheated stoves seemed a special hazard to families squeezed into wood cabins or substandard housing.

In my day, Fairbanks was still a frontier town. No one ever locked a door in his house. It was a local boast. Hardly anyone in the town had a front door key. "Hell, haven't locked my kitchen door in 30 years," people bragged, "even when we go Outside for the winter. Neighbors sorta keep an eye on the place. If they ever need a bottle of catsup or a can of beer, they sure know where to find it!"

I have no recollection of ever locking my own apartment door. Well, maybe once or twice I pushed the little button in the center of the doorknob. One of the bitterest complaints of old-timers about how Fairbanks was growing and expanding, was how many new people came in each summer an' hell, now a fella had to lock up nights.

For all that, we had a serious-minded budding University five miles from town, two important air bases at nearby Ladd and Eielson, expanding development in housing and defense projects. Fairbanks had its own exclusive circle. The military contributed enormously to our town's economic survival, but GIs were lonely outsiders. In town the last original survivors of the 1901–1902 gold rush were still around. When they died, I buried them in the *News-Miner* with grand obituary spreads that were echoes of Jack London. I might add, gold rushers and their descendants found precious little gold, much more harsh reality—hard times and a *hard life*—but grub staking on the rim of the Arctic Circle was a "rich" experience. Descending generations of the original prospectors stayed on, and most newcomers as well, long after the adventure, romance, and the dreams had all been realistically adjusted. *If you were equal to the country, the country never let you go!*

In a frontier society there were surprisingly very strict social acceptance standards. Modesty and restraint—let's say, an amiable silence—were acceptable above all other virtues in a green newcomer. (I never liked and never used that travel guide expression which I *rarely* heard, "cheechako.") Next to modesty, the way to get along when you were an outsider was to let the Alaskans do all the talking.

A boast of past pedigree or social blue ribbons that would have been accept-able in New York or Palm Beach or Boston or London was unmentionable and quite unforgivable here! If you really were somebody, the town would find out soon enough. But not from you. If you were respected for your worth, then your blue blood and even your money would be forgiven. If you were mum-tight on background you would be accepted for what you were, not what you had been. The town knew all there was to know about everyone sooner or later, so all that really mattered was did you get along with everybody, did folks like you, could you produce, did you have any real guts, and were you a giver or a taker? Alaska had an oversupply of takers, but many who came in as takers remained to find themselves givers.

Peculiar thing about Alaska, though. It never made anybody successful who didn't have it all to begin with. Nobody beat the odds up north who wouldn't have been a winner right where he was to start with. Losers in the States didn't get another chance up North, where it was tougher going. Losers lost twofold against the precarious challenge of the North, but in Alaska the people were nicer, and sorrier, and more willing to help the wife and kids.

Girls coming north to snare husbands found the same percentage stacked against them. Alaska's he-man male population so far outnumbered the women a girl might figure that with statistics as well as distance on her side, she couldn't miss. Oh, but she could, and did. Pretty girls had to beat the boys off. They mar-ried from a wide choice and sooner or later, when they were good and ready. Maiden ladies in their 30s with glasses, weight problems, or missionary faces, pure and unpretty, got nowhere. Government workers and schoolteachers who went to Alaska with two-year contracts and high hopes often returned as man-less, intact, and innocent of attack as when they arrived.

Alaskan men may have been lonesome (never for very long!), but they were neither desperate nor blind. Numbers of lone and lithesome ladies were available, too, for the mere pleasure of his company, with no strings. And with a steak din-ner thrown in, the hi-fi soft, the fireplace glowing, and the whiskey in the glasses.

As for Pegge Parker who went North single and left single? Um-m, well, I had my hand held a few times under the great skies, but not so tight I couldn't let go.

The very first Fairbanks dinner party I attended began with an *engraved* invita-tion! "Formal" was noted in the corner. So green, so newly-arrived-from-the-nation's-capital was I that I ignored the formal bit. I did not know that my host-ess, Stella Wann, very handsome and sociable, was one of the town's most seri-ous-minded "nice" party givers. *Formal* meant white gloves to here, gown to the floor.

I arrived in a simple Garfinckel number with a knee-skimming skirt, to which I had added a string of pearls, a whiff of Arpege, and a Washington air. Candle-light and cocktails greeted me, music and the lavish décor of fresh flowers flown in that afternoon from Seattle. There were all the men in tuxedos, like a stack of black-and-white jacks of spades! And by the flickering fireside, all the town's establishment, the wives, arrayed in divine little supper gowns (some air-parcelled from Bergdorf's, having been spotted in the Sunday *Times*), and here and there I caught the glitter of very real jewels. Awed at my error and without retreat, I mur-mured something about my trunks not having arrived and hid in a shadowy cor-ner behind somebody's dirndl skirt.

Formal in Fairbanks did indeed mean just what it does in Washington. You didn't have senators or diplomats or the White House among the black ties, but you had *style,* all you could put on! Fairbanks upon occasion played host to the famed and mighty, and when called upon it had all that any RSVP ever demanded, over-muchly so!

Of course, the inescapable price Alaskans paid for living in one another's pockets, so close together in isolation, was the banishment of privacy, the solace of a world of one's own, the myth of anyone keeping a secret for very long. The mukluk telegraph circulated the news faster than the *News-Miner* and covered trackless miles without telephones from Barrow to Juneau, from Candle to Fox or from Anchorage to Anywhere. Not only did outrageous, shameful, funny-as-hell, real dirty and raw stories crackle all over the place, but old-timers kept the pot hot with warmed-over stories good as new with a fiction twist o' lemon added. One of the funniest, which I suspect was neither new nor true, concerned an Eskimo lady known as Lou. Only this lady was a raving beauty known as Molly who thawed the ice and reheated your coffee with the warmth of her smile and other charms. Molly's igloo sat high upon the barren shores of Kotzebue. Well, it seems Molly was famous for her friendly hospitality all over Alaska's most northern wilderness until one day she got Religion and closed her door to her admirers forever.

Not only did she get religion, she got remorse as well. And things got so bad, Molly sat down and began writing letters to all the boys. "Dear Charlie, I have sinned. I got religion. Here is $10 you give me." Ten-dollar bills in Dear Charlie letters went all over the Territory—not all of them from Molly, though all signed "Molly"! A favorite prank to play on a newlywed couple was to send the bride-groom a Letter from Molly (and a $10 bill) and let him explain it all to his new bride.

The heritage of combined legend and tenacious memory, especially among the ladies, who could positively *compute* their "recollections," once caused me painful difficulties with a routine club column news story.

There is an esteemed ladies' organization in Fairbanks composed of the "original founders," a vintage DAR-type group which shall remain nameless. At the time, the club was planning a large anniversary dinner to celebrate its historic founding. They had programs printed, engaged a speaker, spent a slice of their treasury on decorations, favors, and a photographer. The unfortunate lady put in charge of publicity made a special trip to the paper to consult me in person. "Since this is for our anniversary," she fussed nervously, "we thought it would be appropriate to tell the history of our members and how they first came to Alaska."

Setting a match to dynamite, she bravely suggested we do several drafts of the club members' early histories, put everything in writing, and get it all approved by the club president first. That way we would be absolved of blame, error, bodily harm, and libel! We wrote with exceeding care about how the town's "original" ladies had come to the wild and brassy, boom bustin' Northlands "many years ago" (but not too many), how they had all come as nurses and school teachers and housekeepers and on errands of mercy to retrieve ill or erring fathers or brothers. (Dance hall girls were only in the movies!) Going to Alaska in the early days wasn't exactly like a brave wife in a covered wagon going west with her lawfully wedded husband and kids.

In the gold rush days of the roaring 1900s, single women who went North had their own reasons and stories, all of them personal and intensely private and not to make items for any club's anniversary.

Eventually—on their insistence that this was a good idea—we got a draft approved over the telephone. More names were added, more gingerbread was larded in, but the "histories"—I had the spoken word—were perfectly all right!

When the paper came out a few nights later, my phone jumped two feet off my desk and hovered in midair. The impact of the story was noisy and speedy—but profitable. The *News-Miner* sold out every copy while the ink was still wet. The pity of it all was these incredible ladies from whatever background were genuine heroines of real-life struggles and crises, more pulsating, rending and thrilling than anything Jack London or Edna Ferber ever wrote about.

Speaking of Edna Ferber—when she went to Alaska to do her on-the-spot research for a later and lesser saga called *Ice Palace,* she too heard tales to throb in her notebook. Real tales about real people. But when I picked up a copy of *Ice Palace,* I quickly saw that Edna Ferber's book would cause no one embarrassment or anguish—the only anguish over the whole thing was the fact that so great a talent—and such rich material—resulted in Edna Ferber's rock-bottom *worst* book!

Broadway's acerbic Lillian Hellman also came our way and lingered in the Lathrop apartments for an unplanned stay. We did not shudder at what merciless truth in Broadway play form might result from a visit with the creator of the *Little Foxes* and *Children's Hour*. Lillian Hellman came to Fairbanks en route to Moscow to attend some cultural affairs and to do some *New Yorker* pieces on the Soviet Union. Bad weather grounded her for days. Where to put up a famous playwright in the dead of winter?

A Ladd Field Quonset would not do. The Nordale was jammed. Someone had mentioned to Miss Hellman if she had any trouble in Fairbanks, "go see Cap Lathrop's right-hand girl: Miriam Dickey." The careful Lillian Hellman had written down the name, and indeed she did go see Miriam Dickey and Miriam put her up in her own attractive suite in the Lathrop building. It turned out to be a productive arrangement. Lillian Hellman can cook.

"Nobody believes me," she protested, "but I'm a great cook! I'd rather cook than write. My cooking is a little of this and a throw-in of that, and it's good, old-fashioned Jewish, but try me. I'm enthusiastic; I've got lots of time; I can cook for ten!" And she did. Miriam, delighted with her good housekeeping guest, invited in all of the Lathrop girls.

With the celebrity wrapped in an apron and walking around in the kitchen in her stocking feet ladling up mountains of what she called Jewish-American stew, we were treated to more than six-hour simmered beef. We relished a rare earthy side of Lillian Hellman, off stage. "You know," she confided, soup-spooning her own pungent brew, "I've a Russian book here and I'm trying to cram in a few vital phrases. When I get to Moscow I'm going to have to ask for a powder room in public places sooner or later. Do you know what horrible words you have to learn in Russian to ask for a toilet? Something like 'oo-bor'd-nik!' No wonder they have so little plumbing. No one can pronounce it!"

She was even better than her cooking. We hated to lose her to the Russians.

In my two years in Alaska, I had only one genuine dogsled ride and that was with a young Eskimo driver behind me mushing big white wolf-faced malamute dogs. I had just landed in a Navy plane on the frozen surface of the Arctic Ocean. It was early June. I had joined a group of United States Navy geologists making one of many surveys for wartime emergency oil supplies that could be pipelined thousands of miles to accessible areas farther south.

My young Eskimo on his dogsled had come to meet the plane out of casual curiosity. He wore a light fur parka, head tossed back, and his handsome face was so Asian, so tanned and oriental, I swore the land bridge theory of the Eskimos' origin must be true.

"Do you speak English?" I asked him almost shyly. He was my first real Eskimo, and I simply didn't know what to expect.

"Of course. What else?" my real Eskimo shrugged gracefully, smiling a big-toothed, very white grin. "Would you like a ride on the sled over to the Will Rogers-Wiley Post memorial," he asked, pointing, "just over there?"

The ride behind seven white fluffy sled dogs to the scene of the 1935 crash of two famous personalities (the plane actually went down in icy Walapa Lagoon nearby) brought me to the ugliest memorial I have ever seen! American school children and others had sent voluntary contributions to erect a "fitting" memorial to the dashing, eye-patched pilot and the beloved cowboy humorist. The mercy of it was that the marker, completed in 1938, was probably never seen by the donors. My notebook records that there was an inscription on the marker reading "A tribute to two world heroes from the citizens of Hillsboro, Texas." And at the base of the stone marker an arrow pointed to the location of the crash in the icy lagoon. Mud and a few pebbles and rock—even considering the treeless wild remoteness of Barrow—hardly seemed adequate as a final tribute to such giant personalities.

The wind blew in a balmy gust, the snow and ice all about us was pink-misted and spongy with first thaw. How incredible, I thought: just up there, somewhere not too far away, is the *North Pole!* We were standing just outside Barrow on the extreme northern tip of Alaska, the farthest-north town on the American continent. This unreal settlement is a great tourist attraction in the summer season, and no wonder, but it still seems a far-out trip just to take a few snapshots and to mail post cards from the "top of the world."

Alaska's hinterland survives on light plane transport. Wien Airlines' little cargo and passenger planes went everywhere all winter long in unbelievable weather. The miracle is how few accidents they and other bush airlines had. When a plane went down, there was rarely loss of life. I walked away from a few very minor unscheduled landings myself, dusting the seat of my pants. We just radioed for a spare part. When another plane flew it in, we took off again.

Bush flying in the Arctic in winter, stopping in little villages with names like Yakutat, Nyac, and Unalakleet (I was once delayed a week there) provided a tangy addition to my news beat. In one town I was taught to play something called Pullman poker. What I really learned for a lifetime was how fast you can lose money at poker! There were no "learners" or beginners at Alaskan Pullman poker, only players. My ten bucks was still warm from my timid little hand when it was snatched away from me, *lost* at the first snapping *deal* of the little plastic cards.

Alaskan Eskimo women seemed to me a sad and pathetic lot. If they were young and pretty, some white no-good with a few bucks in his pocket and a bottle in his hand always got them. With or without formalities or much consentin'!

The bloom of beauty vanished fast. They went to fat, toothlessness, and worse, all too soon. A Jesuit priest from Boston (who loved the Broadway Theater and his late-arriving copies of the *New Yorker* second only to God) despaired of what the White Man with his liquor, money, and disease had done to destroy the Eskimo, physically and morally.

There in his godforsaken little Bering seacoast town of Kotzebue, 50 miles north of the Arctic Circle, facing Siberia, he struggled to teach the Decent Life: to baptize, wed if possible, to bury the townspeople, and to keep the women out of white-trash's clutches.

Even he knew it was almost a hopeless task, although on Sunday mornings his little chapel was all but filled with oily, smiling, nose-sniffling, applecheeked native women, with fur bundled babies.

"My hope," the Jesuit confided in a polished Boston accent, "my only hope is the kids. Look at them. Aren't they magnificent! Born up here in this frozen Nothing-and-Nowhere, yet so strong and smart, so rosy with health, so quick and eager to learn! Eskimos make good mechanics. The Army's found that out. And these youngsters, properly schooled and encouraged, can eventually hold jobs and learn to support themselves. It may be hopeless, but I try to get these kids started so that they can grow up immune to the white corruption which long ago claimed their parents."

Eskimo children, the good Father's precious lambs-to-be-saved, were indeed merry-eyed, shrieking, racing, giggly, dolly-faced and utterly captivating. Little girls wore hair ribbons and cotton dresses over their fur parkas. Boys were brown-skinned and handsome, quick to hunt and fish with their fathers, but I observed they were often heartless and abusive to their sled dogs. I have strong Walt Disney ideals about the children of nature and their pets who are wild or near-wild animals. Here, in reality, I found quite a heartless attitude. Eskimos were quite indifferent to their white furred dogs. Only when there were some fluffy white husky puppies around did the children play with them and treat them affectionately as pets. Full grown and trained to haul loads harnessed to the dog team, the animals lost their pet appeal and were treated as beasts to be mastered and commanded with a whip.

The most ambitious assignment of my Alaska days was an observation flight down the entire length of the Aleutians, to the very last dot on the map in that long, trailing, bony finger of islands pointing across the Bering Sea to Russia and Japan. That last dot in the chain was chill, heavily-misted, fog-frothed Attu. You arrive, gaze about in silence, but don't believe you are there.

No Navy man who has had to do an 18-month—or longer—stretch in the Aleutians has a kind word for them. But to a touch-and-go sightseer, they were like a glimpse of original creation: moist island green-on-green, silvered with a gauzy, smoky fog, silent and primeval, without people, without sound.

Although modern development and modern defense have made considerable inroads on the most strategic islands, and we have weather stations, tracking stations, the Coast Guard, Navy bases, fisheries, schools, villages and some sheep ranches, the mood of silence and isolation hovers like the fog. Just beyond the military bases and the runways and trim warehouses and immaculate quarters is another world—primeval, untouched.

These empty islands look today as they must have appeared to Vitas Bering, that Great Dane who first explored this lone sea for the Imperial Russian navy. Bering was not after islands, of course, nor to prove, as he did, that Asia and the American continent are not joined. He scoured the cold, colorless sea and pushed vainly through the accursed fog, straining and driven for what all explorers backed by kings and Tsars seek: gold, land, wealth in any form, something unseen, unimagined, unknown before!

Bering never discovered the Alaskan mainland because he could not *see* it through the unremitting fog. A pity that nothing more glorious than death from scurvy awaited Bering on the way home. Although the ocean of his trial, disappointment, and death was named for him, it was to another crew member that the richest nugget of discovery came, quite by accident. A German botanist, George Steller, observed and studied with intense fascination a beautiful blue bird—surely this bird was the same as the blue birds of the American Carolinas, and if that were true, the expedition had not failed. It had somehow reached the offshore waters of America! The scientist rejoiced, thrilled with his "proof," but a little blue bird is a thin trophy for an entire expedition!

In addition to Steller's bird, the rich, fur-bearing sea otter was observed in the Aleutian chain. If there were no gold, furs would have to provide the wealth for Russian craving, and indeed it did. A fur rush eventually brought more Russians across the misty sea and almost totally decimated the priceless little sea otter.

I was a lot luckier than Vitas, or else I had picked a better season of the year. On Adak we had one full day of sparkling, blinding, radiant sunshine. It was celebrated exactly like wave fever in Southern California when the Surf's up! Everyone ran out of quarters yelling: *"Sunzout!* Hey, you guys—*Sunzout!"*

This delirious shriek sent everybody at the base rushing out of doors. Topless GIs—in sunglasses—luxuriated in the glow of the strange bright stuff on their mushroom-white skin.

There may be nothin' like a dame, but in the Aleutians the sun can strip the Navy even faster!

As though sun weren't enough, that night we had an hour or two of unearthly moonlight before the fog drifted in, wrapping everything in thick grey wool. From Attu our old bucket seat C-47 went north to the remote, rarely visited or even barely remembered Pribilof Islands, St. Paul and St. George. Fur-bearing seals know about them, though, and this well-timed tour included finding them by the thousands, beached for the spring mating season.

We happened to land in the Pribilofs on a Friday evening. I remember it was Friday because of the Russian Orthodox Church service. I have never landed in a strange hinterland of the world and rushed from the plane straight for the nearest church, but this was different. Everybody on board hurried right along with me. On this fantastic seal island in the Bering Sea stands a wooden bulb-domed Russian church where the services are as lavish and as musical as they must have been in the Old World.

Native singing of the Russian mass was a sonorous chorale. Islanders may not have comprehended a glimmer of what it was all about, but they sang in a lusty chorus, thrilling to hear. The church was ablaze with candles and from the ceiling hung a large, glittering crystal chandelier (*where* had it come from? How had it gotten way out here?). Icons, with black-eyed, black-bearded portraits of the Savior inlaid with silver and gold, gleamed from the altar. Most splendid of all was the white Russian Orthodox priest arrayed in all his embroidered gold and white vestments.

The next day I went to interview the tall, distinguished priest in his quite modern and attractive bungalow. Rich Persian carpets covered the floors, fine curtains hung at cheerful windows, a powerful short-wave radio stood on a table in a book-lined den. I have long since forgotten his name and his story, but I do remember being impressed with this sophisticated and scholarly human being so isolated yet so at home on these islands, a local chief among the natives. His range of knowledge of the world was impressive, considering he never left the islands. He read a vast number of books and late newspapers, and he did have his short-wave radio. If he lacked intellectual companions, he indulged himself for that omission with a surprising hobby. He grew orchids. Tenderly, devotedly he cared for hundreds of rare specimens in a large, well-heated greenhouse he had built himself. New plants, ordered from catalogs from incredibly distant places, were flown in whenever a plane was detailed to the Pribilofs. On his bare, treeless island 300 lonely miles from the Alaskan coast this urbane, knowledgeable man reveled in escape to a make-believe tropical jungle brimming with fairy flowers.

I marveled at him as I said goodbye and walked on in unreality down the beach to see the famed Alaskan seals. There on the island's forlorn, black, gritty beach of volcanic ash were hundreds of noisy, smelly, flipping, flopping honking satin-wet blubbery seals! The slaughter season was not yet upon them. Mercifully I saw none of that. I moved forward silently, scarcely breathing as I approached a pile of sleeping seals. Like kittens or puppies they flung themselves in a criss-cross heap on top of one another. I reached down and for a swift moment managed to put my hand on the head of a sleeping baby seal. He was warm and wet and soft as down. Big, soft, liquid brown eyes opened sleepily—then with a shudder and honk of panic he flopped away from me with incredible speed.

I wrote no story about the appealing furry, pathetic seals because I could not bear to hear the details of their slaughter with baseball-type clubs, which was to begin in early July.

The long trip down the Aleutians did not end for me with the assignment completed and the suitcases home and unpacked. I kept thinking:, If that plane had kept on going from Attu, it would have landed in Japan. And just beyond Japan was China.

The Pacific world did not seem so remote from us in Fairbanks. Alaskans, for sheer survival and necessity, were in the air age almost as soon as they got out of dogsleds. The airplane not only held the vast territory together, it linked us to the world. Alaskans thought ambitiously that Fairbanks was the "only" place for a direct link with the Orient, and for coming polar shortcuts to Europe.

Our air importance and strategic location gave Fairbanks two air bases, Ladd and Eielson. And something more in those late days of World War II: the Russian Air Mission. Since early 1942, an airlift of American planes bound for the Soviet Union changed hands in Fairbanks. Soviet pilots and technicians came there and were trained how to fly and maneuver American aircraft. Then the Soviets flew them to Siberia and eventually to the besieged Second Front, against the Nazis. In Stalin's day American crews and technicians were not permitted to deliver and land the planes on Russian soil. Much, much smarter for the Russians to move in on the Americans and learn everything possible about the American airbases, the American defense system and the Alaskan terrain.

Ah, me. This was called "enlightened self-interest." The Russians *were* fighting the Germans and annihilating Hitler's master plan as well as his armies, but it did seem we were leaving our own back door open to future danger. The Russian mission constantly increased. Eventually women and children joined the resident administrative staff. Russian children began to attend the Fairbanks public schools, but their mamas never came to PTA or made peanut butter sandwiches for the Brownies. The Russians brought strong international awareness into our midst. We would see them in pairs or in groups. The pilots in their grey-blue overcoats, fur hats, and boots were so young, so *blond*, so quick to laugh at their own stumbling English. Some of the interpreters were young Russian women who arrived looking like peasants in mourning. They wore black from head to toe. Within a few weeks, seeing female marvels for sale in Alaskan drugstores, they became platinum blondes with peach-beige cheeks and Revlon-red smiles and fingernails. They swooped up nylons, pretty dresses, silly sexy shoes with toe and heel cut out, and they wore their new, dazzling, American clothes on the job crawling in and out of cockpits and up and down hatch ladders.

The Russians, then our allies but never our friends, were restricted and cautious in their social contacts with people in town. But they were the town's big spenders, and as they shopped with U.S. dollars, they were very welcome. They shopped in a typically Russian manner: they took everything in sight! They might move in on a shoe store, for instance. Through an interpreter or speaking English, they would ask for "Shoes, all shoes, women's, men's, children's!"

Rolls of dollar bills came out of jodhpur trousers. What sizes? What colors? What kind of shoes? "All kinds, *any* kinds." Clerks would clean the shelves, and the Russians would haul away everything and load it onto a truck. Once they almost stripped the town of men's underwear, but then the town merchants remembered their regular customers and said no. In winter obtaining replacement stock would be impossible, or twice as expensive coming in by air. They finally sold the Russians only half their demands for BVDs. Supermarkets would also have been stripped to the walls if the Russian demands had been met in full. Sliced *white* bread was like angel food cake to them.

We wondered where they got their money, those fat rolls of dollars they so eagerly shoved across the counter. Then we decided it was just as well no one answered that question. It would be bad for taxpayers' morale. But at least the Soviet pilots got rid of their dollar rolls held together with rubber bands, as fast as the money came in—from whatever source.

Fur coats lured the comrades, and many were sold without any sales pitch for cool cash. The comrades got no bargains, but they did get good quality. Alaskan furs were not processed in the territory. They went outside as raw hides and returned to Fairbanks as the beautifully fashioned finished product. But the round-trip transportation was added to the price tag.

I was once asked by one of those very blonde, young pilots to try on a magnificent beaver coat so that he could get a better idea of how it looked on a girl. I not only modeled it for him but added my own oh's and ah's and "divines." Perhaps that did it. He counted out nearly $1000 cash and bought it. I glowed my assurance that the girl over there would love it. The pilot struggled with his English: "You are her size, leetle bit. Looks like you, leetle bit." Then with a click of heels to the clerk and a warm *"spaseeba"* (thanks) to me, he and the coat were gone.

This whiff of Russian romance was too intriguing. I had to study Russian. Someday, I reasoned, it would be very valuable. We are in business with the Russians forever. A knowledge of the language would get me in and out of a lot of places, I figured, and someday I could operate without government interpreters, if I could handle the language on my own. I had no idea I was stepping blithely into the Grand Canyon of difficult languages. I just made up my mind like a bulldog and sank my teeth into it, furiously determined to take it in through my pores if not through my head!

I found a Russian-born young teacher living in Fairbanks with her American engineer husband. She feared and despised the Soviets passing by on the streets. Bad, very bad. Communist dogs, she would hiss after them as we hurried to a lesson in my Lathrop apartment. "Americans," she dinned into me, "Americans not know these Soviets. But *I* know dem, what dey do!"

The textbooks we used for three increasingly, maddeningly difficult lessons a week (all grammar) had been ordered from New York but published in Moscow. All of the reading exercises contained heavy-handed propaganda praising Stalin and Lenin. They were a windfall for me. The propaganda passages so infuriated my teacher that she would pencil them out and make me skip them. "Lies, lies!" she would cry. "I give you my own sentences about the real Russia."

I continued the struggle with Russian for many years through a series of teachers. Alas, despite all the struggle I never even approached fluency. I had what might charitably be called a "grasp" of Russian, but even this much of the language was treasure beyond price later on.

Alaska was rapidly becoming a bridge to new horizons for me. For one thing, I was beginning to break into the New York newspaper and magazine market with articles then in great demand about the job opportunities and adventure in the northland for thousands of unsettled servicemen just back from the war. Go North, Young Man, Right Now, was a very inviting, sellable theme. (My little frontier town of Fairbanks has since grown to a big city of 30,000.) A large percentage of those Young Men who went north stayed and prospered in their fashion.

I wrote and wrote and wrote, night after night and all day Sunday. I had my goal, the checks were coming in, mounting up. It was now my intention to write my way around the world! I would start somewhere like China. Dig in. Write from there until I made the fare to the next place. If I wrote very well, fine. I would travel far and see a lot. If not, I wouldn't get very far, now would I? It was all up to me. Self-confidence grew giant-sized in the giant north!

What is it that gives our lives their path and direction? Fate? I have never taken any mystic or mysterious forces seriously. Perhaps that Moving Finger writes and having writ moves on. Perhaps like Omar in the *Rubaiyat,* we go in and out of doors already marked and held open for us. Perhaps nothing important in our lives is ever an accident or a coincidence.

I have traveled the world over, lived for times in strange places, and have had unexplained flashes of "Why, I've been here before! I've seen these people, I've been in this room, or hotel *before*—when it would have been impossible for me to have been there before.

I readily dismiss all this and sleep soundly. But I do know how easily one's direction can be changed by a missed plane, a trifling change of plans which leads to an extraordinary meeting, how a phone call, or letter never mailed, or a trip unplanned, or taking that wrong bus can set your life on a whole new track. Accident or mysterious destiny? I do not know, but in a sense Alaska was my unplanned "accident" simply because of a chance meeting with one man.

There have been three men in my life. Two I married, one of whom is dead. The third was Alaskan George Wallace who unpleasantly and ruthlessly tore up all my roots and sent me out in the world to *learn!*

"How dare you write to inform others," he thundered at me, "when you know nothing yourself?" He commanded, and I—at whatever cost—obeyed.

In this age of exploding youth I often think of George Wallace. To the bare feet of moral draft dodgers, protesters, hoodlums, and slobs he would be a nail. And after ignorance and inexperience had *felt* the nail, the rest of the message would be equally tough: everything in this world must be worked for, earned, dug out by hand, in sweat and blood! Nothing is free, least of all freedom—and knowledge—which takes a lifetime. You have an opinion? Show me your proof, your research, and study, tell me what first-hand investigation you have made. Then, maybe, I have five minutes for your "opinion," son!

I was sent to interview George Wallace one dreary dark-skied winter day. A memo had come to my desk from the Lathrop Company's front office! George Wallace, VIP, General Motors, European division, lives in Geneva; his wife is an Italian countess. He's important, knowledgeable, may be difficult, dislikes press. Born in Yukon Territory, self-educated, remarkable success story. Tough.

George Wallace, when I found him, was reading the air edition of the *London Times* and wished not to be disturbed. "I never give interviews," he dismissed me with half a glance, returning to his paper. "Oh," I murmured coolly, turning away, "I've met people like you in Washington."

"Washington?" he looked up. "You came up here from Washington? Why?" He then interviewed me. But at least I kept him talking and I got a little, but very little, out of him. "What do you write in the paper?" he asked finally. "I will look especially for your column tonight."

It had not exactly been my best day. It was the deadly, immobilized winter season. I had no strong grist in my mill for that afternoon's paper, but I did have one little item he found quite unforgivable!

Among the bits and pieces of local news, I had written a little feature story about a young Yugoslav woman who was raffling a handmade tablecloth to aid royalist refugees from Tito's Communist State. The woman had brought the story down to the paper. She had been so appealing and had made out such a hard-luck story about the people who "had lost everything" that I gave her lots of sympathy and lots of space.

It was this trifling space-filler which had the misfortune to come under the scathing eye of George Wallace. He telephoned the newspaper. "Would the young lady reporter come to the Nordale Hotel lobby?" He wished to discuss something in the evening newspaper with me.

When I arrived, he was waiting with the paper folded back to the Yugoslav story. "Tell me," he began, his manner icily restrained, "where did you get your information on Yugoslavia? I see. The woman came in and told you her sad tale. Did she bring along the tablecloth? You say here it is quite beautiful and all hand embroidered. Did you examine the cloth personally before you wrote that? Do you know any more about lace tablecloths than you do about Yugoslav royalists, or Tito, or what happened in Europe? I doubt it!"

I had *stepped* on the nail.

By the time he had finished his briefing on Yugoslavia I could have written a thesis in Croatian. George Wallace had made his point. I crawled home, mouse-sized. The next day I found a slip of paper rolled into my typewriter. The names of books I must send away for, at once, to read. He never *gave* me a book to read.

In fact, he never *gave* me anything but a shove and the certainty that I was totally unschooled and uninformed (but I could work at it, over a lifetime).

He was a man of privilege, power, and influence, but he never wrote a letter on my behalf, opened any door, arranged any interview, picked up the phone and said a single helpful or right word to anyone. I once asked him to. He ignored the request and charitably forgave me.

It has taken a few years, but I am now better prepared to handle a story on Yugoslavia. I have observed Marshal Tito personally at close range and I have, at long last, traveled all through Yugoslavia. I could now face George Wallace and debate socialism, Eastern Europe, Tito, and tablecloths with informed firepower it has taken years and firsthand experience to attain. Which is what he was trying to tell me back there in Fairbanks.

There is a pearl of advice here for parents and teachers, who lament inability to strike fire, rouse *motivation* from the young generation. I owe George Wallace—and the nail—my discovery of the world. I still have a long way to go and am still learning.

I sold an article to *Reader's Digest* that I had been working at on and off since I first arrived and began meeting the last of the original Old-timers. Out of many a pungent interview and from endless yarnin' I compiled the human history of the Alaskan Ice Pool, the still-legal lottery wherein the United States mail may be used to place bets on the day, the hour, and the minute the ice will move in the Nenana River (not the Yukon, but one of its tributaries). The coming of spring, signaled by the thawing ice, after a frozen siege of dreary, dark winter months, creates tremendous excitement. In the North, sweepstake fever runs giddy and high. Money moves. Bets and tickets snap across the counters. Sometimes win-happy gamblers buy a block of "time" as a sure win and lay out a couple of hundred dollars for tickets. Eva McGown is the hottest ticket seller in Fairbanks. Tickets bought from her are supposed to be extra lucky—the luck o' the Irish being an innocent myth. Not a single winner ever placed his bets with Eva.

My Ice Pool history told the stories of the winners, described the wild joy of a sudden windfall of thousands of dollars (the jackpot varied from half a million on up), to the inevitable jolting aftermath, the tragedies, bitter quarrels, legal battles and for some death—like the fellow who bought an airplane and died in its crash within weeks of his winning.

One day an old-timer shuffled into the office of the *News-Miner* with a newspaper bundle under his arm.

"Hey, girlie. You, come 'ere!" he rasped through missing teeth. In a mysterious manner, making certain we were unobserved and no one could hear what he said, he thrust the bundle at me.

"You're the girl writing all about the Ice Pool? Well, I want ya to take this and keep it. No, don't open the paper. Put it away somewheres, not here. Tell ya what 'tis an' why I'm givin' ya this now: Ya got there the first clock used in the first Ice Pool. It's valuable. It's a ship's chronometer. Mos' accurate timepiece inna world, you know that? This clock gotta little hole drilled in the side, done by a jeweler. We attached a wire to the clock. When the ice moved, a long wire attached to a pole dug in the ice jerked this fine wire and stopped the clock. Whoever bet on that exact time, or closest to it, won all th' money, see?"

Charlie paused, glancing again over his shoulder. He had had a few nips, but obviously getting rid of his clock was urgent, like slipping the noose on the albatross. I was to learn why.

"Now, ya know, winnin' a bet is like a game o' cards. There can be no question of fair play. The clock hadda be dead right. So, to make hunnerd percent sure, we made it a rule, right at the beginnin': each year the Ice Pool committee would buy a brand new clock. It would be used only once. We decided to make sure by throwing the clock in the river after the pool was over. I was supposed t' do it. Well, damn—well, now—honnes' ta God, girl—them clocks cos' a lotta money. I dinn' wanna keep it for *myself*, but I couldn't just throw it in the river neither. I threw a cigar box with stones inside and hid this here clock all these years."

The Old-timer glanced at me sharply. I gently tried to reassure him, inwardly thrilled that he hadn't "throwed" so valuable a keepsake into the icy waters of the Nenana. He greatly feared, as the years passed, he would head down that last trail in his sleep some night and when people came and found him they would also find the clock and think he had "stole th' damn thing!"

Charlie wanted me to keep it because I "done a good job a writin' the history" and if I had it nobody would think *I* had "done wrong."

Well, Charlie's conscience-clock, his albatross, stayed with me longer than either of us intended. I still have it!

My intention was to present it with the story of old Charlie Wilson, in fact in his "honor," to the University of Alaska.

But meanwhile, I could make no clock donation because as tough, old Jack Daniel sippin' old-timers often do—Charlie lived on and on for years. I kept up a running correspondence with Fairbanks' famous Eva McGown, each time asking if Charlie were still around. "Indeed he is, and, dear girl, when I mentioned something to him about a clock he once gave you he had a fit! 'For God's sake, *keep it* and shut up about it,' he says to tell you. He was so upset!"

Charlie Wilson's clock—the ship's chronometer used in the first Ice Pool.

Years passed. The clock had no choice but to sit out its days with me—all over the world. First, it went into an attic in Pennsylvania. Then it went by Cunard to England, finally shifting to the Polish liner, *Batory*, for the final lap to India via Suez. It passed through Indian hands in Bombay Customs without a glance, journeyed onward to Delhi by train. From India the clock eventually came home on an Italian liner, an ignored household effect. Back in New York it tarried briefly in White Plains, then set forth again on a bauxite freighter out of Montreal, venturing southward to the Caribbean. For three years in the tropics it resisted white ants, termites, rot and mildew in Jamaica. It never, in all this long odyssey, ever ticked or tocked. I simply polished its mahogany case with lemon oil and left its broken interior for repairs, someday. Now it is back in America. Age and travel and the oil polishing and many tissue wrappings have given the clock a gem's glow. But the time has come for it to go to its true home, back to Alaska.

Charlie Wilson is gone now, so I cannot anger or embarrass him by honoring him. Someday I will take the clock—and I hope the children—back to the land of my heart.

Alaska's Gaudiest Gamble —The Ice Pool

Condensed from

National Home Monthly

Pegge Parker   .

IT was gray and cold in Nenana, Alaska, last May 5. A raw wind whipped rain across the Tanana River, tributary of the mighty Yukon. Yet the banks were crowded with spectators, their eyes glued on a gaily striped red-and-white pole standing out on the river's ice. Nearby a man with a microphone shivered; he'd been camping on the spot for two days, awaiting this hour.

"It's 4:30," he was saying, "and the main sheet of ice is beginning to weave like the deck of a storm-tossed ship. Big slabs are beginning to leap upward. . . . A wave of muddy water just washed over the ice. . . . She's giving way! The center cake is gone! Ladies and gentlemen, the ice is OUT! At exactly 4:40:42 p.m."

Whistles and sirens shrieked; Alaska for the 29th time gave way to the riotous bedlam that celebrates its gaudiest annual gamble, the Nenana Ice Pool.

This year's pot held $108,000, the

biggest ever. The owners of four of the $1 tickets sold had guessed the exact day, hour and minute when the pole sunk into the ice would move 100 feet, thus jerking a wire and stopping the official chronometer.

Eighty-year-old Mike Johnson, who has lived for the past ten years at the Pioneers' Home in Sitka, won one of the $27,000 slices. He said he would look up his partner of the gold rush of '98 and share his luck.

Another ticket, held by "The Federal Eleven," was owned by six bartenders and card-game operators at the Federal Bar in Anchorage, plus four barbers and one garbage collector.

This fantastic guessing game is played each year by thousands of gold miners, homesteaders, dance-hall girls, Eskimos, river-boat captains, and other Alaskans from the shores of the Arctic Ocean to the southern boundary of Yukon Territory.

The Nenana Ice Pool has paid out almost $2,000,000 to winners. It started in April 1917, when a workman in a railroad gang bet the boss, Tom Riggs, Jr., later governor of Alaska, that the ice would go out "before payday."

A nearby linesman threw down his axe, dug up some money. "I say she busts like plate glass hit by a baseball 'long about chowtime Saturday!" The gambling fever spread and a pool of $900 was quickly raised.

Each succeeding spring brought

Copyright 1946, Home Pub. Co., Ltd., 965 Bannatyne Ave., Winnipeg, Canada
(September, '46)

121

Pegge's article on the Alaskan Ice Pool was published in the September 1946 issue of Reader's Digest.

4

China

◆

(1946–48)

The song about a slow boat to China had not yet been written, but it would have been appropriate for my next chapter in learning. I decided to see the world, starting with what was nearest to me across the Pacific: China.

I ordered my first passport by mail from Washington. It came via Seattle, a trim little book with the usual wincing picture of the bearer inside. Then, suddenly terribly "worldly" and self-conscious about anything that bordered on giving away my greenhorn inexperience as a first-time tourist overseas, I booked passage to Shanghai on a freighter that had been used as a troop transport in World War II.

By sheer coincidence, I sailed on one of the most extraordinary passenger ships of all time. That ship of fools Katherine Porter wrote about was heading for Nazi Germany, but my *S.S. Marine Lynx* was going to China during the last struggling days before the Red Chinese revolution reached its climax and conquered all. And with us went hundreds of American missionaries, repatriating themselves "home" to China. The *"Lynx"* was virtually a chartered Ship of God, as the passengers were almost exclusively missionaries, with only a few last-minute vacancies being allotted to "civilians." The *Lynx* was the first to make the crossing after the war ended. Many of the missionaries had been in concentration camps, had survived dreadful ordeals at the hands of the Japanese. Now, here they were, young and very old, whole families, prayerful and thrilled to be going "back," totally oblivious, it seemed, to what drastic changes and alarming events were taking place every day "back" there where most of them had been born. They had spoken the language from birth, but they did not seem to communicate with reality. They had all lived through many of China's "disturbances" in the past, and they had no fear for the future.

As we moved steadily out to sea beyond San Francisco and that thrilling Golden Gate Bridge (I was so excited my teeth chattered!) the missionaries did not even glance back. They were below decks unpacking, getting organized, making plans for daily worship. When they returned to the upper deck where I had remained, straining my eyes, they were all ready for evening vespers with, seemingly, no lingering ties or memories for whatever they had bid farewell to in America.

That God had personally called them and that they had to respond, specifically for China, these sincere, intelligent, well-meaning Christians never doubted for a second.

As I moved among them, lived with them in close confinement for weeks, stood in chow lines, laundry queues, and looked in on their religious services, I began to have disturbed misgivings that 700 million Chinese, with a violent, passionately nationalist revolution well underway, had any place for them in the future of New China.

I was totally unsure and inexperienced, but I heard nothing from the handful of Chinese passengers on board that encouraged me to think the Chinese on the mainland were any less nationalist and racist (China for the Chinese, throw out the foreigners!) or that they awaited or "needed" all these childlike, Bible-ordained naïve people. The Christian Brotherhood on board, particularly some of the Southern Baptists from obscure towns in the deep South, and some of the Holy Roller, hellfire and sin-and-the-devil touting preachers from denominations unheard of, were downright ludicrous.

The prayer and preparation atmosphere aboard ship was like one unending Sunday morning. This could be oppressive. By sheer force of numbers the missionaries set the routine, occupied every lounge, the mess halls and all the cool, breezy leeside deck space. Non-missionaries were driven together in a tight little band of companionable isolation. We met every evening on one corner of the top deck for cigarettes, a drink, and escape. It was on many of these little deck gatherings that we aired the Chinese passengers' reaction to the missionaries. They were Chinese graduate students mostly in their late 20s or early 30s. No longer kids, they had been caught in the States by the war and had remained by simply extending their education indefinitely, taking more and more courses and degrees, usually on scholarships or grants.

Slickly, superficially Westernized, these Chinese were to me a whole new breed. High-strung, garrulous, opinionated, acerbic, and shrilly critical of the United States, they were blatantly ungrateful, unaware that they owed anything to their benefactors. What personal slights had they suffered, I wondered, to make them so arrogantly defensive? That America had sheltered and educated them, honored them with scholarships and years of hospitality, had no bearing on their attitude and point of view. The closer we came to China, the more Chinese, the more Asian, the more emotional they became. Also to us, the Americans, the more contemptuous. With subtle niceties they were even insulting. In their country, rapidly approaching, we would be the foreigners, the racial minority, the outsiders. At times, staring along the ship's railing at a Bible meeting or hymn singing, they would almost hiss their derision: "What good are they to China? Who asked them to come back? Not the Chinese! No Chinese wants foreign missionaries to come back to China. They go, without asking, because they are rich. And powerful. That is the way foreigners have always gone to China."

I listened in offended anger, barely able to discipline myself to observe and listen, not to argue. Because I had never set foot in China and knew nothing about the country firsthand, I remained silent, let the others do the talking.

"Missionaries stuff rice down coolies' throats," the students raved on. "China needs workers who can build, modern technicians, smart people with good education, clever men like engineers, scientists, doctors, agricultural people who can teach modern scientific farming, using chemical fertilizers, and to show us how to make our own modern chemicals. China needs teachers—many, many modern science teachers. Why does America not send us *useful* people to work for China, not worthless missionaries who degrade Chinese culture of which they are ignorant, who are big, protected, tax-free landowners, who eat the poor people's food?"

One added, "The old missionaries return and bring all their old faults with them. They are stupid. They have learned nothing. China has *changed*—as they will soon find out."

Passing the sweltering laundry room one morning, a young Chinese added another comment. Never removing the cigarette from the corner of his mouth, he remarked dryly, "On this ship, and back home in the States, Americans must do their own washing and scrubbing. When they get to China they will use Chinese as their servants and coolies!"

Although it was late summer, the days grew hotter, longer, more wearisome. The missionaries, crowded together without much privacy or a moment's escape, became irritable and quarrelsome. Christian charity was greatly strained.

As the blue Pacific swelled and rolled and the heat increased, petty inter-faith bickering exploded into full-blown quarrels.

Our ship of salvation needed air conditioning, Pope John, late-show movies, or shuffleboard and a swimming pool. It had none of these, and Jesus didn't save!

If the water hadn't been so wet, we might have had "protest marches" as one denomination battled another for the limited, cool shade for their eternal meetings.

Topside we had an Irish tempered, Irish-thirsting, sin-lovin' captain who hadn't set foot inside a church, even the Roman church, since his wedding day. He met delegations in his quarters with short patience. The missionaries had the run of the ship, the entire ship, what more did they want? Of all the crabbin', bitchin', hymnin', and prayin' buncha bastards he'd ever taken aboard, these were the livin' end!

Perhaps it was the overcrowding and the confinement, but as one of our top-deck civilians put it: life on a troop ship of Christian soldiers was a hell of a lot worse 'n a troop ship o' GIs!

Our Chinese students, of course, missed none of this. Foreign Christians couldn't even get along with one another, they sneered, what did they expect from civilized Chinese who have their own superior way of behaving, especially toward their inferiors!

Not long ago, looking up some early background on Mao Tse-tung when the Red Guard movement was at the height of its fury, I came upon a small gem of a book on China by Harry Swartz of *The New York Times*. Most books on China are like Edgar Snow's masterwork *The Other Side of the River*, which, including the index, runs to 810 pages. But Swartz's book is as slim as a pocket edition. Like a volume of poems, it is stripped of all that is extraneous, edited down to vital essentials. In referring to the role of missionaries and their impact upon the many passing eras of Chinese history, Swartz notes that despite all the years of intense, devoted efforts Christianity had "only peripheral and most superficial effects upon Chinese thinking." Even Buddhism, Asian in origin and character, did not survive in China in its original form. Over hundreds of years, the Chinese so ingeniously filtered and modified and adapted it that Buddhism on the mainland became a separate "Chinese" form of philosophy.

After my close association with the Chinese on the ship, I could appreciate the accuracy of Swartz's further observation that those Chinese who did become Christians were considered by fellow Chinese to be traitors—Westernized sell-outs to foreigners for personal gain.

Meanwhile, were the missionaries totally oblivious of the effect their jealous deck wars were having on the rest of us, especially on the Chinese students? Apparently so. They seemed so involved in their own virtual and self-concerned world they paid no attention to anyone else. I would occasionally see one or two senior missionaries refreshing or practicing their Chinese on one of the slick, cigarette-smoking students—the missionary all simpering, patronizing, my-dear-boy openheartedness, the Chinese, momentarily trapped and embarrassed, painfully polite, smiling constantly, exhaling a nervous string of "Yes, yes, yes!" Shipboard contact between the missionaries and the Chinese was so strained that I could easily anticipate what the relationship must be like on the mainland. What a polar gap existed, especially between many of the simple, rural-type missionaries of limited education beyond "Bible school," and the worldly, arrogant, super-sophisticated young Chinese intellectuals.

I was later to discover, of course, American missionaries of a far superior order, many of whom were Asian scholars who contributed vastly to China's culture through their translations, writings, and teaching. Many of today's most respected Far Eastern specialists, scholars, writers, diplomats and teachers are the sons and daughters of these missionaries. But they were not on my ship!

As we drew nearer the offshore approaches and entered the main channel leading to Shanghai, one of the most fascinating port cities of all time, I was chilled with anticipation. Our entrance was slow and tedious. We maneuvered the perilous channel with great care under the direction of a British pilot who had come aboard. The massive, unlovely, grey, scuffy hulk of the *Marine Lynx* slipped up the muddy Wangpoo and finally, with an exhausted moan, docked at a pier on the Shanghai waterfront. Confusion and excitement ran high among the passengers, who forgot past bitter differences in frenzied preparations to land and go ashore. Lining the decks, they pointed and yelled and waved and strained their eyes to recognize welcoming delegations.

The Chinese students were clustered together in a segregated unit, apart from the foreigners. Anticipation of what awaited them returning to their families after years in America was shrilly unnerving. Clinging momentarily together in certainty before they were parted in great uncertainty on shore, disbursing among manifold relatives, the students in a frenzy of confusion then began hauling out luggage and running up and down the decks, up and down stairways, shrieking in Chinese.

When permission to go through Customs was given, they were the first ones down the gangway without a backward glance, parting word of thanks or goodbye or offer of help or hospitality. America was very far behind them, forever.

I kept a diary of my first China travels and experiences. Re-reading it now, I can relive that first fear and dread of stepping ashore, even from the unlovely, unhappy decks of the *Marine Lynx,* into the roiling unknown of Shanghai in 1946! I was overcome with my own aloneness. Along with the missionaries I too felt woefully unwelcome, unwanted, and worse, *unnecessary!*

I was a writer, but no one had sent me to China to write anything. Without a definite assignment, a waiting editor needing 5000 words by cable or even air-mail, I was just sight-seeing, idiotically afloat, in nothingness—attempting to make my way in a country divided between two factions, struggling to stave off imminent collapse or the inevitable yielding to the powerful new force of Mao-style Marxism.

At this low, low point a reassuring young woman—who happened to be a State Department vice consul arriving in Shanghai to take up a new post at the American Consulate—moved to my side and said in a low voice, "Don't look so scared. It's okay. Stick by me, kid. I'll get you off this tub okay. Don't worry. I've stepped off boats before with five bucks in my pocket. If you don't have a hotel room for tonight, you can bunk in with me at the Cathay. Don't panic. You'll be okay. Just don't lose your passport. Keep in between your teeth if necessary, but forgodsake, don't let it out of your sight. The queasies don't last long. You'll get onto Shanghai in a week or so. Just take one thing at a time."

I did have the queasies. Night had fallen over the city blacking out most of the dock area before we cleared Customs and completed all the landing formalities. I was finally "ashore"! Ashore in Shanghai, China!

A group of American newsmen having nothing better to do that evening had come down to meet the ship because the wife of a *Chicago Daily News* correspondent, who had remained invisible during the tedious voyage, was also disembarking.

From them I gained entry to the oddly named apartment-hotel, the Broadway Mansions, the most decorous press club in Asia. The Broadway Mansions was a modern beige-stone tower located just off the Bund by Soochou creek, a Chinese canal teeming with sampans. The Broadway overlooked the British Consulate with its regal formal gardens and the Shanghai waterfront heavily lined with ships of every flag and the fascinating Chinese junks, some with big black eyes painted on the bows!

The first five or six floors of the Broadway were occupied by an American Army advisory group and their dependents, and the top floors were taken over, luxuriously, by the foreign press. The dining room was a modified penthouse with garden terrace and bar and festive strings of colored lights to enhance the magic view of the city by night.

I felt safe and sheltered in my quarters until I learned the tab was $35.00 a day, not including meals!

At that I panicked but said nothing. I had an immediate roof over my head. I would look around tomorrow.

Shanghai in its final days under Generalissimo Chiang Kai-Shek was, even for the experienced and *employed,* chaotic. One heard incredible rumors and could believe nothing. Tension and fear and insecurity permeated everything. We lived from week to week. At a dinner party one hostess quietly let it be known which of the items on her walls, tables or in her den and dining room were for sale, cash-and-carry and cheap.

Outwardly I had been amazed to find an Oriental city looking little different from a hazy postcard picture of London. There were enormous British banks, British-built hotels, office buildings and public administration buildings from which poured British and foreign staff every noon hour. The Bund in particular—in large outline and silhouette—looked very Western. Only at night when department stores, theaters, and restaurants lit up their Chinese neon signs and the streets were jammed with Chinese did the Eastern accent emerge. For all that the great British banks with their superb brass lions out front looked so imposing, around the corner, vendors and merchants in those uncertain times had already reverted to the barter system.

Paper money, wildly inflated, was like play money. You never carried money in a wallet or purse. You toted your cash in paper bags. Filthy, ragged paper notes were tied in bundles with grocery string. No one had time to count it; you judged the thickness with a press of the fingers. If you sent a prepaid cable to New York, you brought your money in a satchel and traveled by taxi. That is precisely what I eventually came to: I sent a frightened SOS to those nice friendly editors back at the *New York Daily News* to whom I had sold so many Sunday pieces in the Alaska days. The "humane society," I called them. I was sure these nice editors would not abandon me, although I had set forth so cocksurily on my own! Just to survive, day to day, I had to be sustained with $100 a week. That was the message I nervously cabled them.

My cable brought an immediate advance of $400 with orders to return home. Rescued? No—I would not go home without seeing China or writing a single story. So I sent off another cable thanking them and returning the four hundred dollars.

Years later, on visits to the *News* in New York, I was still being introduced around the office on echoes of the shock wave that my action had created. "Here's that crazy kid who sent the money *back!*"

Spurred to last-ditch effort, I did indeed land a job. At the press club I heard that a small United States Army unit in Shanghai was without a PRO (press officer) and a situation had developed requiring urgent assistance. They were so desperate they would take anyone, immediately, so they took me.

The story was almost unbelievable. But then this was China in the midst of revolution. What would normally, intelligently be dismissed as totally impossible, in those days had to be examined, given a second thought.

A dramatic search-and-rescue mission had just begun to find and free five American airmen believed held captive in the wild mountain area called the Lololands. The Americans, believed to be lost pilots and crew of a missing World War II bomber, were reportedly being held as "slaves" by the primitive tribesmen. This attempted rescue of the American slaves from the strange aborigines, the Lolos, is about as close to real-life *Lost Horizons* as we'll come in the twentieth century.

The story began with a letter.

A Roman Catholic Bishop who had spent thirty years in the mountain wilderness, which stretches over a vast area between China and Tibet, sent an appealing letter to the American Ambassador in Nanking. The bishop's letter told our ambassador, Dr. John Leighton Stuart, that a small group of survivors of an American plane crash were possibly being held in captivity by mountain tribesmen, aborigines called Lolos. The Americans had been "seen" by native traders who brought back stories that the foreigners were working in the fields and were made to grind corn and carry water for their Lolo masters. They were in poor and emaciated condition, but they were *alive,* and something should be done immediately about rescuing them.

Remembering that China in those days of tension and near-collapse seethed with rumors impossible to confirm, and there was always the risk of overlooking half-truth buried even in the most fantastic story, the ambassador forwarded the letter to the American Graves Registration Service in Shanghai. This ghoulish-sounding agency performed a very worthwhile, humanitarian service. Their amazing accomplishments represented a sad success: nearly 3000 bodies and some cremated ashes of World War II dead were recovered from Manchuria in the far north all the way to the jungles of Thailand. Recovered remains were returned for appropriate burial in the United States, and careful documentation of recovered personal effects and identity tags officially closed the records on what had for years stood in vague, tragic suspense: missing and presumed dead.

Chinese villagers made possible the recovery missions of the AGRS. Many simple farmers braved Japanese punishment to conceal and bury American dead in the dark of night. Village elders who could write kept accurate records, dog tags, wallets—anything found on the body which would prove identity in later years. Sometimes they were paid for this service, but many times they refused money and had to be rewarded in more indirect ways. The important point was that they buried our dead and kept valuable records.

But the Lolo affair was something entirely different. These five Americans were *alive*. AGRS sent a reconnaissance mission into the hills and valleys of the Sikiang River region, the Lolo territory which lies in the general region of the Hump where so many planes had crashed.

Returning from the first exploratory look at the terrain and some careful interviews with the people in the main town, the team reported they were told the same story the Bishop had put in his letter to the ambassador. But American "slaves" after all these years making no attempt to escape? It seemed so improbable that it *couldn't* be true. I thought of how many pilots and crewmen I had interviewed who had seemingly come back from the grave, surviving harrowing experiences when their planes went down in the wild no-man's-land of the Himalayas. Many had walked out or crawled out, but the point was they *got out*, having crossed hundreds of miles, followed rivers when possible, lived on plants and insects—even fried bees, one told me. It had taken them months, but they had made it back alive.

But at the point of dismissal, responsibility to prove the story false fell on the AGRS unit and a thorough search was organized. Rumor it may be, but five men might be trapped out there as well.

A second carefully selected team was organized, headed by a young, extraordinarily well-qualified captain named Edward L. McAllister. I had met him during a briefing session when disguises were being considered. Should McAllister penetrate Lololand on foot disguised as a peddler and "see" the American captives with his own eyes to establish positive proof before a more elaborate rescue apparatus was setup? How could he contact them without endangering their freedom to move about? If contact was made, how could the five be gotten out?

China-born McAllister, who was then about 30, not only spoke fluent Chinese, but he spoke it like a peasant or kitchen servant. Servants were his tutors in his early childhood. He had a quick ear for dialects, and even more essential, he knew and could mimic instinctively every Chinese habit, mannerism, and gesture. Unfortunately, he had American eyes, light and deepset, and he was tall, too tall even by Manchurian standards.

After much private discussion it was decided disguise might not be necessary after all. McAllister was given the assistance of an old Army crony, Sgt. John Fox, a battle-scarred veteran, ingenious and resourceful.

These two alone might have been more than sufficient to carry out the whole operation, but the Army seldom does things with hold-down economy. Before the mission was over hundreds were involved, expenditure soared, and there was an elaborate PX shuttle flight in regular operation!

Meanwhile the mounting drama did not escape the American press in Nanking or Shanghai. Somehow the Associated Press got the world beat on the story and stayed ahead for days. The Lolo mission got sensational play everywhere as salvos went up from rival foreign news editors and wire service desks. Cables flew like swallows at Capistrano. Emotional excitement over the possible rescue of survivors was understandable. Every family in America with a "lost or missing" loved one, who had served in the CBI Theater, flying the treacherous fog-hung Himalayan wilderness, prayed their husband or son might be one of the five men. Letters and telegrams besieged senators and the War Department demanding that the Lolo Captives be found and rescued *immediately!*

But back in China itself there was great division of opinion. Was the whole thing just a wild fabrication that should be abandoned here and now, or should an elaborate rescue attempt be mounted immediately, with lots of planes, men, and supplies? Had too much publicity been allowed to circulate, endangering the mission's secret investigation? At least on this point everyone agreed. The Lolo mission went under wraps, at least officially. No news of their operation and plans was to be circulated to the press at all.

General George C. Marshall, for one, seriously beset with other far more important political problems, abhorred the sensationalism of the whole "American slavery" story and moved forthrightly to suppress it. As he was the highest-ranking, most prestigious American in China, his emphatic clampdown should have been sufficient. It was not, because of the state of affairs in China in 1946–47.

Armies of photographers and reporters from all the wire services and news magazines moved in on the Lolo rescue operation. Fantastic shenanigans, as could be expected, were used for exclusives, beats, new rumors and new leads. Always there were cameras and demands for pix, pix, PIX! Everyone had to see the Lolos, the rescue team scouring forbidden mountains, and, they all prayed, soon the American airmen.

Midway in this excitement I entered the scene as PRO. My job was to tell the press nothing, everyday, without seeming to do so. Elaborate and top-secret plans were made by the AGRS command headed by Col. Charles F. Kearney. If and when the Americans were found alive, they were to be immediately airlifted out of China and flown to Washington, stopping en route only if medical attention were required. I was to accompany them to make certain that the AGRS Shanghai Headquarters, and Col. Kearney's group in particular, got all the credit when the story was released in Washington. That's how promotions are made.

What came of all this, after months of thickly plotted activity among border-area Chinese officials who saw their opportunity and seized it, and cooperative Lolo chieftains who took weird vows to search their hinterland for the fliers, at the same time denying any foreigners were being held slaves, was, in the end, nothing. There were no survivors, not a trace! There had never even been a plane crash in Lololand, so there couldn't have been any corn-grinding survivors held in slavery.

What was finally and conclusively proved when the Lolo saga was officially closed was this: a B-29 flying from India to West China toward the end of the war ran into trouble and began losing altitude over what must have been the Lolo Mountains. In an attempt to save the plane, the crew jettisoned excess weight and the fuel tanks. The plane struggled on for a time and did eventually make a crash landing in Sichang, but the crew, miraculously, all got out alive. Details of this fateful B-29 flight were verified and confirmed after months of investigation. Members of the original crew were tracked down in the States, and they gave testimony that eradicated all doubt and speculation.

To make doubly certain that absolutely no trace of missing Americans remained in never-never Lololand, however, Capt. McAllister did not leave the area until he had offered a big cash reward for provable information on any lost Americans, dead or alive. For weeks the reward of 5000 ounces of silver was posted and advertised. But there were no takers. Absolutely none.

Much has been written about American policy and American mistakes in China just before the end. The end of Americans in China, that is, for at least twenty and more agonizing years to come. Edgar Snow got to the "other side of the river" and found Mao's communism had made many impressive gains, which had to balance out, in our judgment, the ruthlessness of the system and its leaders. But snow and the Chinese have left the rest of us beached on *this* side of the river, apprehensive and nervous as we anticipate future challenge from the Red power which became in the sixties the Red monster with the bomb.

But do we over-anticipate the danger? Can a country so divided and devastated from within be a terrible threat to us? China faces years of survival struggle just to cope with population and food supply, two very human, non-belligerent problems China seems never able to solve.

Economic development, once the regime's proudest show-piece, wellspring of its "achievement" and propaganda, now seems hopelessly mired in irrational and outmoded practices long discarded by other communist powers.

In plain truth, Maoism has proven to be a crushing failure. It produced revolution, a united mainland, reached a high pinnacle of Chinese nationalism and passionate national pride, pride so strong it could defy Khrushchev and Moscow, see the departure of Russian aid and advisors and continue on outwardly unruffled. Its scientists made the world gasp and shudder and search their maps for a place called *Lop Nor* (where the Chinese tested nuclear devices). Then private pressures became uncontrollable and public. The structure ruptured and almost collapsed. The Red Guard movement demonstrated violently and then receded on an uneasy, uncertain land.

When the dust of anarchy settled, temporarily, an enfeebled Mao was still there, but the world could breath again.

What will come after the death of a deity who has lived too long? Can any one man control from a central capital some 800-million disgruntled people now demanding something better, after Mao passes from the scene? Will the army take over? What will emerge from the demands and aspirations of all the restless, impatient university graduates and the professionally trained elite? How can they remain outside the wave of new liberalism sweeping Eastern Europe and even, with more restraint and caution, educated youth in the Soviet Union?

After austerity, incessant boredom, compulsive slogan shouting, and the thin porridge of material rewards under Mao's state-oriented regime, might the oncoming generation want to cut loose and enjoy for a change? Personal freedom and material goods, money in the pocket (instead of in the state bank), pretty women in pretty clothes, all of it made possible by more efficient and productive industries. It is just possible the practical people of China might prefer this kind of change to more of the same. Only the Japanese respond to the profit motive with more natural instinct. Although they will still call themselves communist, or socialist, for years to come, it is just possible China in the future may find it in her own self-interest to get along with the rest of the world, including (gradually, cautiously) Russia and the United States.

My China experiences after this period of the Lolo adventure were all swift-moving and very personal. I had a compelling urgency to explore the remotest areas, especially the vast Central Asian hinterland, to waste no time in trying to see as much as possible, to go as far as possible. No prophetic wisdom of the rapidly approaching ejection of all Americans from the mainland urged me on. I was just utterly enthralled to see everything, having discovered how many different Chinas there were. North China was another country, totally unlike Shanghai. Canton might as well be Bangkok—the food, language, attitudes, physical appearance, and customs were so different.

Every article I sold brought in money (sometimes all of $5 or $10 for a news-paper article and pictures) which went straight to an airline ticket office or to a railway station to buy transportation to some new place which had to be seen *now!*

I never met or interviewed Mao Tse-tung personally or made the usual jour-nalist's trip to the caves of Yunnan. Everybody was going up there, coming back with the same admiring, glowing reports of having found a new order of new Chinese. Communists, yes, but reformers, dedicated nationalists, young incor-ruptible leaders living in a classless society—on fire with one idea, to weld all of China into one tremendous socialist state.

I listened to my colleagues and was impressed, but I felt no personal urge to go to Yunnan to see what everybody else had already seen and written about. Instead I went to a communist-controlled area, then identified as a "liberated" area, far more remote, under highly unusual circumstances.

With a small group of journalists I left Shanghai in late fall. We traveled by boat up the busy, fairly calm Yellow Sea, ostensibly to survey various projects sponsored by UNRRA (international relief organization). The PRO for UNRRA, a cheerful, pretty Southern girl named Ann Cottrell, from Richmond, was our escort. Only mildly interested in UNRRA, we were much *more* intrigued at hav-ing a look at what the Russians had left behind in their rapid sweep through Manchuria at the very end of the Pacific phase of the war.

I recalled the departure of the Russians from Ladd Field in Fairbanks after V-J Day. I was informed at the time that the Russians liberated and took home on our planes everything removable: light switches were ripped from the walls, bath-tubs pried loose, water spigots, toilets, everything. It was the same in Manchuria, only the loot was more impressive: what remained of the Japanese war machine, factories with modern equipment. As someone remarked, "The Russians took everything but the people. *People* they didn't need!"

We stopped at the American consulate in Mukden, a cold Manchurian city the Japanese had made into a vast modern, industrial center. It was rather lovely with neat boulevards, trees, and gardens. We heard about arrangements being made for a mercy flight into Harbin. Several hundred miles to the north, Harbin was in communist hands, a liberated area. An epidemic of bubonic plague, the awful black death of medieval times, was then raging in Harbin. Medical supplies and serum for inoculations were desperately needed and had been officially requested by the communists. A United States plane was made available: medical supplies were packed and ready. The diplomatic snag was the vicious hostility and mutual distrust between communists and Kuomintang. Nanking feared the loss of its mercy plane to the other side if it were permitted to land in a liberated area. Finally, after agreeing upon certain guarantees, the plane was cleared to proceed and we were allowed to go along. With us went one terrified Nationalist Chinese doctor who feared the communists would nab him along with the serum. But surely, we reasoned, the communists would not want to keep him—or *us*. To get rid of nosy, spying western journalists, as quickly as possible, the plane was certain to be released.

Thin sheets of ice covered every river and duck pond. A light November whiteness lay upon the rigid mud squares of peasant land and villages. Winter was rapidly setting in. Our plane had no de-icing equipment, but the crew on the short hop from Mukden to Harbin wasn't unduly concerned. We were allowed no luggage beyond what we could carry in small hand zip-bags. We filled out the usual United States government forms, signing our lives away absolving the government if anything happened, and rushed to board the plane.

Harbin did not look like a frightened, quarantined area under a black death sentence. We did not see dying people or funerals or anything we had anticipated.

We were met at the airport upon our arrival by a young, English-speaking Chinese official of the slick new breed that communist governments often use as front men in dealing with foreigners. No padded-suit comrade he; quite the contrary, he had the unctuous and elegant air of a French military attaché! He wore a military officer's coat of Air Force blue, long, sweeping, and belted, very similar to the handsome greatcoats worn by Russian airmen in Fairbanks. Like them, our Harbin host wore boots, Sam Browne belt, a grey fur hat, and fine leather gloves! He was the most elegant communist I had ever met, and the best looking. Our amazement at him never ceased: he spoke Americanese, without accent or affectation, and he had a mysterious source of American cigarettes. When we asked questions about his American "style," he smiled a foxy, toothy grin but revealed nothing. We could only surmise he was the product of English-language schooling, no doubt at an American missionary school in the old days, which, presently, he did not wish to acknowledge or recall.

We would be quite comfortable, and "safe," our guide assured us, in the government guest house where he had made reservations. The guest house was located far from the "worst sections of town" and, we feared, far from the local scene and conditions we had come to observe.

The car, the great black vehicle that was to convey us to the safe guest house, ran on charcoal burners attached to the rear (gasoline was scarce). Speed was reduced but performance was dependable. We drove from the airport to the residential district of what had been one of the great glamour cities of the old Far East. Early vintage Marlene Dietrich would have been right at home here, and she would have had a few rivals. We paused at the old White Russian Railroad Club on the Sungari River. It was an architectural indulgence, over-embellished baroque with an ivory and gold interior. But even forlorn and empty and in Chinese Communist hands it still reflected goldenly rich robust bygone days at the turn of the century. Harbin had had its golden era when it was a foreign enclave and the Trans-Siberian railroad was a booming artery of modern commerce and transport.

We learned there were two Americans in Harbin: one was a dealer in pig bristles (used for brushes) and the other was a young oilman on his first foreign assignment: A.C.J. McLaughlin, who was well known in later years throughout the Orient. Mack, now with American International Oil Company in Chicago, recalls the dark days of the plague very well. Every day he saw hundreds of Chinese bodies piled high in trucks, hauled to public ditches, dumped and burned with kerosene. Whether the people ever got the UNRRA serum we brought in is doubtful. No public inoculation centers were ever set up, according to McLaughlin. The serum was probably distributed among party hierarchy. Mack's job at the time had been to inspect and salvage what could be put back in operation from the old Standard Vacuum facilities. He departed when the whole country capitulated to the Red regime.

Our guest house had been the mansion of a Russian lumber baron named Kabilkin. (The family, we were told, managed to get out of Harbin in time and is now located in California.) The Kabilkins lived as the families in Tolstoy's *War and Peace* must have lived: grandly, formally, and socially, with a horde of servants. Stripped of its rugs and draperies and most of its Old World furniture, the mansion was still a showpiece.

A lumberman brings the finest lumber and woodwork into his castle, and this one had a stairway an empress might descend for her coronation! Each bedroom was a high-ceilinged ballroom with bath and dressing rooms like adjoining suites. There were bidets in each bathroom, and mirrors like a Paris salon. As we were escorted to these splendid quarters, one could not help observing the ironic pride with which the peasant houseboys displayed the rooms. (I was later to observe communist pride in wicked old predecessors' appropriated splendor in many other communist countries, especially in today's hard-line socialist Poland. The Poles have spent millions lavishly restoring princes' and feudal landowners' old castles and lake-mirrored palaces.)

In Harbin we were served lunch in a vast dining hall furnished with shadowy, carved mahogany. Chinese "boys" wore immaculate white coats. Lunch consisted of chicken Kiev (every day) and cold hors d'oeuvres, beer or vodka, and tea that was as strong as coffee.

How silly it all seemed while bubonic plague raged on in the city that someone also took the trouble to squeeze slightly turned butter into beehive curls!

As we sat discussing our future program with our Chinese guide, it became clear we would be given no freedom to roam about on our own. Although our host went through the motions of asking us what we wanted to see, he knew exactly what we *would* see. It was all organized, part of the package. He never told us, but we learned elsewhere he had somehow gone to school in Washington, DC—to the FBI Academy. Once, during a crackdown on black marketeering in forbidden foreign exchange he had pulled a surprise raid on a popular cocktail lounge in Harbin. The raid had caught a number of foreigners with hard currency in their wallets. Gloating over his rich haul, he had arrogantly boasted, "That was a better job than anything they taught us at the FBI school in Washington!"

As the days passed under constant escort service, we exerted all our wiles to break him down and learn his story. It became clear his mind worked on one track only. He was trained to order inferiors, to record intelligence, but to give nothing away, not even some trifling bit about himself. Conversation with him at dinner was often strained. Once we did elicit from him that he was a great reader and "of course, of course!" read many American writers. Like who, or *whom?* "Oh," [quickly] "Edgar Snow! There is one American who writes the truth about China." He glowed and enthused about Edgar Snow, but one sensed if Edgar Snow in later years wrote more critically of China he would no longer be "reporting the truth."

We dutifully took the unavoidable packaged tours. We saw literacy classes where before there had been no schools at all for peasants. We saw land reform (every correspondent took the same pictures of the same farmer with the same "reformed" land). We toured factories. One factory had been the property of the British-American Tobacco Company. Cheap cigarettes were made in the confiscated factory, but the people did not look particularly happy with their liberated jobs. They stared at us as we took pictures, wondering no doubt what kind of foreigners we were since we didn't look Russian.

Finally we had had enough tours. We begged off. Couldn't we just walk around the city on our own? Our host, smiling, said he would walk with us so we wouldn't get lost. Because of the epidemic, it wasn't safe to walk very far or into crowds. It was clear we could not shake him. Very well, since we were to depart very soon, could we go shopping? We would like a quick trip to the bazaar, since Harbin was famous for its furs. When he could not discourage us, our host agreed to take us.

In the back seat of the car Ann whispered to me, "Let's get out and rush into a lot of different shops, in different directions. Our Guide will be confused and we'll lose him." That is just what we did!

I hurried off alone down a cold grey street lined with disappointingly poor and half-empty shops, called "magazines" in Russian lettering. One, however, bore a large sign in English, ALASKA FUR SHOP! I hurried to the door, but it was locked. I cupped my eyes and peered eagerly through the window. The shop appeared deserted and abandoned, obviously in great haste. I ducked inside one or two of the shops. My long struggle with the Russian language back in Alaska came to my rescue. I could make myself understood, a little, using very simple sentences. In the shops, as I hurried along, I found more than Harbin's famous fluffy kolinsky. I found intense fear among the furs. Seeing I was alone, people in the shops took courage. "You are American, Madame? Where do you stay here? When do you leave? Where do you go after you leave Harbin? Oh—to Shanghai, Madame? All my family is there. You will please take one letter? Please, one small package? I give you fur hat—take what you like, but one letter to my family must go with you. Madame, it may be last chance for me. We are trapped here like rats, you don't know how is it! Stateless we are. No passport. We have only worthless papers. These new Chinese give much trouble. Very bad. Chinese can do anything to us—*anything*. We can say—nothing! For us there is no government's protection."

Could I get out their letters as well as a bundle without being observed or having the hand baggage opened? I hesitated, although I knew I would take whatever they gave me.

Bundle carrying and hand letter carrying is a way of life throughout the Orient, even to this day. Someone always shows up at the hotel or the airport when you are leaving with a few letters or a wrapped bundle. You never know what is inside, but this hand-to-hand delivery service is an obligation that cannot be refused.

"Hurry, prepare your things," I told the fur man. "I will come back in half an hour. *If I do not come back alone, do not give me anything.*"

So that the furman's bundle would not be conspicuous, I though I'd better buy something and have a genuine bundle of my own. I needed no such high-minded reasons to buy a few things. I found a Russian icon and a magnificent pair of opera glasses from Paris. The glasses have enameled paintings on the delicate gold rimmed frames. To whom had they belonged? To what theaters had they been taken, in what white-gloved fingers were they held? (The Harbin opera glasses went with me not long ago to see *Funny Girl,* and my daughter Mary uses them—so casually!—these days on birdwatching hikes in the woods.)

Pegge bought these Parisian opera glasses at a Russian fur shop in Harbin, China.

My parting impression of what communism had brought to this area and to others was hardly optimistic.

I did not catch the fervor, the rejuvenation, the hysteria of rejoicing in change and new ways among the people, least of all from run-of-the-mill or run-of-the-factory, middle-aged or older people. Only for the rising Chinese youth was there that promised bright and glorious workers' future under Marx and Mao.

Returning to Mukden from that trip with its interesting if restricted observations in Harbin, we paused a day or so to write some stories. One afternoon a jeep was loaned to us to take a swing around the city. The Japanese had seized upon a going metropolitan center here in Mukden. In the old days before the rich Manchuko Empire had been established, Mukden had been one of those prospering privileged havens for foreign entrepreneurs on Chinese soil. It was on the main rail line, it had immense natural resources including coal, and there had been an oil refinery, which the Russians totally dismantled and took home as a prize of war. The town still had a very European look, even after long Japanese occupation. The vandals and destroyers were the occupying nationalist Chinese who grabbed, burned, or ate whatever they could get their hands on.

We pushed into the outlying districts where there was a large Roman Catholic institution—a combined school, orphanage, and hospital.

The conversation I had with the Mother Superior there will always stay with me. She was Belgian. She was also a human being of extraordinary spiritual strength. Her manner, her youthful good looks, her eyes blue as the willow pattern on Chinese plates, and her vitality warmly impressed us. We learned she had come from an aristocratic family. In fact, so the stories went, she had renounced a title, like a lady in a novel, to become a nun and spend her life in that remote school in Northern China.

Mother Superior, at the time we met, must have spent some twenty years in China. What kept her so young and hearty in the face of war, occupation, fear for her life and the survival of her school? With a smile she said lightly, "Why, the secret of being young is in being *needed!* I rise at dawn with a hundred things to do! The joy of doing them and seeing the results is perhaps my 'secret' of staying young. I simply have to be young."

I asked her if she had feared for her life during the long years of Japanese occupation, then Soviet occupation, and now Nationalist Chinese. Which had she feared most, I asked.

Mother Superior did not answer. She gazed—with caution?—about the school playground. Nearby a group of silky-haired small tots in crisp blue pinafores gleefully and shrilly played ring-around-the-rosey-an'-all-fa'-down!

"I would say," she replied at last, "I would say most of all I fear the Chinese."

I was puzzled. "The Chinese? But you know them. You speak their language fluently. You have spent years living among them. You know them well. Do you mean you are uneasy, being here alone with all the children, a white woman?"

"No, no! You do not understand," she was suddenly tense, her voice sharp. "Nobody can change the Chinese! Not teaching or schools or religion or foreigners' ideas! *The Chinese are the cruelest people on earth, especially to other Chinese!*"

The outburst had come at great cost. She had spoken a dreadful truth to herself as well as to me. She turned and left me abruptly, but her words haunted me. I have never forgotten them.

Asian cruelty to other Asians, to their own race, their own kind, their own people, in their own country, is a strange phenomenon. That life is cheap in Asia, that the brutal struggle to survive, to eat, to hold onto the land, deadens compassion for anything, or anyone else, save one's own family—I know all these explanations, and more, but they do not tell me *why* in such a way that I understand. We see an unbroken pattern of Chinese cruelty to Chinese, from the revolution to the Red Guards.

But in India it was the same thing, especially after the Partition. How could the Hindu-Moslem blood bath have taken place when the saint of non-violence, Mahatma Gandhi, was still alive to witness it all, and even he was powerless to bring the national insanity to a halt?

Indonesia a few years ago unleashed a slaughter upon its own people that stunned the world, though it thwarted a communist seizure of that troubled but enchanted island country.

Then, closer to us, there is the whole tragic drama of Vietnam. Viet Cong and, certainly—who can deny it?—even South Vietnamese atrocity and terror and mutilation, beheading and sadistic torturing of prisoners?

Not that the white race is without its history of bloody, shuddering horror. GIs tell us there were very few saints on European battlefields or in lonely villages. And to this day there are the scars of the Nazis in still-standing concentration camps, in Lidice, in Warsaw and Auschwitz where summer tourists bring white gladiolas and roses and stare at the ovens.

My observations on China are not intended as material for serious study. I do not pretend that my brief time there, my hasty comings and goings all over the country, gave me any profound insights. Nor am I any "authority" whatsoever on China. I saw a lot, I traveled almost from border to border, Harbin to Canton, to extreme western China, to Sinkiang, almost to the Russian border in Kuldja. I flew across the Gobi and the vast Taklamakin deserts (meaningless geography unless I mention that Genghis Khan came from this wild sandland). I flew many times over the Great Wall, and stared down, too awed to even manage a good picture. And I survived a plane crash, in torrential rains, in Siang. We landed in mud; there was no fire; we all got out alive.

Before the long winter's night of Sino-American relations froze out nearly all communication for a decade, I did indeed explore this land. With what audacity, poor preparation, and ignorance I went out into China, but I am glad I did not miss any of it.

General George Marshall was in China in those days exerting his disciplined and considerable skills in a valiant effort to weld together fire and fire: Mao Tse-tung and Chiang Kai-Shek. In the beginning they went through the cagey motions of a coalition under duress, called a central government in Nanking. But the communists from the beginning had only one goal, one governmental allegiance: their own.

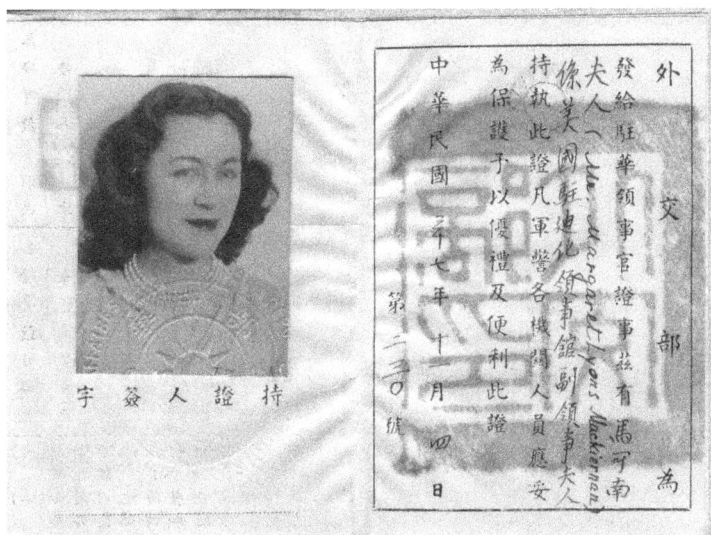

Pegge's Chinese identity card.

On the lighter side, I discovered I had one special asset for getting around and getting know in China: a well-chosen "pen name": Parker. Although foreigners' name are difficult for Chinese to pronounce and remember, just as theirs, with hyphens and apostrophes, are for us, every Chinese official or long-gowned businessman and *every* mayor, had an American Parker pen—a necessary status symbol—clipped to his pocket.

When introduced, I would point to their pen. "My name is Parker, like your pen. Surely you can't forget that name, can you?" No, they couldn't. Being Chinese, they added something more. If my name were Parker, I must be from the *family* of Parker pens. That being the connection, I must be rich and important. "Very number one!" My smiling protests were brushed aside. Modesty! I was always given the best chair, the first cup of tea, and often, offers of a chauffeured car to drive me home!

It so happens the *real* heir to the Parker name and company was actually in China, but before my day.

My Chinese friends and officials would not have expected to find Daniel Parker, grandson of the company's founder, in the Marine Corps, but that was where he was. Enlisting at 18 as a buck private, Daniel Parker was mustered out in 1946 with a first lieutenant's bars, but not until after he had seen considerable service in China. And in all that time I am certain no one offered *him* so much as a peach pit because his name was Parker.

I am *not,* of course, related to the family of the Parker Pens, although my passport has a mighty funny line. It reads "alias Pegge Parker." *Alias*—that's a fine thing to call a byline!

I had a little Chinese amah in those days who took fussy, bossy care of me and my quarters. She was eyeing me, with intense and unusual attention, one night as I dressed for dinner. Being Chinese, she spoke her mind without hesitation on personal matters. Shrilly, she demanded: "How *old* you, missey? Missey got parents? Mother, father living? You no *marry?* Parents, mother, father no worry? Missey not so young but got very good teeth, nice, white, strong. Why missey no marry, eh?"

This jewel of an amah, despite the increasing tension of the times and scarcity of food (well she knew *I* would not let her starve, nor her 10 relatives and 3 half-cousins), had a very cheerful disposition. She hummed little songs to herself, never sat still a minute. She was a reassuring tonic at the end of a weary day, and I was fond of her.

But once I asked her a simple question and she became enraged. I merely asked her what she and her family and friends thought of Madame Chiang Kai-Shek.

Almost hissing, this birdlike little woman cried, "Missey, you ask. I speak you: Madam Chiang no care about Chinese people. What she care? She not know Chinese people. She very big, rich, number one, go Nanking, go all over. Make big speech. Ride big cars. She not know China, missey. *She never know Chinese people."*

When I look back on what it was like living in China, day by day, the political scene blurs. The Nanking and Peking and Yenan of that era are no more—let them go. What I recall vividly is the carnival millstream of Chinese city streets and all those people. I can even smell those Chinese boulevards with names like Bubbling Well Road.

I walked a lot in every city because it was the only way to see sidewalk life. The Chinese are also great walkers, or curious strollers, but always in the street, never on sidewalks. Chinese men and women are avid shoppers and any time of the day one heard shrill haggling or bargaining. Cooking odors: garlic and browning pork and charcoal smoke are the permanent odors of my memory of China, along with the mildew which was the last thing one smelled on bed pillows at night, the first odor of the day when you awoke. But Chinese food: the eye-watering, tender, delicious, golden whiffs of pork fat and meat sauces or roasting ducks; simmering mushrooms and ginger and bean sprouts and cabbage and onions and chicken broth; and boiling noodles in huge black cauldrons; and round pans of rice swelling and steaming and absorbing moisture; rosy pink curls of fresh shrimp in a bed of bay leaves; sweet green peas; steaming chestnuts and brilliant shiny orange jewels called persimmons and clusters of red fruit which look like prickly strawberries but are lychees; the dripping amber taffy mixture of vinegar, brown sugar, and spices which makes the sweet-and-sour sauce for everything from mandarin fish to duck. The most superlative food on earth is prepared in China by the Chinese, from all Chinese ingredients. Had I not dined on such fare in Peking, I would have been content to rave about Chinese food elsewhere. Singapore and Bangkok and Hong Kong, after all, have the same Chinese talents, ingredients, chopsticks, even the savory rice wine from the Mainland. It isn't the same. Peking is just another world, and the food is another-world as well!

In that day, instant coffee, Nescafé, was quite the fad. In the land of tea, the new taste of powdered coffee downed with sugar and canned milk was very popular, even among pedicab coolies. To be seen at a sidewalk stall having a *coffee break* was the newest style in Face! No doubt, pedicab drivers have all been liberated from their pedicabs—and their Nescafé coffee breaks as well!

Chinese children were and still are the most adorable doll creatures in the world. In remote villages, just as I had read about them in old Pearl Buck novels, I often saw a precious manchild, son and heir of his family, disguised as a worthless girl baby, for fear of the evil spirits. Little boys, in padded suits, would have their cheeks rouged bright red, their baby hair braided and tied in red ribbons—all to convince the evil eye that they were really girls!

I did not learn to speak Chinese, but I knew enough to get by. One Sunday morning, I picked up the telephone to inquire the hour of Sunday mass at a little church called the Church of Jesus and Mary. I had no Shanghai directory in my room, so I dialed Information.

A high-pitched Chinese girl's voice came on.

"Wei?" (pronounced "way," meaning "Hello? Yes?"). I asked for the number of the church. She had obviously never heard of it. "How do you spell it?" she asked.

"Jesus?" I began, uncertainly, never having had to spell out *that* name before. "Well, J for—uh, jade, E for emperor, S for Shanghai, U for, uh, U for *you*…" It was a struggle. "Surely," I concluded, "you have heard of Jesus? The Christ, the Christian God, the Son of God—you know, *Jesus?*"

No, she had never heard of Mr. J for jade, E for emperor. And she could find no church listed under "that name." I hung up, grabbed my coat, and hurried down the street. I found the church, but Masses were over for the day.

It did not take much effort to find an excuse or story or an assignment to take one to Peking in those days. We returned to the northern capital as often as possible. The airfare was cheap, the hotels not bad, and there was so much to see!

Peking in late fall was already cold, but the cold was full of sparkle and vitality. Chinese cheeks glowed. Children's moon-faces were round and rosy as ripe peaches. Trees and gardens were still green and fussily cared for. Rows of potted mums lined every doorstep. On bright, warm, sunny days, everyone was outdoors wearing the poor man's overcoat, the sun. After five, when the sun went down, houses were damp, cold, cheerless caves, smelling of age, mold, and mildew. Most families heated only one room in winter. Fuel in Peking was scarce and expensive. Families ate and slept together, in that one warmed room, where, when someone spoke, frosty plumes of breath were often visible.

The atmosphere of the most fabled city of all time, Peking, was then gloomy and uneasy with fear of the way things were going. Rumors fed the tension. Wives began to get out trunks and save old newspapers for wrapping precious articles. More Chinese communist soldiers, in padded khaki, were seen on the streets as well as ranking officials from the Liberated Areas. The Marshall truce teams were still struggling for equilibrium, but no one had any grounds for confidence. Among the foreign business community, the general concern was evacuation and speculation on whether Mao would confiscate foreign holdings immediately, or could foreigners dicker and bargain and at least *delay* the inevitable?

Street bazaars began to burgeon with items shed by refugees. Among the first possessions to be jettisoned were books—whole libraries, lovingly collected over many years, out-of-print books, rare old works on Chinese art, jade, poetry, history, on remote Central Asia. Treasured volumes were going for a song, but the song had to be weighed first. Books were sold by *weight*, balanced on Chinese hand scales! Selling books by the pound (or kilo) amused me—poetry was cheap, dictionaries and histories very dear.

As we read about the wall poster in Peking today, I see China's other walls. Walls around old Chinese houses called compounds, walls for shutting out vulgar street noises and prying eyes, walls for privacy and thought, quiet shelter for reading, for thinking, for a cup of tea and conversation with some honored guest. Walls, too, were there to enclose the family within that precious social order where everyone bowed to the will of the lord and master. Sometimes the women asserted themselves, but on the "face" of things, the head of the house was pampered, a dictator.

Those compound walls and the tenacious family system had thousands of years behind them. How did the ruthless system of the Red Chinese Democratic People's Republic so thoroughly, physically, and psychologically drive Chinese out of their family units into a bullying collective state?

Having lived briefly in China, I have never been completely satisfied with the experts' reasons why. I understand all the long history of Chinese humiliation, conquest, and injustice at the hands of the West. But this was the collapse of the Chinese way of life, of their own customs and traditions, on their own Chinese soil, at the hands of fellow Chinese.

Recalling China's walls, I have a more amusing memory, not of Peking's walls but of the big one, the famous Great Wall.

On our return from the long trip to Harbin and Mukden, our group had lingered on in Peking. One Saturday I was having lunch with my friend Ann, who had a great eye for arty things like screens and scrolls and stone rubbings well worth buying—at panic prices—before it would all be over for us.

On that particular day at the old Wagon-Lits hotel, a famous landmark, Ann had a great idea: "Why don't we take a picnic to the Great Wall tomorrow? It's Sunday, we can spend the entire day taking pictures and looking around, we might even get Topping (Seymour Topping, now of *The New York Times*) to go along to protect us. Who knows, we might even find a few loose bricks to bring back. Think of taking home some bricks from the Great Wall of China—for bookends!"

I laughed. "Oh, Annie, *really!*" But, eyes glazed with the vision of bricks from the Great Wall, she burst out, "You're a Yankee. You don't know how we set great store on historical mementos. Southerners have saved every little bit of the Civil War and handed it down in the family—every little ol' bullet, and shell, and old coat button. Nobody at home ever even saw anything like the Great Wall!"

She went with Topping and indeed she returned, triumphant, with a few smallish bricks. She wrapped them up and sent them right home.

I visited her recently in her present home in Washington where she writes for the *Washington Star*. Her husband is James Free, well-known syndicated news correspondent. I scanned Ann's chaste mantle in her living room. Where, I demanded, are the famous bookends? Where are the bricks from the Great Wall?

"Oh, Peg, how can you remember such silly ol' things? Those damn bricks! They never were bookends, really. I've got them in a box out in the garage somewhere, but good God, they've been dragged around all these years, and now they're all mixed up with stones and pieces I picked up at the Spinx and at Stonehenge—"

I did not study the Chinese language. I was intensely studying Russian, and that was all I could handle. But I did learn phrases and ordinary, everyday words necessary for getting around, shopping, ordering food, or directing taxi drivers. One phrase, however, that I shall remember forever is the Chinese expression for children. The word or sounds translate into "Little Happiness"!

Little Happiness seemed to define China's relations with the rest of the world, but when my own children were born in China, Little Happiness was to have ambivalent meaning for me as well. By 1948 political events were rapidly becoming critical. But they were of secondary importance to me at the time. I was thoroughly absorbed in personal events.

I had met and married a young scientist from Boston, Doug Mackiernan, then an American vice consul stationed at a small American Consulate in the interior of China.

There had been a trip back to the United States and a whole year spent impatiently away from China. Finally we made a last flight back to Shanghai. There, in September, we became the rather stunned and overwhelmed parents of *twins*! Fraternal twins at that: a very blonde, blue-eyed boy, and a brunette, Kewpie-faced daughter. We named them Mike and Mary.

Shanghai, 1948: Pegge Parker Mackiernan with two Chinese amahs.
Pegge's amah is on the left, holding one twin, while Pegge holds the other.
Amah in center holds her charge.

The event was exciting and would have been more joyous had the timing for China not been so disastrous. Newborn twins, with riots in the street and martial law. From there on, nothing boded well for China, or for us. Evacuation and tragedy lay just ahead.

My anxious husband, Doug, spent most of his time in Nanking arranging for our departure to his new post, deep within western China. He just refused to see that it was impossible. The strain was very great. What would happen to us? Evacuation and long separation lay ahead. Wives and children were to go home, as soon as transportation was available, but husbands stayed until diplomatic relations between China and the U.S. were broken completely. My mental state was such in those days that I barely heard the screams and yells of twins.

I hired a little Chinese amah to help me manage two babies, once I left the Broadway Mansions clinic where they were born (the same Mansions where I had lived when I first arrived in Shanghai).

Amah was recommended to me because she had taken care of British twins some years before. When she came to the hospital seeking the job, I was utterly amazed. She appeared at my bedside, carrying a handful of wilted red gladiolas (a red flower symbolizing joy and good fortune). She wore a spotless Chinese gown, her hair was smoothly oiled, coiled, and bunned behind her ears. Her ears were small as a kitten's, and from tiny pierced lobes swung green jade earrings. But most astonishing of all, she had bound feet. When she was a child they had been tightly wrapped to keep them from normal growth. What survived were "lily feet," anything but beautiful as intended, but crippled and shocking to see. She wore black Chinese slippers made to order, and she walked on her heels in a kind of thump, thump, thump. But, I puzzled, how could she walk on those feet carrying twins? I need not have worried. She darted and hurried and got around like a frantic, hobbled bird.

I, who knew nothing about babies, prized above all gifts my copy of Dr. Benjamin Spock. It was never out of my hand. I would stand over the Chinese hand-woven baskets we used for the twins' cribs and read Spock aloud to Amah as the Daily Lesson of divine service. Amah never paused for an instant. "Yes, Missey, very nice, Missey, good, Missey," she murmured soothingly as she went right ahead doing things *her* way.

Amah and I were in total partnership. Days and weeks flew by, and we were alone with the twins. Doug remained in Nanking stubbornly arranging for a plane and supplies to take us on to his post. Just next door to my compound in Shanghai was the headquarters of the Maryknoll Fathers, American priests who each evening sang something in Latin which drifted across to me in a tune I later recognized as a once-popular song: "Through a Long and Sleepless Night." To hear it now and then on the car radio is a disaster. With the twins' early dawn feeding, Amah and I had nothing *but* long and sleepless nights. I always meant to go next door and call on the Maryknoll Fathers and tell them I found their singing very comforting as I heated bottles, changed diapers, and burped babies.

I often just gazed down at the wicker baskets—*two of them*—telling myself it was all a dream. They couldn't be mine! What did I know about the frantic nightmare of caring for a first baby, let alone two, and a boy and girl, one with a diaper flap folded one way, the other folded the *other* way—it couldn't be happening to me!

One evening, watching them as they slept in their baskets, side by side, Amah smiled and observed, "Missey very lucky. Missey catch two babies. Boy baby—piece of jade, very precious. Girl baby, piece of porcelain—very nice, but of little value."

Those words passed into legend in the family. Unreality haunts me still as I think of the piece of jade, now in the Marine Corps, and that piece of porcelain at Barnard, immersed in Far Eastern studies.

One day in the fall of 1948 I was having lunch in the museum-piece apartment of a friend (she was a collector of considerable purse and scope) when the phone rang. It was the American Consulate advising me to go home and pack. Special travel orders were being prepared for me because of the twins. We were to be evacuated by plane to San Francisco. We were to leave the next morning.

My hostess brought a cup of black coffee to the telephone. "Put a call in to Doug at the embassy in Nanking right away," she pressed. "Don't let them scare you, my dear. They can't force you to go. Talk to Doug first."

When I finally got Doug and told him about my orders, there was an agonizing pause. He had secured a United States military plane, and it was already loaded with all our supplies. We were to leave as soon as the twins were able to travel. There was no doctor in our area, but the wife of the consul had been a nurse. No, she had no children, but....

Finally, beaten by the situation, he gave in: "Okay, you and the kids go home, but," he cheered me, "we'll see how things look by spring. You'll come back or I'll get out. Don't worry, darling, it's only for a few months!"

No. It was forever.

Doug was shot and killed making his escape out of the interior nearly two years later. To me, alone with the twins, thousands of miles away, it was a shattering blow beyond tears, prayers, or at times, *belief.* I continued to spin through the days, caring for the twins in a kind of nightmare blackout.

I know what every wife and every mother goes through with a son or husband in Vietnam. The ringing of the telephone at an unusual hour, the sight of a strange car in the driveway, a stranger coming to the front door with an envelope in his hand. *You know before you are told.*

I never once sat down to think. I raced at double speed through the days. I fed the washing machine, made baby food in a pressure cooker, slapped twins in the tub, hurried through supermarkets. My mother came on to help so I wasn't alone. Esther Dodge, an Armenian friend who was a jewel, took me on a long car trip to Carmel, to Monterey, and to her large family in Fresno.

This photo of Pegge with twins Mike and Mary accompanied the newspaper accounts of Doug Mackiernan's death.

California's brilliant beauty in vineyard country was almost unbearable. And the sight of the blue Pacific reminded me that China was out there, and Doug.

One day a letter arrived, in a handwriting I did not recognize. It was a letter with a different kind of sympathy. It was written by Clare Boothe Luce on the anniversary of the death of her only child, Anne. Anne had been a student at Stanford University when she was killed in a motorcar accident. I had briefly known her Anne and had once or twice written articles about her in Washington. Mrs. Luce got across to me one thing—those who experience profound sorrow *are not alone.* Somewhere in every lifetime comes the terrible blow. How well I know that Mrs. Luce wrote from her own experience. Somewhere tucked away I still have the letter—and the sorrow.

About this time another letter came to me from the State Department in Washington. Doug was being awarded a posthumous medal and citation for his last service. A small ceremony was to be held in the Department, and I was invited to come to receive the medal from the hands of the secretary, Dean Acheson.

And, what was far more urgent than a medal to a fatherless family, I was to be given a temporary post in the Department. We left California, and I sold my little house in Marin. The twins went to stay with Doug's parents in Boston, and I went to my temporary job in Washington.

Eventually that job led to one in which I could assume the rank and financial status of my husband. One sparkling spring day in Washington I was sworn in as vice-consul for USIA. It was not the Foreign Service, of course, but it was an honorable status.

Weeks passed as I was being trained for an overseas post, which I expected would be India. Later that was changed to the American Consulate in a northern university town in the Pakistan Punjab: Lahore. I was pleased with my assignment, but what about the children?

Pakistan is considered by the Department a "hardship" post and health risk. The thought of having to leave the children with servants during my working day was not appealing. I decided, reluctantly, to leave the twins with Doug's parents in Boston, at least until I got settled and could see for myself what was best for them.

Choosing grandparents over servants for two-year-old twins, temporarily, with the grandparents' warm consent, seemed very sensible. But in reality, it was a painful, strange, unnatural experience.

Having lost a husband, was I now to "lose" the children as well?

My last visit to Boston was an ordeal. Normally my comings and goings on weekends were part of the twins' accepted routine. The twins would see me off and wave bye-bye knowing I would return soon. But no matter how young they are and what kind of play-acting adults think they are putting over, children have super-acute radar. They always *know* when something is wrong, when bye-bye isn't the same as it always was.

I was taking the train back to Washington. "Don't make too much of the goodbye this time, Pegge," Grammy had suggested wisely. "Make it quick, and be very casual." I tried. But "Mommy! *Mommy!*" the twins screamed in panic, frantically clinging to me, their fingernails digging into my arm. It was a nightmare.

Grammy grabbed them. "Get on the train, Pegge, for heaven's sake, be quick—"

I felt as though I had abandoned them. Put them up for adoption! I didn't *have* to go. Why was I going? Why back to Asia again?

Because Doug was there.

5

Pakistan

✦

(1951–52)

Lahore, in the north central plain of the green, lush agricultural Punjab of West Pakistan, was to be my new window on independent nationalism in young, new Asia!

It was a brilliant, picturesque window through which I watched a young country struggle with old problems, old fears and grievances against the world, itself, and always, India! The United States government had its embassy in Karachi, then the capital, but we maintained a thriving consulate in Lahore, the suburban cultural center and seat of higher education.

Lahore, a city so rich with legend and history in the flamboyant days of Empire, so romanticized by Kipling, so dear to tourists, civil servants, and the military, so British still in its lingering, aristocratic self-esteem and culture, lives on its past. Its progress in the twentieth century lacks vitality and drive, its young students, its rebel hotheads, flay the air and coffeehouses with a charge of the light brigade that is all screaming argument. Violent debate, fist fights of words, torrents of talk, lots of perspiration, noise, torn shirts, little else.

These young Paks are even today only a semi-Westernized, superficially "modern" people. Lip service and lots of outward show dimly conceal a private world that is very Eastern at home. Youth has made its demands, defied custom, shattered the family with free choice in marriage and career, but those who make the break—and for them it is a bigger one than they ever bargained for—are few. And they are mostly from the wealthy, elite 10 percent.

Pakistanis are hypersensitive to criticism, strongly on the defensive when appraised by the West. They can point with pride to the amazing and energetic industrial revolution in their port city of Karachi, for instance. On reclaimed swampland where once stood squalid refugee shacks, one sees thriving modern industrial plants turning out everything from army jeeps and trucks to TV sets and toothpaste. The Karachi docks themselves are a showpiece of modern efficiency and equipment, though the eye is fascinated and the hand quick to reach for a camera when a camel train goes by the ultra-streamlined dock facilities and warehouses. Ah, the unchanging East, one muses inwardly, for in front of the smart, immaculate grey warehouses stands a Pathan guard with pugaree and draped trousers and Grecian vest, idly watching the camels shuffling by with their cheap haul of goods loaded on rattling wooden flat wagons. The camels will go in time, but now they add to the bored eye a warm touch, a reminder that the desert is not far off, with another way of life that is totally outside the space age.

Karachi is extremely photogenic. The pity is, however, that it is like Cinerama, larger than life. Its pictures and facade exaggerate rather than reflect real progress. Towering, ultramodern office buildings push against the Persian blue sky.

Air-conditioned banks hum with activity, and young executives, intent and preoccupied, hurry about in slim-cut Dacron suits. Branch offices of foreign firms look busy and brisk, and the many plush American-sponsored grant and foundation headquarters hire all the Pak beauty queens who are not already working as airline hostesses for their front-office receptionists.

Karachi has one super hotel, the painfully expensive Intercontinental whose front doorman stands resplendent in national costume made of gold cloth. Inside, on a patio, a chlorine-blue swimming pool spans off a shadowy cocktail lounge. As one surveys the surprising array of bikinis in the noonday sun—mere eyepatches here and there—soft music by Musak absolves the traveler of all exotic atmosphere. As a young Pak in white satin trucks cleaves the rippling water and disappears in a wake of bright blue flippers, mask, and snorkel, background recorded music pipes in Nancy and Frank Sinatra with "Something Stupid," and white-jacketed waiters slip among the sunbathing set with trays of iced *limboo panee* (lemonade).

Outside, Karachi's main thoroughfares swim with color. Mercedes, enamel-bright Volkswagen "Bugs," and black official cars, chauffeur driven, swarm by. Motor scooters have replaced tongas and a sea of bicycles have put poor but employed Pakistanis on wheels, but depressingly, most people still get where they are going on their own two feet. Usually bare feet at that, although made-in-Japan rubber thong sandals are almost cheaper than wearing out bare undersole, even for the poorest villager.

Pakistan has its own international airline, operating at a loss no doubt, but flying to London and *Peking!*

For political and military reasons, it was decided under the country's military president, Ayub Khan, to move the capital from Karachi into the cool hills of the interior, to Rawalpindi. The new capital, which I saw midway in its building program, is to be called Islamabad. The natural setting in a bowl of blue mountains was so magnificent that the initial buildings, a hodgepodge assortment of "modern" concepts of architecture and budget restrictions, was not exactly reassuring.

Meanwhile, Pakistan was to be a mixed experience for me personally. It was anything but a career triumph or even a satisfying period of productive work. My reward was knowing the Pakistanis. Muslims are always easier to know than Hindus and far more hospitable, generous, sentimental, warmly responsive, and always good conversationalists.

But much that I saw and read everyday as I made my rounds in graceful old Lahore depressed and appalled me.

In my new position I was uncomfortably, hopelessly miscast as a young lady vice-consul working as a USIA information officer. I was later transferred to the American Embassy in Karachi where I was assigned to the press section. Here I was often given special reports to prepare for the ambassador—news reports, which I could do best.

This ambassador had devastated me upon my arrival. On my very first day in the country, nervous and uncertain, I made my obligatory call upon him as the chief of mission. He took one look, slapped his forehead, and roared, "Goodgodalmighty! Who 'n hell sent *you* here? To Pakistan? A *woman,* for Chrissake!"

Recovering a moment later, he was apologetic and gentler. "My dear, it's not your fault. Any woman—not just you—*any* woman is a horrible mistake in a Muslim country, and especially Pakistan. A place like this is ruled by men. They wear the pants and the guns, honey, and have all the money. Anything that matters or moves is all decided by the old man! Women have never been anything but playthings. All that stuff about women in the government, women lawyers, bankers, college teachers, political leaders—it's all eyewash. This country is run by men, and men only!"

For all his outbursts, this career diplomat, who looked and was a man of distinction, down to the bourbon, later relented from his truthful but brutal welcome. He was always extraordinarily considerate toward me after that.

He sent me to do an assessment of the Red Chinese pavilion at a large international industrial fair in Karachi. Then he sent me to do a report on Pakistani journalists' reaction to a Soviet Union youth festival in Moscow. A group of Russian invitees had just returned and a local newsman's organization was holding a welcome-home reception. This one was interesting. I shall not forget their comments, made in the pained but unblinking presence of two white-shirted attachés from the Soviet Embassy, their recent hosts.

"En route to Moscow," began one of the writers, "we broke the long journey by spending a few days in the Central Asian republic of Kazakhstan. You will be knowing this is directly north of our country. This is the area in which many of our Muslim brothers are living. We observed that these Muslims do not enjoy religious freedom or schooling or have jobs as we do in Pakistan. What is more, we saw much color discrimination in the cities. Everywhere we saw white European Russians had all the big jobs, the good clothes and houses, the motor cars. White people are always the big bosses, isn't it? Muslims were their inferiors in everything. Oh, we saw the mosques are there and they are open, but they looked empty, rundown, neglected. Young people do not attend prayers."

Racial identification—seeing Soviet Russians as white people—has been an acute and highly sensitive point bellowed by the Chinese in their bid for supremacy in the Asian-African bloc. Rival communists constantly hammer home the racial difference. Only caste-ridden Hindu Indians are more hypersensitive to color than Pakistanis. A brilliant young lawyer from Lahore once returned from an international seminar at Harvard University (where he was an American guest) with one comment: *America is a land of white people!*

The brother of this same lawyer left Lahore on an American scholarship after a dramatic tragedy. At the conclusion of a large farewell party for young Munir in the garden of his home, a jealous cousin threw a vial of acid in his face. Miraculously escaping blindness, Munir lay for days in agony under a tent of mosquito netting. His face was burned and disfigured, but doctors were hopeful of full recovery, and his eyes escaped any permanent injury. Throwing acid in the face of an enemy, opponent, or rival is an old and dreadful Muslim tradition. We assured Munir that he would not lose the place reserved for him at a university in America. He left as soon as he was barely able to travel, although he was mortified at the appearance of his face.

I inquired about him when I was last in Lahore. "Oh, Munir has had a brilliant career since leaving here," I was told by a Pakistani friend. "He is now with the international Atomic Energy Commission in Vienna. He is, I believe, also an American citizen. He never came back to Pakistan."

Color, for once, did not prevent a great and exceptional brain from finding its place. Munir, I was gratified to learn, had made his way in the foreign world better than most Americans.

Despite all the obstacles for a single girl I had been warned about in Pakistan, I generally went my way with considerable acceptance. But nothing frustrated or angered me as much as the persistent and hideous custom of Pakistani women in purdah. Wearing the veil here means no delicate wisp of chiffon over the nose, but a huge black, usually dust-caked and filthy *entire body tent!* Unhealthy, unwholesome, and for me unacceptable! When in Rome or Pakistan, I would cheerfully go along with all other customs. I would sit on the floor, eat with my fingers, learn with delight to sample pilau topped with nuts, fried onions, and *real silver foil.* But the *burka,* the black tent, or even the half-burka which just covered the figure to the waist, dismayed me, especially when I saw it on a modern college campus. If education brought no emancipation, the education was pointless. Mentally and physically, the black shrouding of women has been slower to die out than we are led to believe when we are thousands of miles distant and listen to "modern" Pakistani ladies boasting. Wearing gorgeous saris, with eye makeup to match Liz Taylor's, many glittering jewels (*real* ones), smoking cigarettes and sipping Scotch, these emancipated society ladies or diplomatic wives see Pakistan from a long way off.

But there was always the happy exception: my landlady in Lahore, for instance. I rented a small cottage in her large compound. This extremely enterprising, quite worldly young woman who rented various properties to foreigners (at soaring prices she knew their governments or home offices would pay), revealed to me that Muslim women did not feel so oppressed. I made too much fuss over the burka, she laughed. "We comply," she explained, "in public, to keep peace in the family. When the old generation dies, we will do as we please. We usually manage to get our own way. Yes, it would amaze you, but not always by direct means."

My landlady revealed she was a licensed pilot and flew her own airplane! While going to school in England, having money and living a long way from her family, she had taken flying lessons, passed her test, and got her license. Back in Pakistan she flaunted her triumph, a fait accompli. When the shock wore off, the family was rather pleased. In fact, her husband was so excited he bought a small private plane for her. With my landlady's keen business instincts, she justified the plane as an expedient way to keep an eye on the family's large landholdings in far-away Peshawar. But Peshawar is more orthodox than Lahore, she explained, "so I must not be seen up there without my burka. So, fancy this my dear. I drive my own car to the airport in Lahore. In a burka I crawl up into the cockpit. Then I toss it back and fly to Peshawar. There I get out of my plane, put the burka back on, and drive off in the family car which is waiting to meet me."

The mystic East!

Stories like this one infuriate Muslims. Pakistanis vehemently deny them as rubbish, nonsense, untrue, malicious. "Foreigners just do not understand, isn't it?" ("Isn't it" is a localism, like "you can say that again.") What is more to the point: Pakistanis are extremely sensitive to criticism, especially if they feel it borders on ridicule, conveys a backward image, or worse, involves comparison with India. They will sputteringly deny that modern women in their country are still in burkas when members of their own family never leave the house without a black shroud. Religion and custom get a lot of blame for the social condition—the mentality—but I think women's lowly status can be laid at the door of bully-bully, unadulterated male tyranny.

The ambassador was right. Men do run the show on their own terms, and women have grovelled and pampered the Asian male—son, husband, father—for so long they have earned their role of spineless doormats, the despised status of body servants and mindless ninnies!

Faithful marriages in Pakistan are almost as rare as truly companionable, happy ones. The women are as apt to play the moth to the bright light of passing fancy as are the men. Their lives must be so miserable that they are easy prey to kind words and promises and, maybe, some new gold bangles. Anyway, the penalty for getting caught should discourage them, but it doesn't: a guilty woman gets her nose cut off!—another old, old Muslim custom. When I first heard this, I shrieked and cried, "Medieval nonsense!" I refused to believe it! I didn't *see* any nose cutting going on, or scars, or noseless adulteresses, so I just put it down to wildest exaggeration. I was apparently naïve. All this time during my tour of duty in Lahore, an American plastic surgeon was sent as an instructor and surgeon to Forman Christian College, which had a very fine, thoroughly modern medical school. The plastic surgeon told me, with a wry grin, that he spent most of his time doing "nose jobs," putting back noses on errant ladies. And he could congratulate himself on one thing—his noses were works of art, often making the patient more beautiful (and tempting?) than she had been with the original.

I like to recall Pakistan's towering, tough, Marlboro-man soldier-president, Field Marshal Mohammad Ayub Khan, as I saw him last—playing golf on the kind of irresistible, warm sunny afternoon that would have drawn our own golfing president Dwight Eisenhower far from office and onerous chores.

The Rawalpindi Golf Club that day was completely surrounded by police in khaki. I was a guest of a club member who knew Ayub's golf instructor, the club's pro. My escort, a newsman, grabbed his television camera and ran out over the vast green course waving a little white name card in his hand. Burly secret service men caddying a vast array of walkie talkies blocked his path. But Ayub looked up, paused, glanced at my escort's card, smiled disarmingly, and remarked that he had doubts that his golf would look very respectable to far better players back in America. "But come along if you like," he invited John. So, shooting with his Bolex, John joined the party for two or three holes. Ayub was not being modest. His game was *not* very good—enthusiastic, yes, but he's a long way from a cup or the low 90's.

The president's fondness for golf has shaken the flabby, overweight ranks of his cabinet and party elite who shun with abhorrence anything resembling exercise! But whither the Big Man goeth, there they were, some in red Hawaiian-print bush shirts, puffing on the green, struggling to swing the clubs, to hit the damn little ball.

Ayub, relaxing on the course in slacks and comfortable sports shirt, was very friendly, amusing, and at-ease with an American, but off the green, from his capital, from the rostrum, and from his headquarters, he presented a far different attitude.

Toward the United States, the attitude may be privately cordial but not publicly. He is angry that we arm and bolster India, so he woos and encourages China against us and India.

In Karachi, I remember being both indignant and fascinated to see huge billboard advertisements of regular PIA (government airline) flights to Red China.

Pakistan's whole position with the United States and its political ties to the Red Chinese are tied directly to Pakistan's obsessive, never-never-to-be-resolved, hostile relations with India. China is the big stick with which Pakistan seeks to bully her feared and superior neighbor. Pakistan, the smaller country spanning the mighty V of India, assuages jealousy and anxiety by convincing herself that China is really her friend.

President Ayub, who took power in 1958 when the fifth most populous nation in the world was on the brink of disintegration, has been the strongman ever since. Where democratic practices in an immature, semi-educated society threatened to weaken and fragment the country, pitting bitter faction against faction, Ayub did not hesitate to apply the military formula: order at all cost, unity, obedience, and centralized control.

Guided democracy, with all its unfortunate connotations, is what we call military tidiness thrown over freedom's clamor. In Pakistan's case, there are more than 115 million divergent people. A Pakistan-Bengali from Dacca in East Pakistan is quite different from a Northwest Frontierman in the Khyber, and a rich Punjabi looks with scorn upon a Sindi *walla* or merchant from sun-scorched Baluchistan!

From 1958 to the present is a long span of time for a military president whose repeated re-elections were entirely predictable. Maintaining the equilibrium, the balance of power, and moderately good relations among Red China, the USSR, India, Pakistan and the United States has never been easy. Perhaps it isn't even possible.

In 1965 India and Pakistan fought an angry, irrational 17-day war in which India showed surprising strength and Pakistan was outraged and humiliated over her rash, ill-conceived performance. A wild anti-American campaign followed. We were to blame for Pakistan's embarrassment, of course, because we had armed India!

From far away, Americans cannot understand why peace, or at least good neighborliness, forever eludes India and Pakistan. The blister, the nail in the thumb, the shell in the chamber overriding all else remains the irresolvable birthright feud: the Hindu-Moslem separation and the abrasive inequity of The Big Country and the Little Country side by side. The quarrel over unresolved and divided Kashmir, now a huge bore with little merit sustained for either side, is not the only thorn of hate. If Kashmir were solved tomorrow, some other conflict or new, goring passion would be found to keep the two at (fighting) arms' length.

Ah, me…in both great countries there are so many admirable people to know, to be fascinated by, to laugh with and enjoy! So many beautiful and graceful and gifted people with emotions and sentiment and feeling tender as a child's, as *people*. As nations, alas, how different!

Confronted by government, the people recede and are lost to us. We deal not with them but with their powerfully motivated governments. Here are all the fears and hatreds, the propaganda lines (anti-American, anti-Vietnam, anti-Israel, anti-Pakistan, anti-India, anti—anti—anti!) the ruthless power moves, the cynical secret deals to gain, to wedge, to split, or to tighten the fist, the decisions at the top that bring wars and blood and tears and destruction.

My short, indeed fatuous, career as a lady diplomat and my problem of the twins in Boston ended happily if unexpectedly. I married a second time.

I haven't a doubt my new husband John with that name h-l-a-v-etc., married me for the twins! All these years he had been winning golf cups and playing baseball and babysitting other people's kids. From the time he had first seen the baby pictures of Mike and Mary on my desk and at home he had fussed and fumed and infuriated me about them. *"Get the Kids Out Here, Immediately!'* was his relentless tirade and theme song. "I don't care how wonderful their grandparents are. *Here* is where they belong. 'We' can get them out here by Christmas if 'we' hurry and move fast enough!" So "we" did.

John sent out his own news story on the UP wire that Hlavacek had just became the father of twins, having married their mama. It was odd—or was it?—the round circle of fate and events. All four of us in this newlywed family had profound ties to China, but our paths had never remotely crossed until now.

A graduate of Carleton College in Minnesota, John says he specialized in sports first and math second. He must have. In 1963 his ego had a real explosion. He received one of the most elite awards in sportsmanship when he was named to the ranks of the *Sports Illustrated* Silver Anniversary All America!

While playing a lot of football, he was suddenly stricken with appendicitis in his senior year. During his recovery in the hospital, the well-known Congressman Walter Judd, a zealous Old China Hand, gave an impressive pep talk at Carleton. He made a strong plea for future graduates to dedicate themselves to a worthwhile contribution to a better world, specifically to helping modernize China. Young, dedicated teachers were urgently needed, and a reservoir of funds was available for a teacher exchange through the old indemnity settlement that had accrued from the Boxer Rebellion.

They didn't call it Peace Corps in those days, but the idealism to serve, the helping-hands motivation, the youthful moral rally to the cause was all there. The response must have been very gratifying to the missionary heart of Walter Judd, who saw a new program called Carleton-in-China set in motion. Incidentally, several other American universities had also established teacher-student exchange similar to Carleton-in-China, but these days it is just too depressing to ask what they accomplished. More young Americans learned to speak Chinese, many learned a lot about China, and some married pretty Chinese girls, but where are the bridges such vigorous dedication and enterprise were supposed to build? What mustard seed sprang from the gift of education? Where, today, are the students who were educated by the Americans? It makes one a crusty old cynic to speculate that they are either running the newly regrouped Communist government or they escaped and are making money in Hong Kong or Taiwan.

Flat on his back, *John never even heard Judd's* message. But his buddies signed him up in absentia anyway to be a teacher for two years. Then they came by to drop the word.

He hesitated, oh, maybe two seconds (go to China after graduation or home to Chicago to help run the family's pharmaceutical business? What th' hell. China might be great!). It was. He remained in the Orient, all told, nearly 18 years.

John spent all of World War II in China. Language was his wartime contribution. After several years of teaching English in Chinese schools but speaking local dialects every day (he lived in the school with the students and other Chinese teachers) and, of course, becoming fluent in Mandarin besides, his knowledge of regional dialects flagged him for G2 service at the American Embassy in Chungking. There was also a truck driving stint on the Burma Road, which he thoroughly enjoyed. He did no good deeds at all, he insists; he had a ball all the way!

After the war John began working for the UP in Calcutta. Then he moved to Bombay and eventually took over as UP's bureau chief.

Pakistan was as much his territory as India. We met there while he was on a business trip to Lahore. We both attended a meeting of editors and publishers. Only two women sat quietly listening at that dull meeting. I was one of them. The other was an elderly matron tented from head to toe in a black burka. John, the only other American, was introduced to me by the Pak editor of a small but politically peppery and influential newspaper I had long been cultivating to no avail. I had sent this editor American magazines, *The New York Times,* and polite notes trying to get into this paper a fair presentation of American policy and our world position. Nothing doing. The paper continued its almost traumatic hostility. This obstinate man could not just be labeled a communist and a hopeless case. He had a fixation on America and Americans—with one exception: Hlavacek! Not only did he get along with Hlavacek, he bought the UPI service, and the UPI picture service—and *paid his bills!*

Introducing me to John was actually the first time he had ever spoken to me in person. "Madame," observed my resistant editor, "this is my favorite American. Do you know why? Because no matter what I say, he never gets mad. Just gives me a big 'ha-ha-boy' and jokes, and we go off and have a beer. How can you be anti-American with Hlavacek? So long as my paper prospers—*inshalla* (pray God, a refrain heard as often as "isn't it?")—I shall buy his UPI service, although it is too expensive and AP is better—"

Several months afterward, when he received an invitation to our wedding (even though it would have been almost impossible for him to come to Bombay) he took all the credit. His acceptance of one American had to stretch to include two.

Honeymoon in Europe, spent mostly *eating* in Italy!—then home to Boston for the two youngsters who were a bit shy with That Lady, as they called me at first. Worse yet, That Lady had to rush them out for a whole list of inoculations—but we flew almost nonstop back to John in Bombay in time for our first Christmas together as an instant new family. That Christmas for four came exactly two months after our wedding.

In hot, humid Bombay we discovered there were no Christmas trees to be had. Too late, we learned the American Consulate people ordered trees flown down from the north, but orders had to be placed weeks ahead of time. We were frantic. This Christmas had to be better than any the twins could remember!

Finally someone told us the Bombay Zoo *rented* trees in tubs, but they didn't have very many and it was already close to Christmas Eve. We rushed to the zoo. One tree remained. It looked like a crash-landed green stork! Its trunk was a skinny stalk, its branches were like green feathers in the rain. It was ghastly, but it was a *tree*. We could have it for only two days before it went to a party(!) and then to a hotel for a New Year's Eve ball!

Christmas was a wonderful time for the children to get to know "Daddy John," as they called him at first. He called them Mike 'n' Ike because it went together like Mutt 'n' Jeff. Our Indian friends were amused to think we had named our daughter after our president.

Daddy John was not about to waste any time getting the rest of the family going. Our new addition arrived exactly nine months later! I had one of India's best and most famous obstetricians, Dr. Shirodkar, who was so bored with babies that he used to slit envelopes and sort his mail during my visits to his office. He just barely got to Breach Candy Hospital, where I was given an aspirin tablet and little else for the delivery.

Patients who overlooked the sometimes-erratic medical care and uneven standards at Breach Candy (who ever *named* that hospital?) also overlooked the most gorgeous view ever afforded from a bed of pain or childbirth. Breach Candy Hospital by the sea is certainly the most luxuriously beautiful hospital in all India or almost anywhere else, situated like a gleaming white, modern, resort hotel above a terrace of brilliant flowers. Patients could sink back amid the pillows and gaze out to sea where fishing boats and dowhs with their three-cornered sails slipped by as in a dream.

With newborn babies the hospital staff was very casual. I was back in my room with John when a nurse came in with Suzy. Barely ten minutes had passed since her arrival, or so it seemed, and here she was!

"Say hello to your new daughter. Sweet little thing, isn't she?" With this the nurse handed her to me and left the room. No masks, no fuss about germs—we just held onto her, shakily.

Two more babies, both boys, John Patrick (he will have none of that "Pat'rik stuff" these days, jes' *Johnny*, okay?) and Jimmy. These last two made a grand total of *five!* Very grand, very total. No more, thank you, Charlie Brown!

A few years before Jimmy was born, on one of our rare trips home to the States, we changed ships in Genoa. We stayed a week or so in a charming little pension called the Assarotti. There were seven of us on this trip, as we had Tai Bhai along, too.

The Assarotti had nice large rooms, big beds with springy mattresses, and each room had a wash stand. Bathrooms were down the hall. There was even a bidet in the bathroom, very handy, we found, for piling up laundry as we let water run in and out of the tub! Its use as a laundry catch answered the children's questions of "whatzzat?" but not until after they had experimented with the spigots.

The Assarotti was not cheap, but it had an attractive and pleasant atmosphere, the food was good, and we could walk everywhere downtown from the front door. But Johnny Pat was in diapers, and neither Genoa nor the Assarotti, at least in those days, had diaper service or a guests' laundry room. When I inquired at the desk about laundry, a young Italian clerk with sideburns simply smiled vaguely: "Ah, Madame—something—something" he murmured soothingly in Italian. Tai Bhai had no choice but to fill the bathtub and the bidet every day, doing everything by hand. But where to hang anything to dry? Back to the nice young man with the sideburns: Rooftop? Basement? He smiled even more sweetly, shrugged and shook his head. Tai Bhai and I hung the diapers around the room, over the lamps, out the window in a tiny patch of sun. But the manager assailed me the very next day. "No laundry in rooms, Madame! First Class Pensione! No allowit!" Very well, what are we to do with the wet clothing? He stared at us, hurt and offended and angry. "Laundry," he said pronouncing each word like a priest intoning sinners' penance, "Laundry must be dry cleaned! Tomorrow morning, give room maid all baby's washings. We send out. Comes back (fingers snapping crisply) Expresso!"

Diapers dry cleaned? Expresso? Well, when in Rome or in Genoa….

Barely 48 hours later we stood on the top deck of an Italian liner, outward bound for New York. The crossing was to take about two weeks with one or two stops. As we stood watching the enchanting view of Genoa recede in the late afternoon sun, Tai Bhai pulled at my arm. "Memsahib, you have got Johnny's nappies somewhere in your suitcase? Hotel man give you laundry bundle?" she urgently wanted to know. Twenty-alarm bells—panic bells—rang in my head! No—hotel man gave me no bundle. In the confusion and packing I had forgotten the dry-cleaned diapers—"Expresso"—hah!

I don't dare tell how we managed—they will never let us on that Italian line again! Tai Bhai even tried cutting up her 6-yard white cotton saris, but we found sari cloth was as porous as a sieve.

I later wrote That Man at the Assarotti a letter, pointing out that we had had a little problem. Months later, by sea mail from Genoa, three bundles arrived. They had indeed been dry cleaned and still smelled faintly of benzene. But from the Assarotti Man—*not one word!*

6

Golden India

✦

(1952–57)

Our years in India were the best of times for the great subcontinent. India's Golden Age under India's most glamorous, most democratic aristocrat, the gentle and elegant Brahmin, Jawaharlal Nehru, that great humanist, that tremendous politician, that vague, one-side-seeing idealist, so moving and appealing, and so exasperating! His family, his staff, his cabinet and his Congress Party trembled before the occasional wrath of the Nehru temper. But he was a dove to the world, the soul of peace under socialism, with neutrality and civilized compromise for all.

He admired a number of Americans as individuals, and he even listened with respect and personal warmth to some who came to New Delhi, but in the broadest sense, Americans were too much for him. He never, alas, really liked us, appreciated, or grasped the American motivation. He never caught the spirit that was behind the vitality, the whole American compulsion and power drive. He accepted our good office and years of generous aid running into millions, not counting private foundations, educational and cultural exchanges, as our responsibility in our own self-interest. That is largely an unwholesome and unlovely truth. It is true because we would not like to see the hammer and sickle flying from Government House in New Delhi and unwholesome because disproportionate aid, year in year out, breeds contempt and misunderstanding of obligation. India had an obligation to correct those conditions that perpetuated the need, the starvation, the grinding inadequacies of its social and economic order. It did not owe us thanks, let us say on a purely practical basis, but it did have to work harder, it did have to learn a few modern lessons, it did have to set its house vigorously in order!

Perhaps Indira Gandhi understands all this far better than did her father. At the height of his fame, with the halo of saving democracy in Asia around his handsome head, Nehru was in no position to be taught lessons…or to be advised by Americans with their vulgar, odious dollars.

It was a great show while it lasted, a heyday not to be seen again. Nehru had only to beckon and everyone came running: communist, dictator, king, emperor, British royalty or Arab sheik, little men in Mao suits, overweight men in black boiler suits, kings in gold braid, breathtaking ladies in furs and pearls and crown jewels. During those years the world went to a party and Delhi was the "in" spot! No setting anywhere could touch the gardens of Rashtapati Bhavan, the Presidential palace, built for the British viceroys. It was, and still is today, so magnificent it makes the exterior, at least, of Buckingham Palace look like a German railway station.

During the winter season, sparkling and crisp and cool until about March, the Indian spring was afloat with flowers and brilliant colors, bluest skies, green terraces, green fields pushing up the new crop, the greenest trees, some so old God himself must have put down the seed. And roses, roses *this big*, my dear! Not even England grows such bloomers! (Well, at least Indian roses are their equals.) Ah yes, in the cool season great people came and great receptions were held for Nehru's friends. The world was at peace—and at parties in the garden.

Correspondents who covered and filmed all of the festivities were invited to almost everything except state banquets. We even went to those, too, not to dine but to cover. Our cars rolled up right along with the diplomats and our doors were opened by white-gloved attendants just as though we were Somebodies. Amid the marigolds and petunias and frothing fountains; a turn past the Indian President's six-foot bodyguards in coats of scarlet and wearing navy blue and gold-cloth puggarees; amid willowy Indian beauties faintly scented with sandalwood or Chanel, red-dotted on the brow, ears swinging with a dowry shower of real jewels—and strolling just nearby in contrast, a Congress Party *walla* (merchant) type from the provinces in dhoti and sandals and handspun *khadi* cap; amid all this the famous guests moved about at Nehru's side.

Sometimes all the informal, casual mingling was almost too much for the famous guests. Back in the Kremlin, for instance, the Soviet bosses do not stroll about with people near enough to touch. Occasionally royalty did not stroll among the Mortals but remained in a place of honor behind a golden cord, seated upon silk damask and gold chairs making chitchat with Nehru and the Indian president while the rest of us observed from a distance. The Shah of Iran, for instance, sat behind the gold cord. With him on this trip was the green-eyed

Saroya wearing the first really short skirts we had seen in Delhi. When she was seated upon the divan, a "shocking" length of bony leg and knee and a bit of thigh were clearly visible. Bored and uncomfortable, Saroya drew a cigarette from a jeweled case, put it into her red, very full mouth, and turned to the Indian president for a light. An elderly orthodox Hindu, the startled president merely stared back at her. Suddenly the Shah, then Nehru, rushed from their chairs with lighters snapping. Saroya inhaled deeply, then exhaled, sending a cloud of smoke into the president's face. Aghast at such boorish manners, an Indian official's wife standing nearby remarked: "It takes more than marriage to make a queen!"

The most exciting reception was one an American would not expect to be invited to attend—honoring the Red Chinese Premier Chou En-lai. We were invited, not as Americans, but as correspondents, and of course, we rushed off twice as eager and very early. I remember standing for a moment staring down at Chou, not realizing until I stood that close to him how gawkingly tall Americans are among the Asians! (Recall President Johnson on his state visits to SE Asia, towering over toy-sized Asian leaders so tiny even heel lifts couldn't help.) Chou, to be sure, looked exactly like his pictures but the in-person impression was of an older man whose urbane and polished social manner is but the thinnest shell of exterior. Although among the lingering senior elite he is the one Chinese most at ease with foreigners, and he is reputed to be witty and keen in social debate, I sensed the inner man was something very different, much more elusive, not quite so urbane.

I did not quite have the courage or command of French to venture a word or two of conversation with Chou. I did not know, for sure, whether he spoke English. But I did manage two or three stammered words to Nikita Khrushchev, who looked so much like a harmless grandpa. Haile Selassie, Ethiopia's Lion of Judah, was a fiercely erect little man, almost overwhelmed by his military uniform, medals, gold braid, and sword! The dark and regal ladies of the royal entourage lit up the night with their diamonds and Dior gowns, but they were on display: they seemed uncomfortable and never smiled.

Briefly too, in later years, came Queen Elizabeth, and at other times Lord and Lady Mountbatten (*she* was a one, as the British say, what dash, what style, what a smash!). Little wonder she was the light of Nehru's eye and he escorted her about on his arm, utterly radiant, looking twenty years younger! I shall never forget my last glimpse of her. It was at an Independence Day reception in January. She arrived, displaying the total look, in ruby red satin. Yes, *satin*, from a mad little satin cocktail hat down to exact-match gown and bowed slippers. She was an original, and someday Julie Andrews will star in a wide-screen version of the fabulous life and loves of Edwina!

Amid all the glamour, the Dalai Lama came down from Tibet, though with the veiled permission of Peking, to pay a visit to Nehru. He was permitted to leave his own country only because the Chinese were already in New Delhi and could keep a constant eye on him. Incidentally, the Dalai, who had drawn me with a compulsive fascination all the way to the airport for this arrival, was a great disappointment. Swathed in his wine-red robes, with his stubby crew haircut and squinty eyes behind rimmed old-fashioned glasses, he seemed far from the romantic figure presented in the *National Geographic* by Lowell Thomas. Incidentally, the Dalai's mother also came with her son, and she more than took up my slack on the reincarnated Buddha. She was simply marvelous, responding to each new, earthy, twentieth-century discovery in New Delhi with cries of delight. Mama Lama, as I called her, had the face of an English walnut, with bright black-button eyes. She wore a long Tibetan gown, brocade apron, boots, and a fur-lined hat with ear flaps! Aggressive and acquisitive, Mama quickly collected a store of goods. But she really lost her head over automobiles. Off on her own one day, she bought a Ford station wagon, with whitewalls, radio and power steering. She must have paid for it with a brick of gold bullion, of which the Dalai had an impressive supply!

When their state visit was over (Nehru told Mama Lama's alarmed and frightened son to go back to Lhasa and not cause trouble, above all he was not to rock India's boat of friendship with the Chinese), Mama Lama wanted the station wagon delivered "FAB" (Foot and Back) straight to the capital of Tibet. When her son refused, she had a royal fit. The wagon could not go. It had to remain in Darjeeling with two other sons living there as quiet businessmen in the import-export business. It was at their home one day that I not only learned about the car but had a ride in it with Mount Everest climber Tenzing Norgay at the wheel.

I have a passing thought on the Dalai Lama in his present unhappy exile status, as his plight relates to Nehru. If ever there was a case of the weak exploited and annihilated by the strong, or of crass aggression, of the great big grab right out in the open for the world to see—it was the Red Chinese takeover of little Tibet. And there was nothing Nehru feared more than Red China on India's mountainous frontier. But Nehru was a great moralist. A posturing idealist, a vocal umpire calling the world's foul plays. Confronted with aggression's victim seeking shelter and sanctuary, moral support and help from India, Nehru barely had room in the inn. He wanted no awkward houseguests to give China any excuse to move on India. But here was the Dalai, his family, his entourage, and hundreds of primitive Tibetan refugees. Only under strong pressure did Nehru permit the Dalai to stay, far from the capital, in silent retirement in the hills. Above all else was the condition of temporary residence: the Tibetan leader was not permitted to use India as a basis for attack or accusation, or a striking point from which to take any action against China.

The Dalai bowed to Nehru's conditions, and arrangements were made to care for the Tibetans, an added embarrassment on Indian soil. Eventually many of them were resettled in Switzerland. Many more came to India, some of them moving on to Nepal while others remained in India.

Their welcome in India was a very thin one, indeed, and money for the Tibetans' housing, food, medical care, and rehabilitation was provided not by fellow Buddhists in India or elsewhere, but by the Christian West. I recalled Mama Lama's station wagon and I remembered the pictures I had seen of the dramatic flight from Lhasa of the living Buddha and his family—with pack horses laden with Tibetan treasures, gold bullion and rare artifacts. Were the Shepherd and his family to live in luxurious comfort while the flock was cared for by the charity of foreign institutions and Western religions? Apparently so.

Where Nehru was less than the Good Samaritan to the Dalai Lama, his daughter Indira in later years was also, it seems to me, without moral and womanly compassion for Svetlana Stalin.

When Stalin's daughter came to India with the ashes of her dead Indian "husband," she sought to live quietly and in peace with her friends and family. Her initial inquiries were nervously refused. More letters were written to higher-ups. The answer was the same. Where Nehru feared China, now Indira feared the Soviet Union would be angry if India sheltered Svetlana. Even so, before her visa expired, Svetlana met Indira Gandhi face to face. The answer was still no. Indira, also a widow, also a woman alone with many burdens, found no compassion, no hand of sympathy to extend to another desperate human being. I do not think I can bear another righteous moral word from New Delhi ever again.

The supreme irony of this, of course, is that grovelling fear earns only contempt for weakness and opens the door to new danger. Today, as I write, Indian soldiers have been shot and killed on Indian soil by the Chinese on the border.

American children growing up in New Delhi at this time got a sort of animated cartoon of the passing parade of world figures. Mike 'n' Ike were dismissed early from their American school one day so they would be home and off the downtown streets when India put on a big welcome for Red China's Premier, Chou En-lai. But of course John was filming the whole event and the twins were more or less with Daddy. They crowded in with everybody else to see what was going on. When a man went by handing out welcome signs, streamers and little 2-anna paper flags of China and India, no one noticed the two small Americans. They got flags, too, and waved them and yelled with everyone else when Chou rode by with Nehru.

The slogans and banners of that day were ironic and prophetic. Hence my not-so-flippant suggestion of an animated political cartoon: "Hindi-China Bai Bai" the banners shouted, meaning Hindus and Chinese are brothers. But the "bai bai" could also be transliterated as "byebye!"

Mike and Ike brought home their flags. We sent them back to New York with John's film, but I'm sorry about that. We should have kept them. The twins will someday be curious about the China where they were born.

The twins were nine when Jimmy, our last-born, made his appearance near the end of our time in India. When baby production gets up to *five*, the whole thing is almost like another run to the dentist! It's all so yawny and "what—again?" I well recall that day in the hospital in Delhi in the midst of the July monsoons when I was just coming to after producing James M., number five, *positively the last*. John bent over me, shaking my shoulders in great excitement. "Hey—wake up, wake up," he yelled. *"THE ANDREA DORIA IS AT THE BOTTOM OF THE ATLANTIC!* We just got the news! What a story! Passengers overboard—big names, so many prominent people—massive rescue operation—heroism and tragedy—husbands and wives separated—people going down—being pulled out of the water!—Terrific! Like the *Lusitania* or the *Titanic!* We're already getting pictures back by radio!" Not a word about our own "story," a dimple-chinned eight pounder sleeping soundly by my bed.

All in all, we found India a singularly healthy place for raising our large family. We did not live in a village, or Indian style, of course. We had air conditioning, modern conveniences, that even more modern miracle called "Help" (two hands and two feet are *still* greater than anything you plug in), and excellent doctors like tall, gentle, and lovely Sita Sen. I can still see her as she dashed into the delivery room, belatedly, in her white eyelet sari and green satin choli.

In our rooms at the Cecil Hotel I had the home office to keep an eye on. The phone and typewriter were always right by the bed, but I was *at home,* supervising the brood closely or doing things myself most of the time.

But nothing seemed to reassure distant grandmothers in America that India was not a "terrible" place for raising small children. All those *diseases*.

One day I was amused to write my mother back in Harrisburg, Pennsylvania that she could now relax, because we had finally settled the score on diseases. At my insistence, John and I had taken the twins, then about 7 or 8, along with us while covering Nehru's vigorous campaigning for India's first democratic national election. We had decided upon the long car trip from Delhi to Indore, an old princely state in Central India. Arriving late and weary in a comfortable, modern hotel (except that hot bath water had to be ordered the night before) we were too tired to pay much attention to Mary's complaint that she "itched sumpin' awful!" "You'll have a nice hot bath tomorrow morning and you'll" (yawn, yawn) "feel much better," I reassured her. The lights were 10-watt and dim in the dining room where we were joined by all the other correspondents from the wire services, *Time, Newsweek* and *The New York Times*. No one glanced at Ike. The next morning, in broad daylight, I got a look at her itches. She might have been drenched from top to toe, all over her scalp and even across her eyelids, in red pepper or paprika!

Chicken pox! Before we could get her home, Mike came down with them, too, and Danji, our Hindu driver, got a serious adult case of the same itches and pox! Smeared livid pink with calamine lotion, we had no choice but to make our way home slowly by car. A Canadian missionary doctor in Indore advised us to make the trip by gradual stages so that the worst infectious period would be past before the twins got home to toddling Suzy and Johnny Pat. So the recovery trip included a drive through the central plains, past old forts, historic ruins, past peacocks, monkeys, camels, and at the Amber Palace, there was a ride on an elephant (both twins suddenly recovered completely) up the hill to the fascinating, romantic old ruin on the top. We assumed the elephant, gorgeously painted and adorned with flowers on both ears and down his trunk, was well past the age for chicken pox, as was his mahout.

Democratic elections in India were a very moving and stirring sight to see. Alas, one could only realize much later that the poor villagers never got much in return for their efforts at the ballot box. The little paper slips did not bring them food, or water during droughts, a schoolhouse, or an extra rupee. But voting was an exercise very pleasing and cheering to approving Western eyes.

Covering elections and the campaign tours all over India with John brought me frequently into the receptive and friendly company of Indira Gandhi. We spoke together lightly and pleasantly almost every day. Sometimes the conversations were really interviews and she would be careful of what she said. If I asked a question she did not want to answer, she would simply smile and look at me wisely without saying a word. But over a long period of time I could not help establishing an easy rapport with her. So casual and continual was this carefully cultivated tie to Indira that I typed and saved my notes from only one private interview with her.

It is a great temptation for writers who have known highly placed, attractive, and interesting persons informally in the past, to recall a very privileged friendship on an intimate first-name basis later on when that person becomes world famous. John F. Kennedy would hardly have had time to be president if he had spent as much time with all his book-writing friends as they claimed. I would not wish or dare to presume so much with the woman who, as I write this, is still India's Prime Minister. But I lived in India in the days when freedom and democracy and India itself were all so young and exuberant and going somewhere.

Indira was very much a Nehru, every inch her father's daughter. She thoroughly enjoyed her busy life, although it cost her a carefree childhood, normal family life, companionship in a circle of young friends, and even her marriage. She lived in the airy world at the top, and if she was exclusive and alone a great deal, the cost was well worth it. She has *chosen* her life and now pursues it with even more vehement drive and ruthless tenacity.

Her greatest burden was enforced and unending speech-making and social obligations. But public life kept her traveling. The restless Nehrus traveled at the slightest opportunity at home and abroad. Too long away from fresh air, from the countryside, the mountains, his worshipping people (Nehru not only loved them, he *needed* them! Their ardor, their helpless condition fueled his ambition), and the Prime Minister cancelled appointments and took to the road or plane. Indira and the press always followed. Whenever possible, I went along too. Many times on these exhausting long tours to back of beyond, to remote towns or old temples (Nehru was as eager as any tourist to sight-see and discover his own country), Indira and I were the only women present.

Generous instinct and a naturally friendly nature, especially as I was well known to her, often led her to extend to me a very informal entrée. I understood the mere accident of circumstances as an interval, nothing more. I just happened to be there.

Later on, I worked with her worldly and sophisticated aunt, the late Krishna Hutheesing, on a book-length article about the Prime Minister and Madam Pandit for the *Ladies Home Journal.* Editorial sessions with Krishna lasted nearly a year and extended from Bombay to Delhi. Indira often met me casually coming or going during those working days. She saw me as a fixture (pregnant, incidentally) for whom no fuss or bother was required. She was always very much herself with me.

Indira Gandhi with Pegge, October 1968.

That was then. Not so today. When I was last in India on a television filming assignment with John, Indira boarded the plane with us for a regular commercial flight from Delhi to Bombay. I saw at once that the Indira I had known was now understandably burdened, a preoccupied mature woman. The years quite naturally have taken their toll. They have marked me, alas, as well! Indira had not only deepened in maturity but there was about her now a new aura of isolation, which held one at long arm's length, or so it seemed to me, and I kept my distance. She is now 50, and the years have been strenuous mentally and emotionally. She flashed a warm, recognizing smile to John, however, and then turned to me with a polite greeting. But there was, in those few minutes, no recollection of the past. She gestured toward her woman companion. "My secretary," she said, sighing. "This will be a working trip all the way. We shan't even get a bite of dinner to eat." They didn't.

We arrived in Bombay past midnight. Indira, first to disembark, was met by Bombay government officials who seemed eager to heap problems upon her silk-wrapped shoulders the minute she stepped from the plane into the humid June night. I admired her but did not envy her as I watched her vanish in a gleaming black official car.

First reaction to her tenure as Prime Minister from returning friends, United States businessmen, or the chance Indian visitor passing through the States were not favorable. Was the idea of a *lady* Prime Minister too unpalatable to Indians? Was having a female, though a Nehru, at the head of the government just too much for the country at this critical stage? If Indira had been Nehru's *son,* would it have made a difference? I was clearly on the defensive. The world's first lady Prime Minister in Ceylon, Madam Sirimavo Bandaranaike, had badly bungled the job, leaving her country bankrupt and all but Communist, but I staunchly supported Indira.

Other women joined me in her defense. "She's new at it," they would say. "She's coping as well as any man possibly could. Look at the problems she inherited!" Men, however, wasted no time on excuses or comparisons. "Indira's government is weak—has no guts—gives into every tough situation. She'll be out as soon as political power rivals can agree on her replacement. India's an impossible country. It cannot be run by a woman. Indira is impractical, politically inexperienced." (After 17 years of life with father? How so?) "She's still living on all those worn-out socialist myths of the past. Look at the economy—the country's slipping badly. Law and order and national unity are rapidly and alarmingly deteriorating." So the conversations and opinions ran.

To hold to its course, maintain its institutions as the world's most populous democracy, India needs extraordinary, very strong leadership. It needs a giant, a hero-revolutionary to whom nothing, including radical and swift change, is impossible! *This leader has not yet been found in India's cloudy twentieth century.*

With grim forebodings—after the last series of elections that indicate an unchecked downward trend for both Indira and the Congress Party—one can only predict that discipline, toughness, and organizational strength lie as a last resort with the army. It happened in Pakistan. This may be India's fate, eventually. No one seems to have much optimism, *based on realism,* over the enduring prospects for India's once ecstatically heralded democracy.

It would be presumptuous of me to add to this dismal outlook any further assessment of my own about Indira as Prime Minister. I will merely share some personal observations, which provide human insight into her personality and character. People in America are so quick to admire anyone who is seen often enough in the news, on a *Time* cover, in *Vogue* or *McCall's,* or frequently in the newspapers. Indira Gandhi's name is always on the Ten Most Admired list and deserves to be, though I doubt if Indira knows or cares one whit.

I am always asked what she was *really* like when I got to know her. Well, this is what I remember. Few, if any, heads of government are ever really happy with the press. Indira had many occasions to give sharp rejoinder to interviewers she considered presumptuous or downright impertinent. *Time* was her particular cross to bear, and she would quote back to the unblinking correspondent teasing and biting little phrases that had pricked and irked her. But *Time* had no monopoly on her exasperation. We all at some time came in for our share when stories out of New Delhi were particularly critical, which was very often.

But once when she was in a better mood she told me an amusing little story. We were at one of those unending garden receptions, where the weary soft drink (at prohibition parties), an obnoxious bilge called orange squash, was served. Indira had just let the *Time* man feel the rap of her knuckles. He had listened, made a few defensive cracks, then excused himself. To his retreating back Indira addressed an observation. "News people and photographers," she said, "are always following us around but still they always miss the best stories." "Oh, how so?" I was all ears. "Well," she smiled, "we have just had a most unusual Christmas at the Nehrus..." Indeed, as she described it, it had been unusual. The visiting state guests at the time were Red China's Chou En-lai and the Dalai Lama of Tibet, *and* Peking's replacement for the Dalai, the malicious-looking, head-shaved Panchen Lama. As Christmas guests, these three were a bit awkward. Furthermore, Prime Minister Nehru and Indira had just returned from a trip to the White House in Washington.

Communists, Buddhists, and Hindus do not observe Christmas, of course, so December 25 is just another day to them. But all the Nehrus had enjoyed a strong and indulgent Westernized upbringing. Christmas was always a joyous, gift-giving holiday, and Indira told me they had a Christmas tree and lots of presents whenever possible. "No one enjoys presents and surprises and family jokes more than Father," she said. And Indira was the family gift-buyer as often as she could get out to shop. In America, she said, she loved Washington stores, and in New York she was entranced with Lord and Taylor's Christmas decorations. But best of all she had been thrilled to find those noisy, new, battery-powered cars and airplanes, which whirl around the room directed by a small hand control! They had just come on the market. She knew her two boys would love them. With easy candor Indira admitted the two boys were very upset and "put out" that even on Christmas Day, a private family day, very stiff and difficult state vis-

itors had to be entertained at the Prime Minister's. She told them it would just be
for lunch, and if they behaved they could be excused immediately afterward. The
boys had waited for their mother's first signal to escape and had swiftly vanished.
Soon the *N-z-z-z-ZZZZZ* roar of the battery-powered planes drifted across the
terrace. Curious, Chou En-lai excused himself and left the table. Then the Dalai
bowed himself away, and on his heels even the villainous Panchen Lama hurried
off in the direction of the *N-z-z-z-z-ZZZZZ!* Laughing, Indira declared, "Father
and I dashed after them too. And what did we find: Chou En-lai running around
with the airplane and the Dalai Lama down on his hands and knees playing with
the cars. What a picture it would have made. Think of it in *Life!* Without a picture to prove it, no one would believe it."

She told me another story about a visit to the White House with her father.
Dwight D. Eisenhower was then president. "You know," she mused, "I have
always liked Mamie Eisenhower. She is such a modest, thoughtful, *easy* person.
She makes no demands or fuss, and I find her a very warm and comfortable hostess. But one morning she told me she had invited some of the most outstanding
career women in America to meet me at a 'small,' informal White House luncheon. I was aghast. I'm not good at large *ladies'* functions. I was somewhat on
the spot. You know, when I thought about all those women, and what they *do*,
that many of them commanded hundreds of employees, ran huge banks or factories or industries, were responsible for decisions involving tremendous amounts
of money where a mistake would be a disaster, or they made important legal decisions, or were doctors or scientists—well, it was really too overwhelming. I knew
it was an honor to meet them, but I shrank from it. What does one talk about to
such women? As guest of honor I would have to lead the conversation, and I just
didn't feel up to it. I didn't want to say no to my favorite hostess, either, so I
explained I had an appointment and would have to leave early. But I didn't
leave." She turned a radiant face toward me. "I was just delighted with those
women. They were all so—oh, completely themselves, so utterly feminine! First
of all, they came in looking so charming. They wore pretty hats and dresses with
ruffles or bows and white gloves and pearls. You Americans always have those little white gloves and a purse and a string of pearls! Well, there wasn't one who
overwhelmed me. We sat through lunch laughing and chatting about silly little
personal and family things. In fact, we ended up talking about our children and
grandchildren and passing around snapshots. You would never have guessed all
the work they did when they went back to their offices."

Indira would grow quiet and thoughtful after an outburst of conversation. She would be totally silent in a complete mental departure. No less polite, no less friendly, just gone.

Another time an editor of a magazine had suggested I approach Indira, between her world travels, which then were whirling her from Peking to Moscow, Paris and London, for some observations on what women of the West could learn from women of the East. Inane, but requested from New York, so I asked her.

When I mentioned the theme to her on the telephone, she snorted: "*Nothing,* absolutely nothing! Our Indian women are too lazy, wasting their time and their education. They do nothing for India, make no contribution!" But she hastened to add on a more cordial note, "Do come along to tea if you like. I'll be home tomorrow anytime after four...." We did not bother with women of the East or West that day. Or even with tea, which I recall being cold by the time I arrived and the color of California redwoods. The unimportant mechanics of hospitality at the Nehrus were usually left to servants. We discussed two fascinating subjects: her impressions of a trip to Peking and her husband, Feroze Gandhi, the shadow in her life, the most painful and elusive subject one could ever bring up. Only the two of us sat there in the restful, quiet, warm afternoon. A pencil and fold of copy paper (I never owned a notebook) lay in my lap. I did not need them to remember a single word.

Indira was a portrait of softness and grace. She could have been painted that afternoon, as she sat there in her white sari and sandals, with softest watercolors, all the lines blurry and melting into the green terrace, the still trees, the misty pinks and reds of distant rose beds.

When she told me about China, she spoke not as a government official but as an enchanted sightseer. Peking was truly so amazing, such an old and fascinating city, that she had been exasperated with Chinese hosts who infringed upon and rigidly organized her time. On arrival she found every day had been meticulously planned, allowing her time to see nothing! Every day she was scheduled to dash to factories, schools, child clinics, nursery schools, cultural exhibitions, and work centers. This was not her idea of a visit to Peking. Besides, she had a long list of things to shop for and was very, very determined to be left alone. "I just put my foot down after a few days," she declared, "and refused to see any more workers' centers. The Chinese did not understand, or maybe they *did* and simply tried to keep me from being nosy. All I wanted was to go shopping, and I did!"

Heavy programs were also laid on in Moscow, too, but the Chinese had been much more persistent. For someone who had been restrained from shopping in

Peking until the last few days, Indira had many beautiful Chinese things in her wing of the residence. Collector's items, they adorned all the walls and tables of the upstairs social rooms.

Since the original theme of my interview was something new in the exchange of ideas between East and West, I asked Indira what she thought would be the reaction to a *woman* ambassador from the United States to India. Indira nodded her head. "Depending upon the woman, I think it would be an excellent idea." The first name to pop into my head was Mrs. Clare Boothe Luce. What did Indira think of her as future ambassador to India? Silence. She avoided answering for a moment. Finally she murmured that a woman of international personality, someone like Eleanor Roosevelt, would be well accepted in India.

Now that she is herself Prime Minister I doubt if Indira would welcome another woman. Especially from the powerful United States. Despite surface amity, diplomatic relations between India and the United States have always been touchy and difficult whether the issue be *aid* (the most acutely painful one), private investment, fertilizer factories, the U.S.-Israel tie, Vietnam, or Pakistan.

The responsibility of official entertaining as her father's hostess had not been easy for Indira. Her childhood and girlhood in Allahabad had not been spent learning social graces. Quite the contrary. "I find," Indira made a small tent of her fingers, "I find the best way to manage state dinners is to keep guests in small groups at a number of attractive small tables. I loathe big, long tables, although I dine at them far too often! I am personally consulted on the food and entertainment, if any, and our protocol office sends out the invitations and takes charge of all the seating and notes any special formality that must be accorded certain persons of high rank. They are so very good at their job, the protocol people, that I need never worry. They just take over and tell me what has been arranged." No wine is served as a matter of personal choice. "And," she added, "I go along with the official policy of the Congress Party, which discourages drinking at public functions. "But," she frowned delicately, "it is my personal opinion that all this prohibition only makes people drink more and pay more for it!" Also, "We are a poor country and we miss a lot of revenue from excise because of prohibition," she sighed. "I don't think I'm a hostess like the glamorous ladies whose table settings and menus are written up in magazines. My table settings are nothing very special at all. A few flowers or candles, but again, the protocol people do everything. Lately, though, I have been observing how other clever women make a great art of dining, of their food, the service, and the way their banquet tables are set. We have seen some simply amazing dinner tables here in Delhi! One year there was an Italian countess here as the wife of the ambassador. She had a great flair for entertaining, and we loved to go to her parties. One night she led Father and me to a dinner table spread with gold Benares brocade with a lace cloth on top! From Italy had come her own personal service of gold plates. It was all simply stunning, but I was afraid of spilling a morsel of food on that cloth!"

At the height of the political-social season, Indira and the Prime Minister on occasion entertained kings and comrades in swift succession in a single week. How did she manage Right and Left in rapid order? "Well, as a child I was in Europe when my mother was ill. I put the time to good use by studying languages. I'm fairly at home in French and know some German. Most of our foreign guests speak one of those languages, if not English. Visitors ask a lot of questions about India, and that makes conversation very safe and gets us through dinner without awkward pauses." After a light smile, she added that the Russians and the Chinese were her most difficult guests. The Chinese interpreters were very quick to convey the meaning of a sentence rather than every word, but it was still tedious.

Whenever she volunteered any remarks on China I froze, praying she would go on and on, chatting. She did. "Chou En-lai," she observed, "does *not* speak fluent English as I have often read he does. He can manage a few simple sentences. He admitted he was studying to improve his English. In fact," Indira noted, "there was quite an improvement when he was here last. Truly remarkable, because outside of a few trips abroad, when would he use English in China?"

"Our family is very fond of Chinese food," she continued. "We all know how to use chopsticks, too, including Father. Years ago my grandfather, Motilal Nehru (a great lawyer), had a Japanese gentleman for a client. He became very fond of Grandfather and one day presented him with a beautiful set of chopsticks. We really put them to good use. They were on the table whenever we had any kind of chopped up dish, or when we attempted a Chinese or Japanese dinner."

As she found herself so much in the limelight entertaining famous and glamorous people, what was her own little glamour secret? She shook her head. "None, I have none at all. Only once that I can recall did I really want to look terribly glamorous. It wasn't on my wedding day. It was for the London coronation of Queen Elizabeth. That time I went to Elizabeth Arden for hairdo, manicure, everything. I could hardly get in. Everyone else had booked months ahead. Nowadays I don't have much time, and it's so hot that I don't bother much."

The husband of Indira, Feroze Gandhi, was at one time a Congress Party worker, back in the early days when he worked on a small newspaper. In later years he was an arch-critic, perhaps with a hypersensitive chip on his shoulder, as he served vigorously, outspokenly, in the Indian Parliament. He was no relation to the saintly Mahatma; in fact, Feroze wasn't even a Hindu. He was a Parsee, which is as different from a Hindu as a Jew is from a Roman Catholic. Now that he is dead, and his story is such a forlornly sad one, it hardly seems appropriate or in good taste to revive memories of him. But as the marriage reveals another side of Indira Gandhi, perhaps we may recall the remainder of my conversation with her that day.

At the conclusion of our very enjoyable conversation, I delicately broached the matter of Feroze, who was never seen at the Prime Minister's house or with their two sons. I said "never." Perhaps it was really never when outsiders were around.

One problem of their incompatibility had been Feroze's refusal to jump to the tune of his father-in-law. A "yes" man he was not. Strongly on the defensive, Feroze considered Indira his wife, not Nehru's daughter. In this he was mistaken. Indira was a Nehru first and foremost. When it came to a showdown, Indira had simply packed up and left, taking the two boys to Grandpa's house. There she moved in another world with great preoccupation among the elite and powerful. Feroze had his pride. He refused to follow, refused to beg, but he had little to offer Indira that could in any way compare with being the first Lady of India! He had little money or family influence, so he lived his own life almost oblivious of his physical surroundings. The break between Feroze and Indira had grown out of anger, the kind that makes forgiveness difficult. The marriage, which had originally been a romantic young love match against bitter opposition which shook the country, had now ended in sadness and hurt pride and total apartness. Feroze had undoubtedly been Indira's only romantic love, hence the disappointment and emotion over him was profound and intense. I had not guessed *how intense* until I observed the swift change of face and voice when Indira spoke of him. The bitterness had never come to the surface before. Perhaps it is true that women like Indira whose love life goes awry are driven passionately in other directions, usually into politics, culture (what I call Organized Culture), to causes, and groups, and committees which get lots of publicity.

As for Feroze, whatever else can be said, he was no shadow of the great one even in the Congress Party. Far from it. While in Parliament his exposure of a scandal in the insurance business led to a study by a commission of inquiry. Still later he again made Indian headlines with a second exposure of the government's National Insurance scheme. This scandal led to the resignation of the Congress Party's Minister of Finance.

But Feroze's triumph as an investigative parliamentarian did not bring him any closer to Indira. "It had all been clearly understood in the very beginning," Indira said crisply, "that I would have official duties. Even in the early days I was never home, always off somewhere with Father. Feroze used to come to our big affairs if he liked, or he would stay away with his own cronies if he preferred. When he gave dinners for his friends or constituents or his labor people I, of course, didn't go. I had nothing to do with his crowd." (Her tone of voice was so contemptuous that I winced.) "I never got involved in his affairs in any way! It just could not work out, and Father needed me. We were not divorced. That was out of the question. We just separated in the sense that we both went our own ways, and the boys were with me. Please word that—*or whatever you write*—very carefully. *Do not write that we are legally separated.*" She looked away, frowning, turning a cold profile. When the silence seemed unlikely to end, I rose to leave. She walked with me to the driveway and waited until my car drove up, smiling graciously as I thanked her. It was already dark. We had been sitting there in the garden a long time. She was pleasant and friendly, but I was sorry we had parted on the subject of Feroze. He roused emotion in her she would prefer to forget. I looked back as the car drove off in the soft blue Indian night. Indira was still standing there alone. I waved. She did not wave back.

Few of us would care to step into Indira Gandhi's slim sandals, to live her lonely life or face her grueling problems. Yet she seems to me a living example of Viktor Frankl's concept of the ultimate meaning in life: to live for goals. Dr. Frankl's book, *Man's Search for Meaning*, tells us we cannot invent a meaning for our lives; we have to discover it. Obviously Indira discovered hers long ago, and that goal is her weapon and her strength. It is a better human existence for all her countrymen. After that comes all the rest of the national scaffolding: rapid advancement in economic development, in education, food production, public health—a staggering list, an endless list, and all are priorities, all desperately *urgent!*

What stands in her way?

A mountain high as Everest.

A mountain called—India.

♦   ♦   ♦

In an old diary I kept during our Indian days, I recovered a vignette under the title "Headhunters I Have Known Too Well." It would later become a chapter in my book, *Diapers on a Dateline*.

Possessed by possession—are we not, all of us? And in the most affluent, acquisitive age of all times, how *not* to be? I have fought this idea all my life, and I'm still battling. My thoughts fly up, like Shakespeare's king, but my eyes remain below—bargain hunting.

Living in India, I firmly told myself, I did *not* have to rush out and buy anything. I would be here forever, and I could take my time. I could even do without buying anything. I marked off for myself "Buy Nothing" weeks when I would purchase nothing whatsoever. To achieve this, of course, I stayed home the entire week—and was not fit to live with. About that time, James Michener and his delightful and lovely Japanese-American wife, Mari, came to stay at the Cecil Hotel while Jim worked on a manuscript. When he wrote during the morning, he sent Mari over to visit me. We frequently went shopping on my "Buy Nothing" weeks. We were a great pair because the traveling Micheners could not tote possessions either. Jim never gave Mari an *anna*. We walked and we walked through dusty bazaars in the boiling sun, gazing at antique silver jewelry, hand-woven baskets, Tibetan turquoise beads, prayer wheels, furs, rows of sandal shops, not to mention the sari and Benares' brocade shops and the brass and copper *wallas*—but we would go out penniless (rupeeless) to guarantee our coming home without buying a single unnecessary thing!

But in India, even if you stayed home, insidious materialism came right to your door. In fact, most of the big spending is done by the Sahib, right at home, buying an array of art objects or unadulterated *junk*, paintings or gifts for relatives from wandering vendors who go from door to door—usually American door to American door, to his immense profit. All over India, in every major city, as the sun begins to set, little giftie merchants on bicycles set forth with their wares carried in filthy cloth bundles. They wait until the man of the house has had time to get home, shower, relax, and snap his fingers for the boy to come running with a whiskey soda.

I was no easy target, but the Little Men with the Bundles always found me. "No," I would wail to Pana, the bearer, "no more *wallas*. I have trunks full of junk and oddments already." Then I would think: the poor little man pumped his legs off, maybe peddling miles in the boiling sun, just to bring me his fake antiques or his Very Cheap Genuine Persian Carpets or his Very Cheap For You Only Memsahib Kashmiri Embroidery. Well, I would *look* and maybe consider just a small ashtray…

It was a constant struggle, like the addict with this pipe. I said "no," but I "looked." The trouble with most home buying was, as every dismayed housewife discovered, once you or your weak-minded husband had bought the 500-year-old snake charmer's flute or the whatzis made from a cobra's underbelly, you could no more give the stuff away than you could give away the family dog! Most gifts from India, those special weirdies like Jaipur, the 5000-year-old temple bells or dancing Shivas, are *never* given away. They accumulate. And accumulate. I did at least attempt to *resist* and *desist*. But that was long before I succumbed to the Head Man, the big-time operator who brought truly Great Art and forbidden museum treasures in his filthy rag bundles. He did not come tapping at my door. I had to go out and find him.

Esther Steele, the fastidious, intellectual wife of Arch Steele, longtime correspondent and respected authority on the Far East for the *Chicago Daily News* (and more recently, author of *The American People and China*) came to see me one day. Could she entice me to go with her in a taxi to "some horrible little hole in the wall outside Delhi to one of the best sources of genuine old coins in India"? She added that she did not think it safe to go alone, but the two of us should be all right. I had made no serious study of old coins, but they had long intrigued me. Esther had research, experience, and knowledge behind her, so that such a venture, with her, would be productive. Oh, to come upon an authentic coin of Alexander the Great! We set out in the taxi with Esther's vague directions (in India one friend tells another, and all directions come out with a little man whose cave of a shop is "up some horrible little alley with no number and no name."

We found him and were amused to find that this rascal, who dealt illegally under the counter in genuine valuables and museum pieces, lived opposite the police station. Esther did all the talking. She knew what she wanted, and she could tell at a glance what was good stuff and what was doubtful. The old Muslim dealer also knew he was confronted with an expert who meant business. More and more boxes came out of his dank and smelly hovel. Esther ran a finger through the coins, pushed the boxes toward me, and asked to see more. Finally all that he had, or the best of it, was arrayed before us. Esther found exactly what she had hoped to find, but, thoroughly experienced in the art of bargaining, she coolly contained her inner excitement. Time passed, and I picked up a handful of what I thought were rather fascinating-looking coins. Genuine or not, I liked the look and feel of them, particularly a heavy silver piece bearing a handsome, effeminate, profile. Wisely, I never showed outwardly how much I wanted the coins. Esther, also feigning moderate interest, finally came to terms for her coins and mine. We paid and left. As we started to return to our taxi, the coin *walla* came running up behind us. "Memsahib, next time, you not come here. No good you come here. I have cycle, I come see you. I have got many udder tings besides coins. Very old tings, maybe one thousand, *five* thousand year old!"

Esther said quickly, "Thank you, but I must leave Delhi. Only this memsahib lives here." He looked disappointed. Obviously Esther's expertise had impressed him. Her approval, and her acceptance of what he said was "genuine" had given him much face. "I have letter here. Please, Memsahib, you read, you see I not sell you fake." He handed Esther an old but quite authentic-looking letter from the British Museum in London thanking him for assisting a team of anthropologists "in their work." That was neatly put. Nothing was really in writing except that our coin man had crossed paths with diggers from the British Museum and that he had "helped."

"Where, please, Memsahib, may I come to show you udder tings?" Impatient to be going and thinking, well, the hotel is perfectly safe, I scribbled down my name and room number at the Cecil Hotel and we drove off.

A few days later, he rolled up at my door on his cycle. He wore old Punjabi Muslim trousers, so voluminous with cotton yardage they looked like a skirt, a vest (Grecian influence), and *pugaree* with vast flowing streamers. A puggaree is a sort of rimless hat held in place with a long cotton scarf usually starched, very stiff, so the ends, when tied, make a jaunty headsash. Tied to the handlebars of his bicycle was a lumpy bundle wrapped in burlap. Locking his cycle, the old Muslim stepped inside our Home Office, lugging his wares awkwardly because they were so heavy.

When I saw them, I moaned inwardly that Esther Steele wasn't there to cast her experienced eye upon the stone masterpieces before us. One piece was a stone sculpture, partially damaged, its surface weathered and pockmarked, but its contours and its human forms, warm and round and seductive, half-naked and adorned with carved jewels. John and the children and I were speechless. I had no idea *this* was what the little walla meant by "udder tings." Finally, John asked him, "Where did you get it? How do we know it's really old? You fellas are such experts at fakes. If this piece is genuine, it should be in a museum."

"True, Sahib," our salesman sighed, "but Indian museums very poor. Indian museums got plenty stone carvings. Americans very much like old stone carvings, so I tink you like this from old temple way up North. Come Peshawar side, Sahib."

That was the beginning. Temple pieces and a series of marvelous stone heads followed—so many the children and servants, thereafter, announced our vendor as "the Head Man"!

When Esther Steele returned to Delhi, I had her examine some of the pieces the Head Man had brought. She marveled and approved. For months he would bring a few things, leave them, and return a few weeks later. Meanwhile, friends came and had a look and made their bids. I bought nothing. They bought almost every single thing he laid out on my carpet!

Although Esther was not a professional appraiser of Asian statuary, her many years and wide travels throughout that part of the world, plus her impressive general knowledge of Asia, made me rely on her opinion. She pronounced the Head Man's "loot" to be "Quite good stuff. He's probably the Delhi outlet of a syndicate that operates between India and Pakistan, selling pieces stolen or hacked at night from isolated temples. My guess is," she concluded, "he probably works through back-door deals with a contact in some small, impoverished museum. I frankly think most of this stuff is the genuine article. I know our coins are."

We were never able to pin him down or put our finger on his method of operation or his source of supply, but he was too fascinating and too beguiling to turn away. We enjoyed his infrequent visits, and when we called him an outright "temple robber," he laughed. My friends bought—at their own risk, as I forewarned them—so the Head Man cherished my "friendship." Once or twice we were certain he slipped in a few fakes. If I questioned him when there was no one else around, he never batted an eye: "Memsahib, the nose is fake. Just see where it has been repaired—here—but the rest is 500 years old! I swear you!"

The Head Man's prices were strictly for the American trade, real shockers. Even Esther thought him exorbitant, but she added, "He's got the real stuff—really some of the best pieces." Many Americans bought them whether they were fake or not, even at stiff prices, because they were small masterpieces of sculpture, magnificently executed, and very naked!

One day after the Head Man had been coming for many months, on and off, he said to me, "Memsahib, why *you* not buy anyting? Always you and Sahib look and look. I see you want, you say nice, but you no buy? Why?"

I shrugged. "You're too expensive. I have many children, one more baby to be born soon. I love just to look, Head Man. I do not, at the moment, have all that money to buy."

The Head Man said nothing. He bowed and rode off in the warm blue dusk on his little bicycle. I did not see him for a long time, and when he returned and rang his little cycle bells, he carried one small sack only. He had not picked a very good time. I was alone and feeling very low and depressed. Things were not going at all well with United Press in India in those days. The business side was slipping badly. Unless the wire service could get a renewal of its license from the government and a very substantial client soon, I could see our days in India were numbered. And a baby was yet to be born. Insecurity and mental anxiety gave a certain vagueness to things like visits from the Head Man.

Into such an unreceptive atmosphere my rascally vendor came dispelling gloom, very pleased with himself. "Memsahib," he bowed, wreathed in his devil's tempting smile, "Memsahib, this time, what I bring is for *you*. Just see: for you only! I show no one else. I have great honor, Memsahib to show you...."

I stared, catching my breath. He had indeed brought treasure. It was a stone sculpture of a woman's head, small, damaged, part of the nose gone, but he put it down and the lamplight fell on the noble headdress of curls, the expression of tender sadness delicately molded out of black stone.

The Head Man gloated, triumphant that his special trophy had roused the desired effect. "Is head of queen, Memsahib. The Lord Buddha's queen. He was great prince, you will remember, yes? You will be knowing the story? He is marry with beautiful princess who love him very much. They got one beautiful baby boy. But the Prince must fulfill his destiny, which is to become the Lord Buddha. He is very unhappy when he discovers so much bad tings in the world outside palace. So, he goes. He runs away one night from Queen and baby prince and he never comes back to be with them."

It was all there in that piece of black stone, in the universal woman's look upon the face, in the half-smiling acceptance of the half-joy life so often brings: the loss of the husband but the gain of the son.

I was in no mood to talk that night. I was certainly not in a position to buy a treasure, and treasure it was. My Head Man stepped to the door to go: "We talk next time. I leave Queen lady with you. You see everyday, you look well. I no charge you much, Memsahib. You pay little now, little later, I wait. Do not be sad, Memsahib." He was gone.

From that night on, the Queen was a presence in the room. We exchanged many a long glance. I dusted her lovingly. The children *dared* not touch. She lived with us and communicated. Never mind, she seemed to say with that half-smile, UPI worries are mere trifles. They will pass away. The baby will be born soon. A son perhaps. Things will be all right.

When the Head Man finally came back, I was thoroughly possessed by this possession. Unthinkable to him, or to me, that the Queen should be taken away. I paid him in installments. There were no receipts, no written accounts whatsoever. There was no need. I paid, he agreed to wait. I was pleased that John, too, was in complete agreement that we should buy the head. Business was never worse for him; the future had never looked so dark and uncertain, but "Money," John said, "is a cheap exchange for a Queen."

This sculpture of Buddha's queen brought a touch of regal serenity to the busy Hlavacek household.

◆   ◆   ◆

One would like to leave a country one has been at home in for years with a feeling of confidence in the country's future. I owe India a special debt. I rebuilt my life there, and three of my children were born there. Heart ties are forever. But on a less emotional plane, I cannot feel certain India has "made it" or ever will.

Young men pouring out of colleges see little hope of recognition or outlet for their talents. They push half-heartedly for change, but they talk more than they push and usually end up speculating about going to the States. Artists and writers and the intellectual elite are at bitter odds with the old Congress establishment. Tired old clichés of the past—like Cows and Caste—which should have been alleviated or modified or given a modern adjustment by now can still, at a spark, cause violent, bloody riots. It is the same with any government move on the national language issue. Though Hindi is the official language, English is often the only unifying one (the language of Parliament and of the best-paying jobs), thus relegating numerous regional tongues to lesser, diminishing importance. Fear of losing status, jobs, and subsidies divides the country into passionate factions—armed camps of hate and fear one against the other.

On the plus side, the exterior signs of progress are everywhere in today's India. We recently put them on TV film, and they photograph impressively. The cities look modern and luxurious in the residential areas of the well-to-do, in Bombay, for instance, and sweeping skylines are full of striking apartment buildings and office towers and TV antennas. The streets are surging canals of cars, cycles, humans, and animals. We interviewed many officials, documented social reforms, especially India's now accelerated, if belated, birth control program. We were encouraged by the number of new schools jammed with eager-eyed, scrubbed, and immaculate children—though we knew in the villages and on the fringe of the richest cities there was no pretty picture of healthy, happy children in good schools.

The completion of tremendous hydro-electric dams and irrigation projects constitutes a substantial gain, but as you gaze and murmur "marvelous!" to please an Indian host, you know the end product, more food, more and better and cheaper manufactured goods, chemicals, fertilizers seems lagging, muddled, exasperatingly short on production. You become inwardly angry, the need being so desperate, the money and energy expended so futile, and then you sigh and say to yourself "India!" and pass on.

We were pleased to see that our driver, Danji, had a better-paying job with UPI (no small miracle of modern progress in itself!). He told us proudly he had moved to new quarters and had in his modern house a big transistor radio and two electric fans! Even Tai Bhai was doing well. Her new Memsahib is of the Beautiful People caste, one of India's lingering maharanis. Tai looked after her baby daughter, "the little princess." Progress for Tai was shown in her new attitude. I had taken her a gold bracelet as a present from New York. She accepted it with obvious disappointment. I know her so well that I knew her thanks and thin smile meant she wanted something *else* from magic America. I was so right. She vanished into the kitchen and returned with a slip of paper on which the cook had written in English the name of a transistor radio she wanted next time. Rising expectations never cease. A Sony TV will be on the list as soon as she sees one, and before I can get the transistor out to her.

It is certainly true that the years since Independence have brought some change, rewards, and uplift even to the humblest elements of the people. But as soon as I say that and begin to feel more cheerful, into my mind's eye comes the distressing memory of an afternoon in Bombay. We had gone by the Willingdon Club, an exclusive and beautiful golf and swim club for wealthy, Westernized Indians and the foreign business community. In John's bachelor days he had swung a neat golf club and had won a number of silver cups. We wanted to shoot some TV footage and see for old times' sake how the club looked these days. The club was filled with sporty Indian golfers and the pool was achurn with a splashing, noisy young crowd. Waiters served tea, nannies in white saris held towels and robes for young charges who ignored them. Nothing had changed. This was how I remembered it.

As we were leaving we swung the car out of the driveway, and then I saw them: the people in the pipes! Living in a stack of abandoned water pipes, a small community had set up housekeeping. Flowering pink oleanders screened them from view of the (shattering contrast) Indian golfers in shorts and bright T-shirts. Not even in my day had people been reduced to this. "Stop the car. Let me walk past and get a good look at this. I can scarcely believe what I'm seeing," I whispered to John. I got out of the car and walked slowly past. A few women were cooking over small fires. Old pots and pans were littered about. Half-naked children ran about. Laundry hung on a branch of hedge. Adorning the exteriors of the large black sewer pipes there were even one or two gaudy posters advertising Indian movies with pictures of sleepy-eyed, bosomy Muslim movie stars. The little clutch of human beings obviously slept inside the pipes by night. The scene haunted me. Later that evening, gazing from the balcony of the apartment where we were guests, I saw the wrapped forms of Indians sleeping on the sidewalk. No—India, in terms of its human beings, 70 percent illiterate after all these years, still has a long, long way to go. I left India with no assurance it would be "better" if I ever came back.

7

The Caribbean

✦

(1958–61)

We were about to leave India when John won a fellowship to the Russian Institute at Columbia University. This prize of an academic year came from the Carnegie-endowed Council on Foreign Relations in New York. I had not heard of the Council before, but this influential, serious-minded organization, which has branches called Committees on Foreign Relations in every major city of the United States, publishes many books and the prestigious magazine, *Foreign Affairs*. I had dipped into this magazine occasionally, although I often found its valuable store of information buried in the heavy sand of dry reading.

As the resident fellow during his year at Columbia, John attended all of their black tie, and their more standard knit-tie, dinner-lecture gatherings at 68th and Park. These were men-only affairs, like Cabinet meetings for members. I believe the only woman they ever let in was a guest speaker: Economist Barbara Ward!

From far-off New Delhi to this exclusive, elite group was, for us, flying high in heady company. Following one of those little intellectual dinners, a fellow member asked John one night for a ride home as far as Scarsdale. Thus, in our battered, secondhand station wagon John took home an interesting traveling fellow whose "wife always had the car": Dean Rusk!

We lived in White Plains, and John commuted every day to Columbia with an instructor from West Point. When John had mastered some Russian, had studied intensively under some of the shrewdest, most astute analysts of the USSR in this country (the Russian Institute for *thoroughness* must be on a par with what their opposites put out in Moscow!) we did a complete about face!

We went about as far from the Soviets as you can get: into the land of palm trees, cruise boats, cha-cha-cha and calypso, blinding sunshine, mask-flippers-and-snorkels, blue marlin fishing, paradise beaches—the Caribbean! More specifically, we went down to those jewel-like little islands in the warm blue sea on a wholly new, very risky venture: to open our own news bureau.

We didn't know at the outset what ugly and violent things lay thinly screened by the lush setting. The Dominican Republic looked troubled, there were chilling noises from street mobs in booming Puerto Rico, and *The New York Times* kept running more and more articles about a bearded guerrilla in the hills, who was not a communist, named Fidel Castro. But I merely skimmed all this as I was whirling around doing things like buying Keds in five sizes and, for the future, in graduating sizes, an electric iron and coffeepots that would plug into whatever plugs they had down there.

The Caribbean move gave John and me many other things to think about, too. We were going into the news business entirely on our own. We paid all moving expenses. And there were a lot of us: eight in fact. We still had our little Indian aiha Tai Bhai with us, going bravely into the Caribbean and the Unknown with memsahib and her "childer."

We went down on a Canadian bauxite freighter we boarded in Montreal. Lazily, inelegantly, but inexpensively, all of us, our car, and all our possessions sailed for Kingston. We were to remain there for three eventful, productive, financially successful years and to leave only when John, unexpectedly, received a rare, rare resident-visa for Havana, the only one the Cuban government issued to an American correspondent at that time.

Our fledgling home office for our new business was not entirely without the promising weight of an anchor on the leeside. We had two exclusive clients: *NBC News* and *Time-Life*. This sounds pretty impressive, but the hitch was in the arrangement. We were not staff employees. We were not paid a salary. We were only humble contributors, called "stringers," who were paid for what is published, put on the air, or ordered in advance from New York. But the trade winds were blowing our way. With the Caribbean moving into its most critical era, we arrived just in time for Act I and had all the news we could handle and lots more.

Professionally, the news bureau was to be the most valuable if most ruthless experience of our lives. It cost John an ulcer, wore me down to a bony size 10, and there were times when nerves, noise, kiddies, sweat-wet heat, a huge dog and several cats, the cables and overseas operator, and marriage rocked the boat, splintered the oars, and sprang leaks! But there were plenty of sweet rewards too!

Jamaica is the most expensive island of the Caribbean. Hence, getting down to business immediately was very urgent. We wasted little time finding and renting a huge, furnished old-fashioned British-looking bungalow with sagging, green-and-white-striped canvas awnings over a veranda. But the house had a large garden and a lovely lime tree whose graceful branches poked through my kitchen window. There were also a privacy thicket of pink oleanders and red hibiscus and some neglected rose beds. I remember the address. It was so easy to direct guests or interviewees to Winchester Road. "Winchester, like a shotgun, at Half-Way Tree."

Jamaica is greatly enhanced by the names of some of its towns, coves, and beaches. My favorite was Big Bottom! A town named Big Bottom sounds quite improbable, I know. I learned later that the name referred to a *river* bottom. Half-Way tree got its name from another age. Years ago a huge tree had spread vast branches of welcome shade just half-way from dockside downtown to the cool residential foothills. In our time, Half-Way Tree was a busy intersection or roundabout over which presided a strikingly uniformed, white-toupéed Jamaican traffic policeman. Progress has not only robbed Half-Way Tree of the tree, but the colorful policeman and all its charm and atmosphere as well. People cross the street at their peril, traffic lights blink, cars race heedlessly by. Only the name remains.

Back at the home office, we first made certain our lifeline to New York was working—the telephone. Jamaican phone service is a part of the local legend and lore, but overseas calls from Kingston were remarkably quick and clear. When that phone was working, a familiar cry ran through the house: "Quiet, kids! Quiet…QUIET…"

Next stop—a hardware store for some cheap, ingenious office furniture. The master bedroom of our bungalow was ballroom size. As in India, bedroom and office for us was all-in-one. A pair of desks had to be devised immediately. We looked around at hardware miscellania. Then John had a great idea: a pair of doors with legs nailed on would make us big editorial desks. Into the back of the station wagon went two pre-cut, unpainted, lovely creamy-beige pine wood doors stamped: CZECHOSLOVAKIA. With them were 8 legs, nails, and brackets. To this day I would just as soon have a DOOR desk as any other. Standard desks never give you enough space for junk and clutter. Never mind drawers: *Space* is the essence.

Next stop: cable office. Second only to the telephone in importance, the cable office with its night and day working staff became virtually our downtown office. And we got our cable address from "our" Jamaican staff, too. Business firms who transmit frequent communications by cable register a special cable address, usually one word made up of several words from the name of their firm. "Nobody," observed John as we walked into the cable office, "will ever suspect that 'HLA-VACEK' is a personal name. I'll bet we can get a cable address like 'Hlavacek

Kingston'." The friendly Jamaicans in their calypso bush shirts, with dazzling-white grins, would have given us anything, but regulations wouldn't. We did some figuring, trying to think of something close to the name that wasn't a name.

"How would yuh like HATCHECK, mon?" suggested one of the clerks with a radiant smile. Hatcheck it was. *Life* once sent us a cable of congratulations on a story: "Tip hat to Hatcheck."

Whole volumes, incidentally, could be written on colorful, inventive, highly original Jamaican speech. "Mon" or sometime "man," went at the end of every sentence instead of a period. "Sure, mon. Ah tink so, mon. One mo' Red Stripe faw yuh, mon?" And there was the constant theme song: "Ah come soon, mon." Instead of Memsahib, I became Mis'tress.

Working assignments on Jamaica's truly spectacular North Shore, after so many years on the other side of the world, were to give perspective a jolting dislocation. Here we found an elaborate organized business of fun and fantasia for the world's wealthiest, the Kennedys, the British peers, big names, too many of the gaudy, jetty set, those full-time play people with private planes, bored to suffocation with pleasure but with time and the season to get through. There were faceless, non-famous Canadian millionaires as well, a surprising number, who came not for sun and sport but to buy up land, hotels, factories.

In our India days celebrity status rested upon the burdened shoulders of Prime Ministers. In Jamaica we had Prime Ministers too, but it was all very different down on the sunshine island. Only one Prime Minister, Britain's Harold Macmillan, came to discuss pressing matters of state (such as telling Jamaicans that their imminent independence would mean the sunset of many "colonial" benefits like unlimited immigration and economic subsidies). Other Prime Ministers who came were Winston Churchill, who painted his pictures quietly, and Canada's colorless and dour Prime Minister Diefenbaker, who caught a blue marlin. He disdained a single smile because the marlin failed to weigh enough to make it a prime trophy!

Even if events on our island were far from world-shaking, as long as *people* made news we were in business. The great and very good life of the terribly rich as we observed it in Jamaica, the day-to-day existence of those blamelessly born to great names and fortunes, often gave lesser mortals philosophic thought: are they really happier, we used to ask over the rim of our rum punch, than ordinary mortals?

After meeting, filming, interviewing, and dining with many, as the occasional brief guest in a lavish "cottage," I must conclude, to my chagrin, that the answer is really *yes!* Yes, they really do have a very good life. They know it, and love it just that way!

Life hands the peers and beautiful people the same jolts and blows and tears and heartaches and disasters as the rest of us—but oh, they can suffer and reach for a scented Kleenex in such surroundings. They can wring their diamond-laden hands gazing out over such gorgeousness: gardens bending, brimming with flowers melting into the blue and bluer sea, a gentle footstep bringing a maid with a breakfast tray, with the newspapers, with a Bloody Mary, with a Vogue silk gown, with a cable and two aspirins or a sleeping pill.

Pegge and Tai Bhai in Jamaica with Jimmy, Johnny, Suzy, Mike, and the family dog.

And damn-it-all, if a husband has run off with a best friend, there are other husbands and many, many more "friends." Meanwhile, William has a car ready anytime, and the sailboat rocks as gently as a well-fed swan upon the water just at the end of the private pier. Or if it's just too much and you want to go home, the chauffeured plane awaits at Montego Bay. Oh yes, there's a lot to be said for the rich way of life.

Once we took a beachfront census for *Time!* A complete word and picture story of just who lived on Millionaires' Row from Montego Bay to the terribly exclusive private residence area called Tryall. Discussing the people and the assignment later with my favorite North Shore mentor Liz Pringle, whose super salesman Britishy-Jamaican husband John had originally built Round Hill, I mused that in all that opulent stretch of property not one intellectual, humanitarian, or creative profession was represented. In all those dream houses there was not one brain that had benefited mankind in some inspiring way. There was not even one doctor, one scientist, one great artist, or even an architect or lawyer.

"How true, luv," Liz Pringle nodded her head with its long, long fall of wheat-gold hair. "The great brains," she observed, "are too busy working for anything like this. The closest we have come to someone creative owning a house here has been dear old Oscar (Hammerstein), but even he came only for a short time."

"You'll discover, she continued, "there are lots of people down here who do work, work their heads off, but not in these resorts. You'll find them hidden away in little places without phones or flush johns. They don't want anybody to bother them, so they go where no one can find them. When they do want a bit of a bash, they come up here for a day, then vanish again."

Back in Kingston, the real world always awaited us. The children loved their new Jamaican school, Priory, spread out like a plantation, with each class in a separate little cottage under the trees. School began early in the morning and was out early, usually by 1 o'clock. As the twins had begun their schooling in India, under the lingering British standard, they fit right into what was then the Jamaican-British system. Priory's headmaster at that time was a rare, wise, and humorous Mr. Chips in the modern manner—Henry Fowler, a Rhodes Scholar. Who will replace him, one wonders, and what will survive at Priory under the intensive Jamaicanization of all educational institutions, already evident before we left.

We had a good example of how Headmaster Fowler's Priory coped with difficult students. Our own problem child was Mike. He came home, day after day, in a shambles. He had been ambushed at the corner of Winchester Road, and we would see him coming in the driveway blubbering, bawling, eyes red, shirt torn, his book bag ripped and bashed.

What small boys' ruckus was behind the repeated ambush attacks was never exactly clear. Mike was no haloed lamb, and he was no doubt being pelted for something obnoxious he had done. But what was the real problem that set so many against him repeatedly? We went to see Mike's teacher, a protégé of Headmaster Fowler cast in the same admirable mold, Pat Burke. "Mike," we were advised, "is a born maverick. He is very bright without having to work at it, he produces poorly in class (C average) out of boredom. Perhaps he needs a jolt?" With this, Mike was advanced one full school year. It was hoped tougher assignments would spark him to work a lot harder just to keep up, and a whole new class would circulate him among new and older boys. The full grade jump hardly fazed Mike at all. He continued to throw a few more punches and raise hackles among classmates, but the advance work was a snap. Perhaps Mike isn't so different after all. The years have passed, but he hasn't changed that much. He surprised and pleased us recently by becoming a National Merit finalist, but Mike, along with many others of his generation, is still threading his way unevenly on a long, confused road to self-discovery and to that out of-date lodestone: responsibility. But I am grateful for the interval of special concern and guidance from Pat Burke who is still at little Jamaica's Priory School.

There were many other general advantages in what remained of the British system. Schooling in private institutions is an expensive commodity. Space is limited and reserved. Hence, even having a "place" is a special privilege. Perhaps all this adds up to the special attitude, the resolve to get on with the learning, to skip the frills that sometimes clutter our own system. Priory's attitude was simple and strict. Homework was essential, and there was never any question about its being done and done well! Students knew exactly what was expected of them. Oh yes, and I think they even said a traditional prayer or two, and there may have been a God Bless the Queen and "Our Hi'lun" (island) and this did the children's souls no more harm than breaktime "thruppence sweetie" did their teeth!

Above, Johnny talks with his Jamaican friends.

Below, Jimmy and Johnny play "airplane" with bamboo wings.

Have I mentioned the Jamaican currency is based on the pound sterling? Hence the colorful island lingo was further enriched with expressions like: "Cost yu' two bob, mon!" or, "Lovely paw-paw, mistress, two and six, all right, take it for two—"

I am grateful to the British Commonwealth for its practical application. At an age when young Americans were learning about Washington, DC, and Boston and Philadelphia as merely big cities, within the Commonwealth we took in the whole globe: Africa, India, Australia, New Zealand. These far-off places were not just names on the map to be memorized, tested for, and forgotten. Jamaican markets provided an abundance of commonwealth products. When you eat your geography, you remember it a lot better. I could go to the "fridge" and show the children our roast leg of lamb stamped in purple ink: New Zealand, or tinned Kraft cheese from Australia, the chocolate from Ghana that went into a pan of brownies, our tea and spices from India by way of England for pretty packaging.

There was no television on the island when we first moved to Kingston. They have it now, and I wonder if it has changed the children's attitudes toward homework. Do they hurry to finish it to get to their cartoons and cowboy movies? In our day, the slack was always taken up by reading. The back of our station wagon always had a stack of books coming home or being returned. Kingston had model free public libraries and friendly, interested librarians whose whole purpose was to circulate books. A maximum supply of books going *out* pleased them more than neat books sitting on shelves in perfect order.

Our three oldest children have been voracious readers, but our two youngest boys, growing up in the American school system and exposed to American television, look upon reading as a chore. (Exception: After a bicycle accident landed Jimmy in the hospital with a severely cut gum and lip, a friend made him a present of Ian Fleming's *Chitty Chitty Bang Bang*. Not only was the story of the magic car thrilling and exciting, there was that *fudge* recipe in the back.)

Jamaica, as my lovely friend Liz Pringle had pointed out, was one of the writingest islands of the Caribbean. Mornings and afternoons hundreds of novels and plays, song lyrics, histories and theses, even political speeches, were wrung from sun-warmed Olivettis.

The word output from Jamaica was exceeded, I suppose, only by newsmen putting out the news across the way in Havana, "Kooba," as the Cubans called it or "Cuber" as the late JFK pronounced it. (A small note in passing: I recently took a tape recorder to a meeting at which Senator Edward Kennedy gave a Democratic fund-raising speech in our town. He is amazingly like his brother, but I did not realize how much he resembled JFK in his speech until I played back the tapes. I heard not only a passing reference to how the Democratic Party handled "Cuber" but how it would always win in "Nebrasker"! The Kennedy myth brought home no bacon. Democrats were defeated in a clean sweep at the next election.)

The writing business is fascinating when the writers are even more famous than the books they put out. I recall that our very first HATCHECK story for *Time* was a visit with Errol Flynn, then working on his autobiography. He and his very able pro ghostwriter from New York were mildly "hard at work," as the saying goes, in a remodeled version of the famed old Titchfield Hotel in Port Antonio. This used to be a sleepy banana-boat town pulsing with life in the days of the United Fruit Company. In the good old days, Errol Flynn had won the Titchfield in a poker game. Then he swapped the hotel for an island, an intriguing gem of a little offshore island not far from the Titchfield's poolside bar. In another game of poker he lost it all.

The day we spent with Errol was one of his best, just before the end. He had peaceful spells when he "dried out" and was his better self, and our Sunday lunch with him took place during one of them. Full of amusing conversation, Errol talked about skin diving, showed us his equipment, he talked about his acting, his family, even his detached wife, Pat Wymore, and his new home then being built some miles down the coast in a rather remote hillside area called Castle Comfort.

A year or so later we spent a day there with Pat Wymore. She had flown down to see what she had managed to legally inherit at Castle Comfort. She walked through an enormous stone-on-stone hillside fortress of a home built to erratic specifications by a Texas boy-wonder architect who had also designed Frenchman's Cove: William Taminga.

Pat Wymore eyed a cascading waterfall flowing through the house, a swivel of swimming pool just below a living room, which extended from the foundation like a ship's yardarm. Her only comment after a profound silence was: "Why—there's not a single broom closet in the whole place!" Where to hide the Pledge and the Hoover and the dust mop at Castle Comfort? One can understand why Errol and Pat spent their marriage in wholly separate worlds.

Beyond San San and Port Antonio lay a far more serious and successful writing lair. Completely hidden behind a heavy wall of pink flowering shrubs was perched the most fascinating writer's retreat in all Jamaica: Ian Fleming's Goldeneye.

It has always amazed me that James Bond's Maker had to wait years before his books—the whole 007 mystique—really caught on. Fleming came to Jamaica and Goldeneye every winter for 14 years. He came to do a whole book at a season's sitting. He worked like a man possessed, relentlessly pushing himself to grind out one complete manuscript each winter. Day by day he poured out pages of Bond, never pausing to rewrite or check detail, facts, or spelling. Much later, whole scripts were meticulously re-studied, rewritten, revised before the final draft went to print. Yet all this output, for years, attracted only a very small circle of faithful readers and admirers. It wasn't literature he was turning out, and he couldn't have cared less. Fleming wrote his life away to make the big time: the mass market. He sought above all public acclaim, popularity, and *money!*

I stopped by Goldeneye one afternoon. I recall being about to sit down, having been handed a drink in his rather rumpled, knocked-about looking library-living room. "No, no, my dear, don't sit *there,*" my hostess warned, steering me to safety. "That chair's got no seat! Meant to get it down to a little chair man in town, but, you know, somehow…" Well, if occasionally chairs were missing seats, Goldeneye's atmosphere was still legendary and very picturesque. There was a white marble bust of Julius Caesar staring out to sea, and at that hour in late afternoon the sun was indeed a blinding Goldeneye, going down like Thunderball!

Ian Fleming is gone, and Goldeneye is for sale. Or may even have been sold by this time. It must have cost someone a frightful tab with the view, the name, and the lingering traces of great and illustrious guests (and tree planters), including Anthony Eden when he was Prime Minister.

Speaking of names, it always seemed to me the supreme irony that the real James Bond survived so coolly, even having to live with the real name, worlds removed from the jazz of 007. The original James Bond is an American ornithologist from Philadelphia whose book, *Birds of the West Indies,* had years ago caught Fleming's eye. Not for the birds, but for the neat, two-syllable name: James Bond. Bond, the ornithologist, eventually came to meet Fleming at Goldeneye. The two found the twain involvement highly amusing.

Jamaica had another special bond for Ian Fleming and his London socialite wife, Anne, the former Lady Rothemere. Theirs had been a sophisticated romance. When her divorce became final, they were duly married in the unlovely, beige-and-green north coast town with the pretty name Port Maria.

A quiet marriage in an obscure island parish happens frequently to famous visitors in the Caribbean. Dipping into the past, I had not been aware that even Lord Horatio Nelson once put into a small island bay and married a captivating widow named Fanny! The marriage signatures in the church registry are preserved for tourists' scrutiny to this day, but it is unclear whatever happened to Fanny after Horatio sailed out with the tide.

Thinking historically for a moment, associations with Columbus are very prevalent in Jamaica. I recall, too, that there was one famous writer who came down not to write but to dedicate a statue of Columbus at Runaway Bay: the renowned Pulitzer-prize-winning biographer Samuel Eliot Morison. The statue of Columbus stands slim and white and graceful above a circle of pink and purple petunias near a small Catholic Church at Runaway. How calmly Columbus now gazes out to sea, not far from where he was once miserably marooned an entire year. His noble profile gazes in stony wonder upon sand beaches he knew in yesteryear where today New York secretaries on package-vacations romp in too-small bikinis and where tired businessmen boil themselves pink as French veal, remembering only to protect and cover their *noses* with those hideous little plastic noseclips!

Now I had a cable from New York to quiz Morison on the latest controversial angle on Columbus: that he was a Jew, or was at least part Jewish! I put in a long-distance call to his hotel in Ocho Rios and asked for his comment. I got a snort of outrage and a shout: "READ MY BOOK! Don't annoy me with such rubbish!" before he slammed down the receiver, deafening me momentarily.

There was yet another controversy I never had a chance to ask Morison about. It seems the first landing place of Columbus in the New World had raised a furious but more gentlemanly debate between the great authority and a mere amateur with the temerity to suggest Morison might be wrong. The upstart was no less than Edwin A. Link, inventor of the Link pilot trainer and serious Columbus buff if not a biographer.

Where had Columbus actually landed? Columbus himself was of little help. Morison contends *he* knows a lot more than Columbus himself where he first landed, and that was on a remote island in the Bahamas called Watling or San Salvador. Morison's authority is based on nautical experience and personal investigation in a small plane and in a shrimp boat. Link puts Columbus on East Caicos in the Caicos Islands, some distance from Watling.

The interesting Link study and its conclusions were published by no less an authority than the Smithsonian. However it was, and *wherever* it was, Columbus fulfilled his destiny, he pointed the way, but he personally was ill blessed by fortune. As is the case with so very many who come to the Caribbean, then and now, he found no fortune, and he personally was no winner.

Most holiday visitors to Jamaica unfortunately see only Montego Bay or Ocho Rios during their week or two-week stay. A pity. In all the time we lived on the island I became so accustomed to Montego I barely saw its oddly mixed shops, the square with the over-priced straw market, its few new air-conditioned cells filled with luxury items at in-bond discounts, or with rum and Tia Maria. The Jamaica Shop had brilliant beach cottons made from the hand-screened original designs of the shop's American owner, Ruthie Claridge. Dorothy McNabb had taken an old rum warehouse on the waterfront and made it into a high-fashion boutique for the season's celebrity clientele, but, as a place to see and shop in, I often thought the town offered little of what people had escaped from at home. Prices back home might be high, but you got what you paid for. In Montego, I thought, the prices were just outrageous.

The breathless beauty of the whole island setting; the harbor, the sea and the Blue Mountains and the most inviting coves and cream-sand beaches were largely in private areas, far, far from tourists. Only the lucky outsiders with friends, or letters to friends, ever got to see the private splendor hidden away. The day of the great house and vast estates is rapidly slipping away, but what remains is a memorable glimpse of another world. An old house in the foothills came on the market from time to time simply because working a large property required a large and costly labor force. In recent years the best workers went to city jobs or all the way to Ing'lonn (England). Often what remained wasn't worth having.

We visited a number of the few, lingering hideaway great houses, thinking one of these days with five children, we would buy one as an ideal place for weekends. What we finally bought was not anything like a house in the hills. Instead, we got a side of a steep hill hung with rocks and trees. Upon our side-of-a-steep-hill we built a beach cottage like a birds' nest on top of heavy pilings. The view from this odd house (which John after the first year rightly named the "Bin Took!") was unbelievable. As I sloshed dishes in my small kitchen sink I could look down the hill, into the water, even *through* the water and watch the fish! (This is known as 120-120 vision!) I did this looking through the green branches of avocado trees. When the lush avocados were ripe we got a Jamaican to climb the tree (they have the knack and never fall) and shake the avocados into an outstretched blanket the children held up. Our view from the right side of the terrace looked right into the Blue Hole and the tiny cottage of Robin Moore, author of the Green Berets. Eventually Robin and his family bought our place and made it an extension of their own.

This is the house the Hlavaceks built on a steep hillside near San San, Jamaica.

We became so attached to the San San—Frenchman's Cove—Port Antonio area of the island (our cottage was 72 curlicue, sickening miles from our home in Kingston) that a longer trip the other way to Montego meant a special assignment. We went there only to work, to interview someone special, and to take a lot of pictures.

But it had been a pleasure to go to Round Hill to do a story on the strange togetherness—how they fought!—of the world's greatest song and lyrics team: Rodgers and Hammerstein. Legend has it the two wives, both named Dorothy, maintained the peace as far as they were able. But the struggle to get *The Sound of Music* down on paper had been full of tougher bristles than "whiskers on kittens"! As I write this, the movie is *still* running in our town, although the prices have not been reduced and Julie Andrews has since come and gone in *Hawaii* (a sad fizzle, that) and even *Thoroughly Modern Millie*.

I was charmed with the thought that when Oscar H. was thrashing about with ideas and words and emotion and tenderness and the soaring lift-off of "I-go-to-the-hills-for-the-sound-of-m-m'-YOU-zeek" he wasn't gazing at the Austrian Alps at all but at the blue, coffee-growing hills of Jamaica. Behind Oscar's cottage the hills would be but small inspiration, a mere blue brush stroke darkening the horizon, but on the other end of the island, and beyond Kingston, the hills rise to surprising height and to great dreamy beauty.

A nicer, more gentle man—at his ease and leisure between bouts of work—than Oscar Hammerstein one could not imagine. He looked like the bear-sized battered remnant of a prize-fighting career. His voice, following his last sad operation and illness, was hoarse and gravelly. But when you looked into this hoary, lined, and pockmarked face, you saw there a startling contrast: compassion, gentleness, defenseless kindness.

When I interviewed both Rodgers and Hammerstein they were in quiet repose seated in deep shade on the beach. Rodgers seemed not inclined to communicate, so I let him think his own thoughts and moved over by Oscar who sat there thoroughly and carefully shuffling and reshuffling and stacking and cutting a deck of cards. Chess was his specialty, but cards were quick unwinders. As he swiftly flaked the rattan beach table with a deal of cards, he commented that he was glad to be finished with the "R & H oriental cycle." Casting South Pacific and Flower Drum Song had been a helluva job. Never again! Finding Chinese actors and singers for the lead, in Flower especially, had been difficult. They had had to use Japanese for Chinese. "I dunno why," he drawled, "but Chinese, even when you can find them, freeze up on a stage. They're inhibited. They don't give, they can't project."

Did Oscar have a favorite show or song? "Well, you got a favorite news story? People ask us how we get 'ideas' for songs. They look surprised when I say my inspiration is all a lotta hard work. I just sit down and work and keep on working till it's right. If it doesn't come out right, I just throw the whole damn thing away and start all over. That's not my idea of 'inspiration'. Sometimes things come quickly. The words just fall in where you want 'em, but not very often! It's crazy. Like no other business in the world, not a damn bit glamorous on the writing, rehearsing, rewriting end. Oh I like a couple songs I turned out in the early days, but not the most famous ones."

Many months later I found myself in New York with the twins. Their birthday loomed so close that I decided they should see their first Broadway play.

Mary Martin, in the *Sound of Music,* of course. (Mary Martin should always be in the first play your children see!) In this case my own Mary had shyly met Oscar Hammerstein one Sunday in Kingston, so he was very special to her. There were no seats available for this hit musical. It seemed to have been sold out forever! I decided to try the standee routine. Oddly, the day we went to see the play, a wild hurricane struck New York City. By late afternoon windows had been blown out of office buildings, and the streets were deserted. Broadway looked as though it had been scoured by a sandblast machine! We were staying out in distant Mt. Kisco and all trains were stopped!

If I must face a natural disaster, I would prefer not to hold tickets to a Broadway play on the same night.

By five o'clock the hurricane swept over White Plains and moved on up to Boston. Life and transportation restored to normal, we just made it to our dark corner at the rear of the theater. I had momentarily thought that big wind might be the ill wind which blows some good, like a few empty seats for standees to slip into when the lights dim…but like a rendezvous with destiny, every ticket-holder was solidly in his seat that night.

Our first Christmas in the Caribbean was a novelty. We had a tree and presents in the early morning. The evergreen tree stood on the front veranda and in the background was a solid wall of natural blooming poinsettias, the only natural Christmas touch in tropical Jamaica. After breakfast, John said, "Who wants to stay home on a day like this?" We phoned some friends and asked them to join us, packed the station wagon in minutes, and drove to Ocho Rios for an all-day Christmas swim-picnic on the beach. Snorkeling for Christmas isn't quite like ice skating or going downhill on a sled, in fact it wasn't Christmasy at all, but hauntingly unreal and also adventurous.

Runaway Bay was deserted. We had the fish and the reef and all the blond-sand beach to ourselves and our close friends. The wives all agreed this was one wonderful way of getting out of the kitchen on a holiday.

Venturing into the Silent World, we were timid beginners. We stayed in fairly medium-deep water, this side of the reef, until we were almost pros with mask, snorkel, and flippers, until we knew how to handle curious barracudas and sea urchins, black, spiny, and evil. Eventually we even got our Indian Tai Bhai into an XL cotton bathing suit *and* into mask, snorkel, and flippers and let her take a panic-stricken look at the fish. Jimmy and Johnny, though still pretty small themselves, took great pride in teaching Tai Bhai *how*.

The time spent on sunny beaches was very brief. Other events awaited us that first Christmas, almost from the moment we got home. Across the way in

Havana, it was literally all over but the shooting. On New Year's Eve, Dictator Fulgencio Batista fled Cuba after a getaway flight which was pure Cuban melodrama all the way. Most of the women fled in their ball gowns, jewels and furs, the *best* way to go. Down they raced, in the night, to the Dominican Republic. Here the Cuban exiles settled in temporary security until it became painfully clear that the United States would *not*, after all reconsider and permit Batista to enjoy safety and asylum there. His wife and children, yes. Batista, no!

John builds a campfire with a little help from Johnny, Mary, Jimmy, and Suzy.

Dictator Trujillo, whose own hour was not yet nigh, was not pleased. He was already reluctantly hosting another strong man in exile: Juan Peron of Argentina. Three dictators on one little island was enough to make any strong man nervous.

But if Trujillo wasn't pleased, we were. *Time* sent us an assignment to fly at once to Ciudad Trujillo to interview Batista for a cover story they were rushing into print on Fidel Castro! The interview we eventually got with him—after eight horrendous days of trying to break the machine-gun ring of silence surrounding Batista—was our first big, exclusive story from the Caribbean.

Looking back on that strange meeting, all I remember now was Batista's haunting refrain. "They call me a murderer," he intoned in a voice emotionally husky and strained, "yet I had Fidel Castro as my prisoner and let him go! Now you will see who is a murderer. Now you will see prisoners dragged to the wall! Now you will see who is the real murderer."

In the months that followed, amid endless celebrations and marches and the notorious public trials, Fidel Castro dominated the news. NBC kept John commuting constantly between the two islands. Finally, they advised us to move to Havana.

Take five children to Cuba? Uh-uh. I firmly refused. NBC then invited me to go over and take a good look around before I rejected Havana completely.

Cuba in those heady days of liberation was still luxuriating in the residue, the lingering fat abundance of an economy that had been the second richest in Latin America. Greedy and heedless of the future, Cubans had even permitted the sale of their prime cattle which were promptly bought up for a good price and flown off the island to Venezuela before Castro and his inexperienced ministers had time to realize the gravity of their error. The island's food supply was the least of the young revolutionaries' problems in those green early days of the Takeover.

I remember being impressed with Havana's gleaming supermarkets, especially the large chain of American-styled Mini Macks, which still had ample supplies of food in them. I priced meat, eggs, butter, bread, jelly (from Bulgaria!) and took such a thorough look around I even discovered in one corner what no one else had seen: Castro beards for sales! They were really children's party favors, play beards attached to large rubber bands.

John not only shot an amusing little film clip of Castro beards for sale in the supermarket, but we bought up the Mini Macks entire stock of the beards. John was due to make a trip to New York within a few days to appear on NBC's Today show. He thought the beards would make a good gimmick on the air, which they did. Frank Blair playfully put one on when he read the news. (Off camera, Blair is almost funnier than Johnny Carson. But since that man for all seasons and all persuasions, Hugh Downs, has become the Big Star of the program, Frank sits in his corner doing his bit strictly as the straight man. Pity!) We returned many times to Havana but in the end wisely never moved the family to Cuba.

Meanwhile the Havana experience grew more agonizing. Batista's grim predictions came true. Justice was swift. The rule of law entirely disappeared. Youth in olive drab, kids in their twenties with guns, ran things. Revolutionary tribunals became the ruling force that substituted for what might have passed for Cuban law. The exodus of refugees began rapidly, with the wealthy, elite and upper classes, many of whom had helped bring Castro to power, being the first to go. Noisy parades and sports spectaculars on the Moscow scale distracted attention from events that would bear no exposure at the time.

Physical deterioration of the rich jewel of a city which was Havana was shockingly apparent when one made return trips after a brief interval. The revolution began to look grubby, its downhill grind depressingly evident. The atmosphere became chilling with uncertainty. Rumors flew; you dismissed them as wild, but you listened to all the new ones. On one short trip John and I were houseguests of old India friends, AP correspondent Harold Milks and his wife. They lived in a wealthy residential area where the streets were often used as parade grounds for students marching. They marched to school, they marched home for lunch, they marched back—the little league teenage army!

Women of the revolution were often touching and amusing. They marched as though their feet in clumsy boots were killing them, which doubtless they were. Olive drab did not suit their Latin complexions, so to compensate they daubed their great liquid unmilitary eyes with green eye shadow. They also passed muster, Cuban muster, with pink plastic roller curlers in their hair. The dainty hands gripping the drill rifles were manicured, with nails polished.

My last unforgettable trip to Havana was just before the missile crisis when John, exerting supreme effort through the Swiss Ambassador in Havana, succeeded in getting me a visitor's visa. I was then in Fort Lauderdale. Permission to enter Cuba came to my door via Western Union: a Spanish-worded telegram. I sent this with my passport to the NBC office in Washington where further State Department processing and stamping entitled me to buy a round-trip ticket from PanAm, then running shuttle flights from Miami. The planes went in empty, or nearly so, and flew out packed solid with refugees.

From the air as we approached this most alluring and once seductive, lavish city I was surprised to see it still looking very handsome and intact. Closer inspection told another story, but from a distance Havana was a glittering gamblers' prize. I was treated courteously at the airport. Although the armed guard ring of steel gave me a chill, I could not complain about my reception in Customs. At John's urgent request I had brought in more than $100 worth of food—all of it passed without objection and a polite apology for the brief delay for necessary inspection. I saw the Russians, lots of them, looking self-conscious and awkward and exceedingly camera shy, in sports clothes and open-toed sandals. Technicians, we put them down as, but then the island was full of Czechs and other foreigners, many with wives and children. (The Chinese were there too, but rarely seen.) So although it was true they were technicians, we had not the faintest glimmer of what was really going on. No one *knew* until the U-2 pictures were shown by Defense Secretary MacNamara on television.

On that last trip we made long risky tours into the country. We stayed with Cuban families far from Havana, heard and understood their fears and anxieties. We went everywhere with many cameras; if we were spied upon and watched, we didn't know it. No one stopped us. We tried to be careful, but we also tried to get our pictures and our story. We spent an afternoon at the home of Ernest Hemingway, which had been left as it was after his last visit. There were letters and bills and many personal items scattered through the house. The bar was amply supplied. Tins of food stood on the kitchen shelves. I remember being amused at what a reading room Hemingway had made of his king-sized bathroom. There were built-in bookshelves and magazine racks everywhere. I explored the separate little workroom in a tower just off the main house where it seems the Master spent his time. Its collapsed and beaten furniture reminded me of Goldeneye and Ian Fleming. I found no lingering evidence that Hemingway wrote standing up at a high desk. Or maybe toward the end he did not work in that lonely tower. Flowers bloomed in a weedy deserted garden. The swimming pool was green and ghastly with algae and neglect. But above all, the final unforgettable impression of the house itself was the overhead jungle of mounted animals' heads, on the walls, the glassy-eyed stare of African wildlife covering every wall in every room save only kitchen and bath. Down every corridor one passed under the shadow of those trophy heads. Perhaps we were especially sensitive because of the late, warm afternoon, the haunted emptiness, the guilty feeling of intrusion (a Cuban guard had let us in and vanished). There was an odor of decay and emptiness, that empty desk, the bar, and no sound anywhere. We hurried away. I have felt uncomfortable reading Hemingway ever since.

A guard keeps watch inside Hemingway's house in Cuba.

I remember another event that occurred while I was in Castro's Havana. Astronaut Scott Carpenter was orbiting the earth and in those days hundreds of Cubans owned and played, at ear-shattering volume, their transistor or short-wave radios. On the particular morning of the big American space orbit, I had gone to a Cuban beauty shop to get my hair done. I had chosen this particular shop because the young woman operator was running her small business from her own home in an upper-middle-class neighborhood. Woman-talk in a beauty shop was what I wanted to hear.

As she began to brush out my hair, I noticed she had a large short-wave radio on a nearby table. "Oh," I asked, "may we tune in a Miami station so we can get the news on the American astronaut?"

"Ah, si, si! Why not?" With this she tuned her radio to a Miami station. Soon two or three other ladies drifted into the living room salon. One pointed to the radio. "Did you hear him?" she cried. "Did you hear the American speaking

Spanish in space? Oh God—I will never forget it! I am turning on the radio early this morning and what I hear—very good *Spanish* coming from the American Carpenter! He is speaking to ground crews, or somebody, but I think, no, he is up there and I can hear him, so he is speaking to ME! I pray for him! God bring him safely down!"

All the women were very excited. When the operator pointed to me, American, they surrounded me with friendly, excited squeals. "How you come to Kooba? What you tink of Kooba? Is good, is terrible, eh? You hear your American Scott Carpenter this morning?"

Rollers flew into my head, but the women would not let me sit under the operator's one electric dryer. More and more they wanted to hear about "Miami—New York—tell us, what is it like now? You know many Koobans?"

There was an interval of music on the radio, so hairstyling preoccupied them for a half-hour. Then again, a newscast from Miami. The radio was turned up to full volume. Carpenter would be descending soon, but he was miles off course. "Oh," cried the señora who had heard the Spanish exchange between the astronaut and a ground crew in Mexico. "Oh, maybe Scott Carpenter come down near Kooba!" Laughing, she turned to me. "You know," she wagged a finger playfully, "You know what happens if the spaceman goes in the water near Havana? Fidel goes personally in a boat and fish him out and bring him back to Havana and give him big welcome. All Havana go wild!"

As it happened, Scott Carpenter came down nowhere near Cuba or his designated landing target. He was the astronaut who landed farthest from his designated recovery area, and I hear he will never live it down. Later, I dropped him a note to tell him his little bit of Spanish spoken way up there had made him a big man in Havana beauty shop circles.

The children went into orbit when he wrote an amused reply several weeks later ("Hey—that's his *real* autograph!"). Astronaut Carpenter explained he had studied "some Spanish" as a special tribute to the great guys who ran the tracking station in Mexico. The letter went to school with the kids and was read aloud to three different classes. I was delighted. What better proof of the "people bridge" defying political barriers: from a beauty shop in Havana, to outer space, to kids in sixth grade English? Communism builds the walls, but human beings never cement the bricks.

NATIONAL AERONAUTICS AND SPACE ADMINISTRATION
MANNED SPACECRAFT CENTER
HOUSTON 1, TEXAS

IN REPLY REFER TO

September 14, 1962

Mrs. Pegge Hlavacek
2600 Northeast 26th Avenue
Fort Lauderdale, Florida

Dear Mrs. Hlavacek,

Thank you very much for your good letter. I regret
that the mail load prevented my answering more promptly.
I can only hope that the address is sufficient to find you.

As you may know, I spent some time in Guaymas, Mexico
during the flight of the Mercury-Atlas 3, and had a chance
to brush up on my high school Spanish; at the same time making
many Mexican friends in that area. It was my promise at
that time that I would send a message in Spanish to the
friends I made in Guaymas should I ever be given an orbital
flight. When it turned out that I was to get MA-7, I took
great pride and pleasure in putting the message together
with some help, I might add, on the grammar, and I am most
pleased to hear that it was received with such good favor
in Cuba and Mexico.

Thanks again for your letter and your interest in
what we are doing.

Sincerely,

M. Scott Carpenter
Lt. Commander, USN
Mercury Astronaut

Another American who found walls abhorrent, who fought them and whose golden image crossed them in every country of the world, Communist included, was John F. Kennedy, who flew over Cuba many times on his way to a quiet, peaceful holiday with his family in Jamaica.

When he came to Montego Bay or Round Hill for long weekends he relaxed in total privacy, but he usually brought plenty of work along. He was never really "away" from Washington, even on his honeymoon, according to Evelyn Lincoln! He was once on the phone at Round Hill for almost an hour, dictating a speech. There was only one working phone in the manager's office. The resort was closed to everyone but the Kennedys, so he disturbed no one as he shouted phrases and paragraphs and spelled indistinguishable words.

I watched him swimming and noticed he usually went in alone and spent most of the time either casually paddling face down with mask and snorkel, or gently floating on his back, face up to the sky. Warm seawater must have provided excellent therapy for his back, but until he became president his ailments weren't public.

Occasionally the Kennedys stayed in a private house at the farthest end of Half-Moon hotel, with Caroline, the nanny, and the Radziwells. More often they preferred the borrowed William Paley (CBS) cottage at the most secluded extension of Round Hill. What an exquisite setting for Jacqueline Kennedy—that white, white cabana with its tall peaked roof, perched like a white camellia blown in by the trade winds against the coral rocks. The house had a swimming pool at true horizon level. As one strolled through the cottage toward the terrace, the pool's shimmery chlorine blue blended exactly with the blue line of the sea upon the horizon.

My meetings with JFK were friendly, easy, and informal chats on events and people of the day. Looking back now, it seems all our conversations sooner or later turned to one thing and to one man: Richard Nixon. He seemed obsessed with Nixon and speculated at length on his speeches, his public image, his motives, and his political craftsmanship.

As for Jackie? Even there on the beach, barefoot, wearing faded blue jeans and T-shirt, without makeup, hair uncurled and 1000 miles from Kenneth, she was a puzzling paradox. She looked very unwound and at ease, but obviously she was not. I talked with her one sunny morning when the Kennedys and Radziwells were spending the week between Christmas and New Year's Day at Half-Moon. Appreciating the sunshine switch from the traditional Boston Christmas, and observing Caroline digging in the sand nearby, I asked Jackie Kennedy, "How did your little girl enjoy Christmas in Jamaica?"

Jackie replied, in a tone of voice totally unrecognizable from the breathy, shy, little whispery one we know so well, "She's only two! What does *she* know about Christmas?"

Billy Graham came down to Round Hill one winter in the fashionable season when the place was packed. He and his young, collegiate-looking wife Ruth immediately became the most talked-about celebrities in the area.

What was a religious evangelist doing in a deluxe sea spa for the richest of the rich, where the few cabana rooms available in February or March ran from $60 to $100 *a day*, and where the land upon which the gilded private cottages repose costs the price of an immortal soul?

When John was taking some pictures of him for *Time*, Billy himself brought up the unlikely setting for a preacher's holiday. Pausing in his hand-in-hand beach stroll with Mrs. Graham, Billy gazed at the hillside of flower box cottages.

"Sa-a-y, this place must really be expensive," he drawled with a mild note of anxiety in his voice.

John raised an eyebrow. Billy hastened to explain: "Oh, *we're* not paying for this! Some good friends brought us down as their guests, so, uh, you see, u-m-m-m—"

Billy's innocent blue eyes were still apprehensive as they swept the boat dock, the private houses with private pools, the Jags and MGs, Austins and Hillmans in the parking lot, the Riviera-style dining room where even the waiters were imported from Italy.

But Billy Graham could have room and board anytime at Round Hill or anywhere in Jamaica on the strength of his remarkable personality alone. Corny or square old hat he may be ("God bless you real good"), but like that song about people who need people, many, many people apparently needed someone like Billy or enjoyed him as they found him. Few celebrities so jolted the regulars or wrung from the super snobs such awkward admiration.

Billy Graham and wife Ruth on a visit to Jamaica.

As the Management remarked later, "It's simply this: Graham's a great guy. His racket may be Jesus, but he's got something there. He's even believable, yuh know? He is also a rare breed these days: a *gentleman*. A real Southern gentleman."

The Negro Jamaican staff could hardly have welcomed de Lawd with any more ardor and reverence. At every turn they were at the feet of the Master's man. When Billy and his affluent sponsors entered the dining room, water pitchers and butter pats went down and the Jamaicans raised their voices in spirituals. Hands clapped, hips swayed, eyes rolled, the chorus rose, hallelujah! They sang early in the morning, they sang on the beach, and they "put de whole worl' innezz hanns'" before the Bloody Marys and double martinis had gone in the glass or the filets had turned on the grill.

Billy appreciated it all. He understood, he warmly gave his blessing and his Amen. But in between, he reached out to the unsettled regulars. He may have preferred privacy, but instead he circulated. He talked to everyone, he met the cynical, the curious, the amused and annoyed and unaccustomed—all of them. He accepted every invitation, including bids to cocktail parties. ("I went because that's where I'd meet everybody. I would just ask my hostess to give my wife and me tomato juice.") He was lionized by the worldly ones who soon called him "a doll" and "a storyteller almost as funny as Bob Hope!"

Then word went around that Billy was ill. He wasn't seen anywhere. What was wrong? Nothing alarming, only painful. Second-degree sunburn. Because of his popularity, everyone was concerned, offering advice and cures. The most amusing story told about Billy's sunburn was this:

A solicitous friend came to Billy's cottage to offer him some Scotch whiskey. He said it was the latest cure for a painful overdose of sun.

"Aw, come now, my friend," Billy Graham shook his head. "You don't really expect *me* to fall for that one? You don't really think I'd take a drink for sunburn, do you?"

"No, no, Billy," the friend protested. "You don't drink the stuff, you rub it on all over like a suntan lotion! The alcohol's supposed to cool the skin on the outside!"

Billy handed back the Johnny Walker, still grinning. "My friend, that would be an awful waste of good Scotch whisky!"

No celebrity and no event on the island in my time was to cause as much commotion as the Independence Day visit of Princess Margaret and Lord Snowden, Tony Armstrong-Jones. If the island never forgot Princess Margaret, neither did Lyndon B. Johnson and Lady Bird, to whom she delivered a royal rebuff, a public and petty prima donna snub!

The Princess, Lord Snowden and a royal entourage representing Her Majesty, Queen Elizabeth, came to Kingston and added such splendor to the event that most Jamaicans completely forgot they were celebrating *independence* from all that!

In marking the severance of ties to colonialism and the mother country from whom all blessings had flowed in better days, Jamaicans went lightheaded into spirals of excitement. It was the biggest party, the wildest ball and Mardi Gras of them all. Independence, it seemed, was just an elaborate excuse for Princess Margaret and Tony to have another holiday when the formalities had been disposed of. Jamaican servants in my house talked more about getting new clothes for the celebration than about this doubtful thing called freedom, which would probably mean tighter immigration quotas to England, higher prices, and fewer jobs.

Composing Jamaica's independent constitution was a mere chore in contrast with the protocol arrangements made for the royal princess. Nothing was left to doubt or chance; even the princess's favorite brand of cigarettes was hastily provided. They were, oddly, American Chesterfields, but who can say she hasn't changed or stopped by this time?

Jamaica, and in fact, all the British dot-sized islands had had royal visitors including the Queen and Philip from time to time. But this visit was different.

Jamaicans were going beyond all bounds not only for independence but also because "de Prin'zuss Meg she really love a good time, mon." She was to their mind a real calypso fun girl. The word swinger hadn't yet come into the language.

A tall Texan named Lyndon B. Johnson, then vice president, his wife Lady Bird, and Lynda Bird were also coming. With them they brought a United States gift of $3 million for new housing as an Independence present. They might just as well have sent a cable and the money and stayed home. There wouldn't have been so many hurt feelings and angry words.

Royalty is never so royal as it is on the occasion of retreat and withdrawal. When the "colony" from which the greatest empire of them all is resigning is small and its people African in origin, the British really spare nothing to put on an unexcelled, proper show.

I have seen many an airport arrival of the celebrated and powerful in my time, but nothing compared with the formal arrival of doll-dainty Princess Margaret. This tiny island might as well have been the greatest and richest country of the entire British Empire. All the trappings were there in the noonday sun, blinding bright and splendid: the gorgeous array of gold braid, medals and swords, the army, the band, the bagpipes, the booming of cannon, and the air salute of low-flying planes.

Serenely in command of the occasion was this tiny, graceful figure in pink polka-dot chiffon, long white gloves, and a towering bobby hat of white flowers. Far from wanting to be free from her, Jamaicans were hers to command. Such coos, such ahh's, such crooning of adoration were heard on all sides. But Lord Snowden, with sideburns, in his dove-grey Tom Jones suit complete with grey felt topper, really tickled Jamaicans. "Lordy, jus' see 'im now, mon! De Prin'zuss man look jes' lik' li'l boy all dress up fo' Easter Sunday mornin' ta' get his pitcher taken."

As the visit and manifold ceremonies and garden teas and ribbon cuttings proceeded, Jamaican officials scurried to wait attendance upon the royal party. As wives and daughters and sisters and cousins exhausted themselves with fashion extravaganzas, many worried that independence might also mean the end of the queen's honor lists. Would it also mean the banishment of titles, held by many Jamaican politicians and high court judges—sires, lords, and ladies? No matter how much financial aid the island could hope for in the future from the United States, it wouldn't be the same. There are no frills in the world like royal ones!

Before long it became very clear that there was a royal distance and coolness toward the American delegation, particularly toward the conspicuous tall Texan and his family. Princess Margaret made it increasingly, embarrassingly clear that the Independence was a family affair between a British colony and her people who would be future members of the British Commonwealth. There seemed a painful touchiness about the reality of the dwindling British financial position and the inevitability of American influence and next-doorness simply taking over. It is all well and good to be cool and rational where one is an outsider, far removed from the emotion, tradition, and the thinning status of royalty in the twentieth century. But there was in Princess Margaret a surprising well of emotion clearly evident in yielding even this one small, shimmering, and beautiful island.

Keeping the small tempest in perspective, it would barely have mattered to anyone except the small handful of Americans who bristled with resentment at the royal Margaret's attitude. But as the official representative of President Kennedy, it mattered very much to LBJ, who suffers no slight slightly! He had ordered in a horde of USIA men, photographers, and reporters from Voice of America from Mexico City to give maximum publicity to America's close tie to a friendly island close to Fidel Castro's Cuba. This corps of government-publicists rushed forward to do their leader's bidding, only to be solidly resisted by both Jamaicans and the Princess's entourage. It seems too ridiculous, too trifling to mention—but so simple a request as one picture of the Princess shaking hands with LBJ was turned down. It was turned down even when personally requested, by Johnson's team, of the Jamaican Prime Minister.

As one Jamaican civil servant put it to me, "If the Princess won't shake hands with your Mr. Johnson, we don't dare insist. She could just pack up and fly off the 'hilon if the Americans give her any more trouble!"

Retreating to obscurity, Lady Bird and the Vice-President spent their time visiting hospitals, schools, and the rather depressing American Peace Corps camp for homeless boys in the Blue Mountains. The princess granted one brief audience to the Johnsons, but barred photographers.

I was luckier than the Johnsons. I had my own moment and my own little chat with the Princess. A reception was given for all the foreign and local press covering the Independence. Here Lord Snowden, walking like Philip with hands clasped behind his back, was confronted with all his old British photographer cronies. They knew the Tony of another day only too well. Easing herself gracefully away from the photographers, the Princess chanced to walk straight over to me. I quickly asked her about her well-publicized attempts at water skiing. "I'm rather awful at it," she laughed. "I'm down as much as I'm up, and in England the water is so frightfully cold. That's why I love to come out here. Only here I would rather snorkel than ski."

She went on to say that she was "absolutely mad" about going down to look 'round at the silent world and all the "ittie" tropical fish on the reef. She wasn't mad about going down with a lung and all that, just perfectly safe shallow water would do. Besides, you can see just as much in safe water as in great depths. (True almost anywhere in the Caribbean.) She rushed on to say, "You know, it amazes me how you can put on a mask and dive right down among all the fish and after a few minutes they don't pay any attention to you. They just swim round or come back and stare at you. They are so curious they even poke at you and nibble you!" (If those little Jamaican angelfish or red snappers only *knew* on whose royal limb they nibbled!)

My last glimpse of Princess Margaret was equally memorable. She swept into the new Jamaican sports stadium for the final night of the celebrations, the first flag raising at midnight, in all the royal raiment she might have worn for a crowning in Westminster. She wore a diamond tiara, and glittering beaded, cleavage-baring white strapless ballgown, and the royal blue sash. Decorations flashed under the stadium lights, as did a fantastic necklace of emeralds. About the princess' swanlike white throat was a necklace of emeralds of such size and green fire amid a white blaze of diamonds that we all stared, open-mouthed, through our opera glasses. No one else so short, and already aglitter, could have carried off the endowment of a British throne's worth of emeralds so well! When she reached the royal box and raised a white-gloved arm in acknowledgment to the bedlam of the stadium, she was positively a princess in phosphorescence.

The band struck up the traditional "God Save the Queen" and the proud new Jamaican national anthem. I turned and swung my powerful little opera glasses on the princess. *She was weeping!* I thought I must surely be imagining things, carried away with the drama of the moment. I said nothing to anyone around me, but I never took the glasses from that white oval face. The blond head of Lord Snowden bent momentarily toward her. For one swift second, a gloved hand swept her face and cheeks.

It struck me with a pang of understanding that no matter how much ceremony and dazzle was elaborately staged, for her a flag coming down was a flag disappearing after a long and glorious history. Suddenly it was midnight. All the stadium lights went out. There was an almost panicky, strained silence as Jamaican youngsters who had run a marathon race with the new flag struggled, all thumbs, in the darkness to securely fasten the new Jamaican flag to the flagpole ropes. When the lights went on again, the band played, and the people screamed, I took one last look at the royal box. The Princess's face was a frozen mask.

I had seen it all, I had my story. Hurrying from the press section to a waiting car, I sped to the cable office. By pre-arrangement, I had engaged a circuit to New York to do a short colorful broadcast on Jamaica's Independence for NBC's "Monitor."

New York came on the line, but something was wrong. I could hear voices and typewriters and phones ringing in the background as the night editor wailed, "Say, Peg—we can't take a damn word on Jamaica tonight! We're going crazy up here on this Marilyn Monroe Story."

It was that weekend.

In the span of three years, our Home Office turned out many stories and pictures which were fascinating and important at the time. It was a tremendous event—at the time—when John got the world beat for NBC on the gory assassination of Dominican Republic dictator Rafael Trujilla and the front page of *The New York Times* quoted "NBC's John Hlavacek" on all the details of how the detested tyrant had been "done in." For the *Times,* the most unforgettable story was our report on the Rastas—a minority sect, often weed-smoking and violent, a sort of indigenous Hippie group—which created enough havoc for the Jamaican government that it sent a delegation back to Africa to investigate a possible "repatriation" of unabsorbed Negroes back to the dark continent from which they came. (The Rastas vociferously insisted Queen Victoria had set aside something like fifty million pounds in her will to send the blackman back to his native home!) The back-to-Africa team included more dignified and representative members of Jamaican society as well as a few hand-picked, washed-up, and dressed-up Rastas. Traveling first-class all the way, via England, the delegation received polite hospitality and many gifts from officials in emerging Africa, but no welcome mat. Emerging Africa has enough problems, and quite enough people, without opening its doors to unschooled, unemployed "foreigners." African nations wanted engineers, doctors, teachers, agronomists, and capital investors—not outsiders, even black ones, who were non-contributors.

Island politicians who seized upon independence as a vehicle to personal power have been struggling ever since with its awesome problems. Freedom never had so perilous a beginning as in an uneducated, over-populated society without industrial training or skills, cramped onto land space with meager natural resources and critical water problems. Jamaica, with rich deposits of bauxite from which aluminum is made, in addition to booming tourism and its abundant agricultural produce, is by far the most fortunate of the Caribbean islands economically. Even so, it is in reality anything but its fondest boast: an island of peace and contentment in a troubled world.

To the anger and consternation of many Jamaicans, the freedom they had shouted themselves speechless to proclaim and wildly celebrate had brought no free beer, no free TVs, no more jobs, and no more or cheaper peas 'n' rice, mon!

Inter-island relations throughout the Caribbean are jealous and scrappy. All of the islands have the same problems, produce the same crops, need more water and skills, and must survive on the same tourists, outside investment capital, and jobs. Competition, intense pressure, and borderline economics produce no working togetherness. Social evolution comes slowly. Educational systems have been revamped but modern skills do not come out of books overnight. Petty squabbles, in close quarters, often become violent and bloody.

Occasionally one still hears weird tales of African Voodoo, or "obeh," as Jamaicans call witch doctoring. I always strongly discounted all this talk of black magic seances and carryings on at night in secret voodoo chambers as pure bunkum. Since leaving Jamaica, however, I have been on a long tour of West Africa, natural and original homeland of most Negro islanders. I now see I was perhaps naïve and quite mistaken. Superstition and belief in spirits, good or bad, is so ancient, so profound a tradition among the Negro race, I now believe it far more widely practiced and secretly believed in, clung to, resorted to, often for impressive cash sums, than white outsiders ever really comprehend.

In retrospect, it is heartening to see that the embroiled islands never went the way of Cuba. Not that the United States would have allowed it, but even before Castro completely bankrupted his world cause and prestige there were no other Cuba-style revolutions. Our U.S. Navy base with its fleet of planes and submarines remains intact in Guantanamo, at the extreme end of Cuba. Puerto Rico progresses and enjoys its tourist and factory boom despite internal rumblings and boisterous politics. The Dominican Republic is a special problem; Trinidad is another. Haiti is a nightmare in a class by itself, but no threat to us. So—despite all the manmade hurricanes of trouble in the Caribbean, all the islands have survived except Cuba. And these days we don't even worry about Fidel. Left to his own devices, he is doing a far better job of killing the Fidelista movement than could any of his enemies, hundreds of Miami liberators, or even the CIA.

As events pass from phase to phase, more personal island experiences remain. One of the serenest, most worthwhile stories we sent out during the entire Caribbean period was not about Castro or islanders or their temporarily important, hot pimiento politics at all.

It was a nature story, part of the continuing saga of people rushing to save vanishing species from extinction. In this case an unlikely species: the green sea turtle. Mr. Ugly, Mr. Unromantic and Unheroic. Just a big blob, a seaweed-green, 200-pound floating saucer with only the half-recalled rhyme of Ogden Nash to give him anything like a lovable personality. (With all that armor-plate to be so fertile, Myrtle!)

Some years before Ogden Nash got so curious about the turtle, an extraordinary zoologist from the University of Florida, Dr. Archie Carr, made a study of what the ravages of man had done to the last remaining herds of green sea turtles. In a subsequent book, the *Windward Way*—a kind of *For Whom the Bell Tolls* for turtles—Archie made an impassioned plea for conservation of the vanishing reptiles. After all, the unlovely critters had made a considerable contribution in the past to man's history and survival. In the perilous days of long sea voyages and discovery, it was the abundance of harmless green sea turtles which provided fresh meat supplies for seamen thousands of miles from home; thus, turtles made world exploration possible simply by keeping seamen alive! Wasn't it only fair, at this late date, to repay the debt by keeping the remaining species going—with legal sanctuaries and scientific protection? Absolutely, thought a number of adventurous amateurs and well-wishers who read *The Windward Road* and came to know warmly likable but powerfully motivated Archie Carr.

Turtles may be fascinating, but why the struggle and strain *now* to save them, aside from the strong instinct that keeps modern man from letting any creature of nature pass to extinction? Turtles should be saved, pleads Archie Carr, as an abundant source of food for the population explosion (mature turtles, brought back to herd strength in plentiful quantity, could produce well over 100 pounds each of pure protein). Properly cooked, as islanders and our own American colonial forebears knew how, turtle meat is delicious. It helps if no one *tells* you it's turtle until coffee and dessert! In addition to its nutritional importance, the turtle is possibly even more valuable to science as a superb direction finder and navigator in trackless seas. In the space age, science would like to know the turtles' secret direction finder.

Decimation of the herds began ages ago, but what has more seriously imperiled survival was the crowding of people onto once-deserted beaches all over the Caribbean. Those warm beaches were the turtles' breeding grounds, secluded maternity havens where the females could crawl out of the sea and safely lay their eggs. Turtles usually return to the beach from which they were originally hatched, although they may spend intervening years many hundreds of miles away. In our day the human occupation of beaches has spelled annihilation for the turtles two ways: every two or three years when the females crawled onto land to lay their eggs, they were slain and their eggs devoured. No hatchlings, no more turtles. This devastating process continued for years until along came Archie Carr and after him the first group of turtle-savers, calling themselves the Brotherhood of the Green Sea Turtle. (They now have a duller but more dignified and official-sounding name: the "Caribbean Conservation Corps." Pooh!)

At the outset of the project a government—conservation beachhead was urgently needed. But what Caribbean Island could afford to shoo rich tourists off its golden sands? Finally, far away from the usual vacation run, little Costa Rica found it had a spare stretch of black sand beachfront once used by the old United Fruit company, now abandoned and nearly deserted. The name of the place was Tortuguero, and it won't be found on any tourist map because its offshore surf is unswimmable. A heavy prevalence of sharks has proved mighty discouraging. Years ago at a nearby port town, Limon, the United Fruit Boats brought employment and activity, but now they are gone and only a small lumber industry survives. Otherwise the Tortuguero beach was ideal for turtles—and for the Brotherhood and Archie Carr.

For nearly ten years now on this remote strip of unpeopled, jungle-edged beach the turtles have been protected and carefully observed in the summer season by lingering members of the Brotherhood or by squads of students from the University of Florida. Accurate reports are written on the number and condition of turtles in a season, the number of eggs laid and "saved" from human predators and dogs. Then, before female turtles return to the sea, the active shore patrol turns them over and painlessly attaches or clamps a small metal tag to their hind flippers. (I had to be reassured it "didn't hurt." They told me it was little more than the sensation of clipping on an earring.) The tags give the place of origin, and date, and request that anyone who recovers both turtle and tag mail in the tag for a cash reward.

Over the years more than four thousand turtles have been tagged and nearly two hundred tags have been returned, some coming from astonishing distances more than 1000 miles away. Scientific research into the mysteries of migration—birds, mammals or marine reptiles—is greatly enhanced by the results of the turtle study.

Every possible and very fanciful means of breaking down the mystery of turtle direction-detection has been tried. Assuredly the Brotherhood had a lot of fun-and-games trying these: to track the re-entry trail of the female after she has laid her eggs on shore and made her way back to sea, helium-inflated balloons were attached to their flippers. What a wondrous sight to see—a confused bevy of lady turtles all strung up in huge red balloons flapping out to sea! Although a great stunt as an experiment, the balloons proved too perishable and flimsy to yield practical results. Phase two was more sophisticated and costly, but even more fanciful: small transistor radios were tried to track on a beep signal the migration pattern of the turtles. Archie Carr, this time assisted by the Navy, really thought he was onto an infallible device. If it worked on the turtles—and it seemed absolutely foolproof—it could be tried on birds. (Think of tiny transistors attached to thousands of migrating birds, tracking their long flight over enormous distances on a special peep-beep!) But even the radio experiment proved disappointing and costly. So the migrating mystery remains mysterious, although science continues to bore in, slowly.

John by this time had interested *Sports Illustrated* in a story on the Brotherhood's rescue of the turtle at Tortuguero, so he was sent down to film the operation. Upon his arrival, the hand of the Brotherhood (or is it the flipper?) was extended. If he passed the initiation—downing one raw turtle egg—and made his contribution to the shore patrol, he too could be a Brother, could tag a turtle, and could even put his name on one. Somewhere, I wonder, doth there rock upon the bosom of the ocean a 250-pound, big-eyed, money-green lady turtle named HLAVACEK? Tagged turtles have paddled their way as far as the coast of Brazil from a launching shove-off at Costa Rica, so why not ours?

Those who joined the turtle brothers from irresistible fascination gained a lot more from the experience than beach action with a difference. Personal participation down on that cruddy, smelly old beach at Tortuguero, living in unplush and unflush quarters with assorted companions of age and background gave the semi-scientists keen insights and enjoyment. In spite of their sophistication, they found themselves deeply caught up in the green world of nature, the ageless survival struggle and the sea.

Have they saved the turtle? Nope. Archie Carr admits, "Hell, no! I'm sorry to admit defeat. But there are just too many factors against us and the poor old turtles. Oh, we've saved some. We keep trying. We've learned a lot in the process, but in time—" he squinted hard in the Island sun, his lips pressed into a dry, thin line, *"the turtles'll be wiped out!"*

We took the kids to see the turtles at Tortuguero near the end of one summer. They scoured the beaches with the students, working at night with flashlights. A full moon came out one night and the turtle watchers cursed it. No smart turtle would expose herself in a spotlight like that, they predicted, but being experts they were wrong. Our moonlit watch yielded twenty turtles at widely scattered intervals. The next morning the turtles were recorded, measured, tagged and then permitted to drag themselves back into the frothing sea. Their eggs would be carefully dug up—they were like warm, moist ping pong balls—counted and reburied inside a protected corral, fenced off and guarded against all predators, dogs, and villagers.

Island and tropical people have for centuries relished the taste of turtle eggs—as we enjoy oysters—and it is hard to explain to them that now their government is protecting the turtles and taking away their delicacy. (Human nature being truer to its own instincts than to distant governments, the people snag as many turtle eggs as they can get. Being forbidden makes them twice as tasty, I'm sure!) But the protected eggs finally hatch, and when the amazing little critters dig their way out of both their shells and sand pit, their race to the sea is eagerly watched by a ring of cheering, bearded, and barefoot American godfathers!

What a happy sundowner on life in the Caribbean! Although all odds are against survival and success, here was man for once acting as the defender, the helpmate, and the servant of nature. However futile the effort, it was encouraging to see new life returned to the sea. However small, of what marginal importance in modern times, the whole experiment provided wholesome balance for all of us.

It was nearly two o'clock in the morning. We all stood there in the ghostly neon-whiteness of the Caribbean moonlight. In silence we waited for more turtles to come, a dark, rounded hump to emerge like a moving rock out of the luminous white surf. Awed by the sight of a process old as evolution, we urged the turtles on to safety, temporary safety, because we were there.

We did not breathe in that silence lest the faintest sigh scare the turtles away. Quiet, kids, I thought in that rare and breathless moment—listen to the sea.

It is the rhythm of life itself.

Save the turtle if you can.

In comes the tide, like a claw upon the land, violent and threatening, out rushes the tide, and all is calm.

In balance, give and take, hold and release.

Give back to the sea.

Give back to life.

Give and give and give..........

Addendum: "Lost and Found" Chapters of Diapers on a Dateline

[*Editor's note:* In April 2001, John Hlavacek asked me to look at a book manuscript that his wife Pegge had written during the early 1960s and never published. The title of the book was *Diapers on a Dateline.* John had rediscovered the manuscript while preparing for a possible move, and he called me because he knew that I had done quite a bit of editorial work for his friend Ted Peacock (John, Ted and I are alumni of Carleton College). John told me that he thought his wife's manuscript was well written, but he wanted an "unbiased opinion." After reading a couple of chapters, I enthusiastically agreed with John: Pegge's book deserved to be published. Before anything could be done with it, however, the manuscript needed to be transferred to computer files. The chapters were typed on fragile "onionskin" paper and held together with rusty paper clips. My job was to retype each chapter on my PC, do some minor editing, and communicate with the publishing company, iUniverse, during the book's production. Four chapters were missing, and we chose to recreate them from Pegge's diary and letters rather than hold up publication. Copies of the book were available by December 2002, and about six months after publication the missing chapters turned up in John and Pegge's house. They are included here for the enjoyment of everyone who has read *Diapers on a Dateline.*]

Happy Birthday—Floored with Spaghetti and Kids

Happy birthdays for small children are always glorious blowouts surrounded by balloons. Birthdays for husbands are another matter. Balloons don't quite make it…

John was usually the forgotten man on March 13. He even forgot his own birthday until heavily stamped, air-mailed greeting cards arrived from the home folks. This time I decided to remedy all that—I'd give him a really great birthday party, including his pet ingredient: *kids!*

163

You can get on this doubtful wicket by taking kids into your confidence and planning. Ask them, "How can we give Daddy a wonderful party?" They'll tell you. Mine said, "Oh, gee-willikers! Let's have a treasure hunt—a buried treasure hunt so everybody'll get *presents!*"

And so it came about. On a Friday night, with no school the next day, we had a spaghetti dinner and treasure hunt birthday party for Daddy. Fifteen children strong, and a minor percentage of parents. But kids have the best ideas, I tell you!

What made the evening really boisterous fun was the fact that whole station-wagon-loads of families rolled up as one package! In a government center like New Delhi (or, I suspect, even Washington DC), where social demands set Mother and Daddy rushing out the door night after night, this was a time when nobody stayed home with servants or a babysitter.

Also, as far as comfortably possible I made this a servantless party. Everybody helped, everybody functioned at something, glass in hand. First there was a pirate treasure hunt in the hotel's front garden for the boys, led by Big John. There was a second treasure hunt in the rear garden for the girls, led by one of the mamas who was strictly given no helpful hints or backstage secrets.

The bushes and the trees of the vast, sprawling hotel grounds had been heavily seeded with treasure-trail clues which went a step beyond the bent twigs and the bear paw-prints of the Brownie Mother's Manual. Some were easy, while others were confoundin' hard, almost impossible to find, half-buried. Some of the trail props were scary—soup and stew bones begged from the hotel kitchen after lunch, washed off, and made to look "human," then left in tree hollows with grisly notes. There was a lock of hair snipped from an underneath section of Mary's thick bob, a cowboy gun, a garden worm in a matchbox, an old Zorro hat, a "bucket of blood" (ketchup thinned with water in a mayonnaise jar), even a human tooth (one of the children's, which I had found in my desk drawer).

At the end of this sordid trail there was the foretold pot of gold: a bushel basket the children had gorgeously attired in yellow crepe paper and gold tinsel from the Christmas decorations box. The treasure within was a basketload of Indian violins, one for each boy, which they all rushed back to play for us. Indian violins, which cost about *char annas* apiece (translation: not much) make a hideous racket. With all the boys tuning up, we had the night air curdling with gruesome sounds until the food arrived.

The girls found silent treasures in their bushel basket: silk scarves, fake jewels, even toe rings from the bazaar.

After this twofold treasure hunt, which had been timed to end at the last bone before dark, came chow for umpteen people of all ages. I was experimenting, but

I found this worked fine: we spread out on the ground, Indian style, about three big bedsheets. We dragged up no chairs—everyone got down on his bazooka, took a paper plateload of spaghetti and tossed salad, with a cup of coffee, tea, or milk. Ice cream and cake followed. John's cake was a glorious thing with Irish-green mint icing, the homemade offering of a friend possessed of an American cake mix who had bent over her hot little oven to produce it.

Although the hotel kitchen prepared the food and the servants delivered it in quantity, the staff did nothing more. Determinedly, this was an American party. In the words of the poet, "Do it yourself, dear." The mothers agreed afterward that the evening had a certain horrible quality of nostalgia about it, and hastened to add, "Let's not carry this too far. Once is enough to remind us—let's not start any dangerous trends!"

It did not occur to me then that to an uproarious evening like this I had invited no Indians. The corny informality of this pitch-in night of family fun was strictly American. It would be unfair to say that many Indians would not have enjoyed it, too, but the minute you hand over the dinner plate you're in trouble. Spaghetti and meat sauce or meatballs gets you into beef, and that of course is off limits. Serving a second menu of curry or chicken or some "safe" Hindu food would be an expensive extra and a nuisance when you must attend to other important hostess jobs like laying out a treasure hunt in two huge gardens.

I am sure there are times when Indians abroad feel the same way—that occasionally it is a blessed relaxation to have a purely Indian *tamasha* in which they let themselves go as they would not normally do when mixing with Europeans—when they can wear what they like, eat with their fingers, even suck in a good *pan* or beetle chew…

When another big birthday for the children rolled around, I tried the same idea: spaghetti dinner picnic on the floor covered with easily washed bedsheets. The children had invited their schoolmates, some of whom were Indian. Without thinking, I handed one little fellow a supper plate of spaghetti with one small meatball on top. He looked at it. "Beef, Mrs. Hlavacek?" he asked, handing back his plate. Another mite of a girl refused to touch her cake as well as her dinner because—as she lisped through missing front teeth—she wath not allowed to eat eggths. I turned to order some cheese sandwiches, but another spunky chap stopped me. "Never mind, it is quite all right, Mrs. Hlavacek. We ate dinner at home before we came!" I hugged him, for clearly he'd had a good time playing mystery games blindfolded with a red cowboy neckerchief. Food was the least of his worries, as long as he didn't touch anything.

Giving birthday parties for kiddies when you have five spread around the calendar means scarcely is one behind you than another is coming up!

A birthday party for a jillion moppets in a hotel met its severest test on the twins' "We Are Six" occasion. Their entire class from school was invited, including their adored teacher, a raving beauty in a magenta-and-gold sari. In Delhi few birthday parties were given at which there were not at least 20 children—often many more. The haul of presents was fantastic—to be matched equally with the loot the little lambs fully expected to take home, in addition to balloons, candy, and prizes (if any)!

Anyway, this time I planned all the games and food very carefully, for John Patrick was due any day, and should I not be there I wanted all to go well. To make doubly sure of entertainment for so many, I arranged for two Dettolled donkeys to be delivered to the hotel by 4 o'clock. (Dettol is the main disinfectant used in India; every home with a bathroom has got a bottle of it.)

By 4 o'clock, just as the hotel driveway became choked with cars and kiddies, the rains came! They came as never before. They even made a front-page story the next day as the worst for September within living measure or memory! The vast lawns on which we had planned the games and donkey rides had become pools. They looked like overflowing paintboxes in which mud browns, grass greens, and brilliant flower colors were all a watery wash under sheets of driving rain.

In the hotel's formal Music Room, John rescued me from an island of panic surrounded by sodden, screaming children—Indian, British, American. The Dettolled donkeys (in plastic raincoats, yet!) arrived as ordered at 4 p.m. and waited in the garden, standing in water that was almost up to their knees.

As we stood amid the bedlam of the Music Room, the face of a friend appeared in the doorway—the *Observer*'s Mike Deane. "My God! John, Pegge—how can you manage this—*this?*" he cried. "Here, let me help. Let's turn up some music—*louder* music—grab some chairs—line them up. My God, I haven't heard such noise since the war!"

I faded away feebly to make preparations for refreshments in the adjoining room. Games ended in a screaming shambles. The rain roared down outside. We had to ring a bell to sound the "alarm" for ice cream and cake.

I moved toward the window, eyeing the sky, which I couldn't even see through the sheets of water. "Dear God," I prayed, "Can't you stop this accursed rain and help us to get through this birthday party?" A mother's heartfelt prayer is always answered. The flooding showers suddenly tapered off to a fine drizzle. The donkey *walla* saw his chance. He moved up close to the Music Room window, dragging his nags behind him. Even if there were no riders, he was eager to be paid and get home before he and his horseflesh were washed down to Calcutta.

It only took two little boys to see the donkeys.

"Hey, you guys! Look! Me first!" and two Zorros went right out the window into a flower bed and up onto a donkey's back. After them went every mother's darling who minutes before had been contentedly stuffing at the refreshment board. They squeezed on the donkeys six or seven at a time and trotted away screaming.

"Well," I thought, "I cannot say them nay," but I thought of pneumonia the next day, coughs, sniffles, wheezes, and sneezes.

When cars finally came to collect the lot of them, not a single parent even murmured at receiving back a child so dripping wet as to need wringing out. "My dear—a party on a day like *this*—all those children! How brave of you!"

The Deanes really endeared themselves to us that day. In addition to Mike's fieldwork, they gave each of the twins a small Brownie camera, which thrilled them so much that they took the cameras to bed that night (after first marking which was which with a dab of my nail polish).

"Goll-ee, Mommy, what a wonderful birthday," Mary purred from her pillow.

I was pleased. Spontaneous thanks at the age of six makes it all worthwhile. As I kissed Mike goodnight, I whispered a gentle hint: "Don't you think it would be nice to thank poor Daddy, too?"

Mike hopped out of bed, then awkwardly patted John's shoulder as he asked, "Did you have a nice birthday party, Daddy?"

◆　　　◆　　　◆

The twins have just had their twelfth birthday party, and those original Brownies are still going strong. Makes you wonder about the $200 jobs…

Anyway, on children's birthdays generally the wisest rule of all seems to be one I heard somewhere: the young child should invite as many guests as his age. One friend at a one-year party, two at age two, three at age three, and so on. Few mamas can hold back like that, but from wide experience the rule is in the best interests of the child.

Letting the children invite *their* friends of their own age makes for happier parties than those odd assortments that are created when children of business contacts or customers are invited irrespective of age, together with the children of one's adult friends. In India, 16-year-olds attend parties for 3-year-olds, the connection of course being business, relatives, or favors.

Unless one is really desperate or terrified, it seems to me that renting movies as the entire program, next to serving refreshments, is an admission of defeat and not really a party. There must be some run-around game, and you do not necessarily have to think them all up. Kids are perfectly happy playing the same old game they played that morning at school.

Experience has equipped me to have rain-or-shine plans made. If you have a small living room or patio, a game of "hot potato" can keep them going a long time. Seated in a circle, the players pass something around until the music stops. Whoever is caught holding the Something has to drop out. The pass-around Something can actually be a fine Idaho, washed off, or a rubber ball, or a gift-prize buried deep inside a wad of newspaper wrapping, with each player being allowed to remove one sheet of wrapping when the music stops.

If the children are of an age where they can write and spell without strain, here is an excellent living room or apartment game, tried and tested. I call it Scotland Yard because I dug it right out of a book about the training methods used on police and detective rookies to train them to make accurate observations.

This game was first tried out on a Cub Scout pack as a merit-badge project for memory training, on one horrible rainy afternoon when our outdoor program washed out. So popular was Scotland Yard that the Cubs promised to "be real good" so they could keep playing it.

You need little equipment for this game. Pencils and paper are passed around. Two youngsters are chosen to be the subjects for observation. You whisk them out of sight and dress them up in any kind of rig you like, crazy or clever. Don't take too much time to do it, or the pencil-and-paper outsiders will get restless, break pencil points and make hats or spitballs out of the paper.

Next, you return your two objects of observation and clock the children on how long they may look. Observees then vanish. Observers begin quickly writing down everything they can remember. At the right interval of time to get the main points down (let the children's age be your guide on the length of time allowed), call back the two dressed-up specimens. Check the observation reports against the living image. Boys, especially, just eat this game alive. Competition is fierce, because nobody wants to be a dumb detective. They scream to play it over and over.

Every good party must have lots of prizes, all of them if possible being wrapped in a *big* box. No matter what dime store oddment or notion is inside, pack it *big*, lady!

Refreshments for young children tend to be an appalling waste. Oh, the bowls of melted ice cream I have fed to cats after a birthday party! And I am always amazed by the cake that has one bite taken out of it and then is left, maybe because forking up the entire piece was too big a job. Cookies, by contrast, are always devoured, but of course every party must have the cake as a holder for the candles! Lately I have found that cupcakes made as miniatures of the guest of honor's cake (i.e., with the same icing), with a tiny wax candle in the center of each one, are a great hit and a beautiful table effect. As soon as the candles on the main birthday cake have been lit, you light up all the little cupcakes for each guest to blow out and make a wish, too! Children's faces in the momentary candleglow up and down the entire table make a lovely sight.

While we're on the subject of refreshments, has anybody found the answer to handling all the parents who come to pick up kiddies and are so happy to linger on for a cocktail or two? By the time a good, hard party is over, Mama should not be asked to start mixing up a second one at which *she* gets no chance to sit down. Passing out drinks with one hand and balloons and prizes and take-home loot with the other is just too much! If a hired helper is doing all the runaround work and the dishes afterward, and keeping an eye on dinner, too, or the party has been one of those age-of-the-child small ones, this is another matter.

Now, regarding that take-home loot (party favors, if you prefer), I'm dead against it. The idea of the ready paw outstretched expecting More (than a balloon) is not the right spirit. I would rather give out enough prizes that almost every child has *won* something he is bursting with pride to take home and show off.

I love birthday parties and knock myself out planning them. Come to think of it, everybody in our family gets a birthday party of some sort except me. Lovely cards and checks come in the mail on my June day, but from John, no presents.

Trips. I'm a trip girl.

And that's where all the trouble begins…

I Was Dreaming of a Snow-White Christmas— For My Birthday, Which Comes in June!

My birthday comes in June. I hoped to collect my present in December, as I always did, with a trip. And with Christmas near and giving me ideas, I decided I'd have mine snow-white this year…

This business of having gift days—anniversaries, birthdays, even Christmas—can sometimes find you not really "needing" anything (or wanting anything "for the house," with a handle on it especially). I solved all this long ago by buying what I "need" in the right size and color, when I need it most, and when my Gift Days roll around I simply say to John, "A trip, dear. Where haven't we been, and when will you have time to drive us there?" I sometimes wait months, but I never miss, or forget, ever, or let two trips pile up until next year and take a bottle of perfume instead. The system isn't easy; I hesitate to recommend it, for twice while taking my birthday-present trips to unlikely places John has missed sudden news breaks: once, an assassination attempt on Nehru's life when no one ever suspected it, so calm and undisturbed was the occasion of Nehru's visit to a South Indian town. Despite all this, trips I have accumulated over the years are not only my most cherished intangibles, but I can take them with me (wherever I am "going"), and I have shared the trips with John and often the children too. That's more than you can do with a stole or a new hat or (one friend's birthday choice) contact lenses!

Trips, however, hinge on many things under the heading of Time. This is what causes all the trouble. Though I wait weeks and months, the time we always set aside is just the time somebody else picks to Do Something newsworthy.

This time, my snow-white birthday present ran afoul of Dag Hammarskjold, who was due to pass through Delhi on a UN Mission to Peking. His visit was loaded with big, news-making issues. For one thing, it was hoped and prayed that Dag would persuade Premier Chou En-Lai to release long-captive American airmen. The second angle on this visit was Jawaharlal Nehru taking a pointed attitude of winter's chill toward the prospect of Dag's visit. To Nehru, China is his particular bowl of shark's fin, and he strictly prefers to do all the talking, negotiating, and dog-watching himself. Call it The Long History of Friendship Between Our Two Countries.

When I first mentioned a white Christmas to John, and snow—real snow—for the children, which in December is just a day's drive away in the Himalayan foothills, he gave me an editorial growl. "Oh, come now. You read the papers. You know Hammarskjold's coming. Scram, woman, don't bother me!"

I do not scram or take no with my name on it, ever. I just bide my time and watch. I boiled the sterilizer, changed diapers, stirred formula into boiled measuring cups, did the Routine as usual, but I had Dag on my mind, and those American fliers in those cold December jails. If Dag would only hurry. The quicker he got through Delhi and on to Peking, the quicker the boys might make it home.

I read the papers with intense interest, watched incoming cables, put down many an Evenflo in a hurry to grab the telephone for any hot or revealing messages. Finally it was officially announced that Dag would pass through the Indian capital immediately *after* Christmas. He would pause here long enough for a few chats with Nehru (and rather chilly chats they turned out to be).

John worked at all hours in a tight little pressurized world of his own, and soon I knew why. "Look," he told me one afternoon, "we're having one guest for dinner tonight, but don't ask anyone else to join us. This is strictly a private deal. If it works out and Hammarskjold comes through on time, we might yet be able to run up to a hill station full of snow for you on a one-day shot."

What was this mysterious private deal all about? I wanted to know.

John sat back and explained. "UP would love to get a man into Peking on this American airmen story. Chou is certain to release them as a grand gesture if Dag makes an appeal on their behalf. UP cannot send in an American, of course. God knows how many angles have been tried on that one, so we've been shopping around on the Q.T. for a neutral but not commie correspondent who can get a Chinese visa and get to Peking immediately. We want him there ahead of Hammarskjold, working on officials who might permit him to see or interview the prisoners, take pictures if at all possible. While he's baiting the line for the prisoners, UP wants lots of Peking datelines rolling out: what's going on there, how the city looks these days, how many Russians are hanging around and doing what, and how chummy they are with the Chinese—local color stuff and pictures. All of this will be wonderful material while the Chou-Dag talks are going on and hard news will be tight."

"Well, who did you find?" I asked. "Who's going to Peking? The private party of one who's coming to dinner tonight? Anyone I know?"

John named a senior editor of the *Times of India* whom we might call Jai. Ostensibly, Jai would be going for his own paper and the *Times* would, of course, be printing his daily dispatches on an exclusive basis. UP would simply be footing the bill and publishing the Peking stories on a worldwide basis. The *Times* was delighted with the arrangement, and Jai himself considered the job a real plum, which it was. His reports from China would be appearing under his byline in newspapers from Tokyo to Topeka. He already possessed an Indian passport, he had never given the Chinese cause to blacklist him, and he was certain he could get a visa simply by walking into the Embassy and asking for it.

He was quite correct. He brought his passport along to dinner and showed it to us. We marveled at it, for both John and I had known Peking way back *when,* although we had, of course, not known it together.

Obviously the Chinese were banking on a friendly, highly favorable report from Jai, and they did not in the least suspect he was planning to release an inside story through an American wire service.

All through dinner, John and Jai discussed tactics for handling Chinese officials, what seemingly innocent questions to ask the prisoners in order to yield the greatest amount of information, and so on. When they had exhausted all of these topics, John instructed Jai on his best picture possibilities and checked him out on operating the Rollei he was loaning him for the assignment. Then, over coffee, we sat back and recalled famous streets, the bazaars, Jade Street, Silver Street, hotels, eating places (especially the thousand-year-old restaurant outside the city, where you picked out your duck or chicken as you entered). Oh, I could smell the sweet and sour sauces, the pork, the North China garlic, pale dishwater soups with 10,000 flavors, chestnuts, mushrooms, ginger, almonds, mustards livid hot, and steaming rice wine. There is no nostalgia like acute attacks of Old China Hand—and even more acute is Old Peking Hand.

As Jai was leaving, I asked if he expected to pass through Shanghai, and if he did, would he please snap a picture of the Broadway Mansions, the zany name of a quite smartly modern apartment building at the end of the Bund on the waterfront. The Press Club had once occupied the penthouse and top floors, the American military and dependents the remainder. On the first floor was a small Army hospital where the twins had been born. I had no picture of it save one on an old menu from the Press Club, which I have framed. Jai promised if the Chinese would permit him to wander about freely taking pictures he would not miss the Broadway Mansions. Yes, but the only picture you're going all the way to Peking to get is the American prisoners," John put in his long oar, "and remember if you get the pictures don't sit on them, boy. Move fast. If you can't radio them out, get the first plane to Hong Kong. A good, fast, exclusive picture of the airmen is well worth the entire trip, and UP would be happier with just one picture than with an interview with Chou, who probably wouldn't say anything anyway."

Jai, terribly excited about his trip, was to depart the following morning for Hong Kong, where the UP man would meet him, expedite his through passage, but remain discreetly in the background. Jai was due back within two weeks unless important developments detained him. As he was shaking hands, he remarked, "Don't come to the airport tomorrow to see me off. I believe some chaps from the Chinese Embassy will be on hand."

We knew when Jai had arrived, for the first of his articles began to appear in the local paper and were much commented upon. The *Times* was congratulated for its initiative in having sent its own man for an on-the-scene report.

But soon we began to wonder what had happened to Jai. The things he was writing he could have turned out from New Delhi just by rewriting handouts from the Chinese Embassy. What marvelous progress, what tremendous drive, what dedicated industry on the part of every Chinese, who, although regimented, felt proud to exert his utmost for the people's economic revolution. No divisions of caste or religion separated the people. All worked for the common good, "joyfully."

John read all these stories with some misgivings. Not a line had been written thus far about the American prisoners or the in-field work of the U.S. with a power it did not recognize, the neutral role of the UN, or Hammarskjold's delicate job parlaying between two camps.

As he rolled a cable form into his typewriter, John said, "I think I'd better tip them off that Jai's probably playing it very cat's paw careful, buttering up the Chinese to get to the Real Story. If they think he's a good boy, they might let him in to see the prisoners and take pictures. London had better print all his stuff exactly as he's writing it, but it sure is a lot of eggroll for their money."

Meanwhile, Christmas came with all its bounteous joys and trimmings. We borrowed an Indian custom from *diwali*, the festival of light, for our outdoor decoration. Tai Bhai scurried to the bazaar and brought back a hundred very cheap little clay bowls (lamps, strictly speaking, although they looked like kiddies' cereal bowls). Into these, the children and I put little twists made of cotton, about the size of a swab. This created the wick. Then we spread out the bowls, putting them on the doorstep, windowsills, door frame, garden banister—everywhere we could find. Into each of the bowls Tai Bhai poured a little cooking oil. The cotton twists were set aglow, and when every "lamp" was ready, our hundred golden eyes on Christmas Eve brought out everyone in the hotel.

"Happy Berse Day, dear Je-zuz," Suzy lisped in great excitement.

"Santa Claus *couldn't* miss us tonight," Mary chimed in.

The next morning it was obvious Santa had seen the "hundred watt" welcome on our door (and alas, the oil made 100 oil smears on the hotel cement). The children were one with others the world over on Christmas morning, and that night we elders tripped off to our own Christmas Ball. Even in Hindu India December 24th and 25th are the biggest days of the year. Sparkling Kris Kringle in the glass is nothing to the excitement in the heart if you make it so.

Barely was this past until Hammarskjold finally arrived and was cordially and politely received, but although amiable outward show was made, Nehru was far from happy, and Dag was a closed book with a Nordic smile and a bright bow tie.

Hardly had his plane become a tiny speck in the sky than I sprang into motion. "Okay, he's finally gone, and godspeed. Now can we make a dash for my snow-white trip?" I begged the Father of Many Children who also wanted a snow-white trip. We had tentatively selected Ranikhet, a snowbound little hill station just above the lovely lake resort of Nanital.

John had his doubts. "London wants some reaction pieces to Dag's talks with Nehru. And I hate to leave Delhi until Jai comes through with something. He's just not delivering as we expected. He does not seem to be any damn closer to the prisoners than I am. Can't figure out what's gone wrong with his switches…he seems so dazzled with China he can't even remember why he was sent and who he's working for! If Chou announces the prisoners' release, I've got to be here for Nehru's statement. Don't look like that! I promised nothing. Lemme watch the story for another 24 hours, and we'll see. Above all, don't build any snowmen yet with the kids."

My yen for snowballs was a long way down the line from events of the day, but this is how a newsman's family lives, orbiting like a minuscule cinder-speck around the maneuvers of Nehru, Dag, and Chou.

Finally John said, "Okay, I guess we're 80 percent sure of a safe breather. I've made an arrangement with a man on the *Times*. We'll make it a three-day jaunt. One day driving each way and one day there. We'll take Danji and the twins only—too risky for the smaller ones. Wonder if I'll need tire chains—imagine *chains* in the land of the high-noon sun."

Ranikhet, a sometime military hill station in summer, raises its roof to an elevation of about 7000 feet. It is no fancy chalet or ski spot and has no special attraction save its spellbinding views of the Himalayan range. There are a number of comfortable hotels and guest houses that close in winter but maintain caretakers year round. For those who insist on coming to Ranikhet when it's freezing and almost snowbound, the caretakers will open one wing of the hotel and take you in. We had reserved our quarters by long-distance telephone and had even "rung up" a second time to give the exact time of our arrival so that a warm fire would await us, with a hot meal if possible. All of this was agreed to and "promised" ahead of time, but on arrival we discovered that the caretaker had waited to see the whites of our eyes and hear the chatter of our teeth before tossing a single log on the fire.

We got all the snow-white I could have wished for on my birthday trip. We arrived in a swirling blizzard that was nightmarish to drive through but fantastic to see. We rolled down the windows and gazed in dazzled amazement at snow falling while the sun was shining and the sky was aflame with the setting sun. How many times have you watched a summer shower while the sun was shining on large, pelting drops? Fancy, then, a feather float of snowflakes tumbling down among towering trees that had been mighty pines when Buddha was a babe.

"Hey, Mommy!" Mike hung his head out the car window and plumes of frost rose from his mouth and nostrils in the cold. "Hey, look, the snow's all *strawberries!* It's all *pink.* Lemme out, lemme out! Daddy, stop!"

We had never seen anything like it. Possibly it was the high altitude or the intensity of the setting sun just then, but for those fleeting minutes before almost total darkness (there were maybe four streetlights in Ranikhet, each about one watt to save electricity), the snow was indeed a strawberry pink.

We circled around and around, trying to find a smoke signal to indicate a direction to our reserved hotel, but we saw nothing. One blanket-wrapped passerby finally indicated with a jerk of his thumb that we were right in front of the hotel we were looking for, although we could not detect a glimmer of light nor the faintest sign of habitation.

Shivering and stumbling across the crusty, crunchy snow, we made our way to the hotel lobby, which was colder than the outdoors. The place was forbidding and eerie, with the chill of a tomb and the silence of a grave. We shouted, we rang, we went calling and exploring to find "someone." A little man finally shuffled out with an unwilling sigh of "Oh, you're here." (Where had he been—in his tree trunk?—we wondered, for he did not even have a spark glowing in the wood stove in the kitchen.) John and Danji fell to immediately, trying to get a fire going faster than the confused caretaker. But no heat came even from the roaring yellow-orange blaze. The old-fashioned fireplace was truly British, a vast, deep cave in the wall that sent all the heat roaring up the chimney. Only when the fire had been going night and day did any kind of reasonable warmth fill the half-moon circle of the room immediately in front of the grate. We stomped our feet, and I rubbed the children's legs to keep the blood circulating. We were invisible to one another, our faces marooned in frost clouds! John remarked that I might venture to glance at things in the kitchen or we would not get so much as a swallow of tea until the next day.

I hastened to find the distant kitchen. On my way, I chanced to glance through a frost-framed pane and stood stunned, stock still—

The snowy peaks of Nanda Devi—over 25,000 feet—were blue-white against the deepening blue-black sky, and piercing pinpoint stars hung diamond-white in the freezing night.

Awed and quite overcome with the magnitude of this view, I stepped outside to a summer veranda. The silence after snowfall on a December night moved me to profoundest wonder. Is eternity like this? Overpowering as those great mountains and the orbiting stars…so vast but obedient to nature and the Plan of Things…and withal, so *silent*…silent as this night. I stood there a long time and did not know that I was cold and that everyone inside thought I was cooking dinner.

Our day at Ranikhet was spent wallowing in snow: rolling, tumbling, throwing, making snowmen (one for each Hlavacek at home and abroad—grandpa snowmen, baby snowmen). What delicious luxury to be *cold* in India, to wear woolies, heavy mitts and snowsuits.

"Hey—are we still in India?" Mike would ask. "Seems more like the States, huh? Snow's nice. Gee, aw gee, we gotta go back tomorrow when we only jus' come? Awww geeeeeee!"

I bounced a snowball off his noggin. "Look, my boy, your little brother and sister didn't get here at all. I spied some ponies down the way a bit being trotted around for exercise. If you stop moaning, we might beg you a ride."

Mike and Mary in the snow at Ranikhet.

In the afternoon we left the twins napping with Danji on guard (napping, too, no doubt). John and I drove on to the next hill station, Almora, a far-flung hideaway for writers, painters, thinkers, the religious. The view of the Himalayas from Almora would almost bring an atheist to his knees. The eye and soul are one in Almora.

This quiet little town clinging to the side of the hills gives one wistful, dreamy thoughts that "someday" it might be heavenly to have a tiny cottage tucked away here in which one could live in perfect peace and let the world go by.

I found one American who had done just that: Gertrude Emerson Sen, who is something of an institution in Almora. To her white cottage with a view have come a stream of visitors from Nehru on down. Gertrude and her Indian botanist husband, Boshi, had us to tea and in addition served us popped corn made from Boshi's experimental garden hybrid strains. We were given a bagful to take home to pop for the children in Delhi. One can only marvel that the tired, old, worn-out soil of India can produce species of farm-catalogue perfection in every variety of produce, as Boshi showed us. But hybrid cultivation has to be sold to farmers, zamindars and peasants. Chemicals and fertilizers and controlled irrigation and growing processes are costly new ideas. Tillers of the soil resist high cost and change everywhere, I suppose, but especially in India where the food supply is a matter of life-and-death urgency.

Gertrude and Boshi had no children, but the bright, clever son of their cook had so endeared himself to Gertrude that she had elected not to adopt him (which would have taken him away from his natural family) but to educate him. As Gertrude was a brilliant historian and writer, the cook's son was indeed in gifted hands.

For all her years in India, and China before that, Gertrude Sen had remained as thoroughly American as cinnamon and clove-spiced apple pie. For an intellectual, she was a cozy, comfortable homebody, a great attribute. There are times, after all, when apple pie hits a spot no genius can reach.

It came as a mild surprise, therefore, to find this sweet, practical little homebody had a secret room in her house. While searching for the powder room in her crisp and spotless New-Englandy cottage on a hill, I came by accident upon a Buddhist prayer room. Gertrude was at my elbow immediately. "This," she said, "is our private prayer sanctuary. We are both devout Buddhists."

What a paradox, I thought. Here were two extraordinary persons who dealt entirely with the modern mind—Gertrude in her writing, Boshi in his science of the soil—yet they followed a philosophy that was ancient. Here were two who lived away from the world but continually sent lifelines out to it in their working professions. Both were thoroughly outgoing, concerned with world events and the daily news. We even discussed Hammarskjold's visit, Nehru's reaction, and the preponderance of Red China "just over there," Gertrude pointed across the neighboring mountains. Buddhism had not in the least carried these two to misty distances beyond the wheel of the modern world. And, I further marveled, for two persons past middle age, what eternal youth their religion or their way of life had given them.

We headed back to Ranikhet for dinner. John was full of hustly-bustly Organization, mostly directed at me. I kept dragging behind, looking back over my shoulders, lost in the mountains and their winter-white, spellbinding fascination. One day of this—one day only!

I heard John's signals as from a great distance. "We pack everything tonight…leave early tomorrow. Hear that, memsahib? *Early.* I don't know what's been happening in Delhi."

In Delhi, things were happening. Hammarskjold did indeed use his Good Office, as they say, to get Chou to use his Good Key in the jailhouse lock. The fliers were eventually, if not immediately, released and sent home. Also, Jai returned home from Peking.

He had not seen the prisoners, he had gotten no advance information about them whatsoever, he had taken no pictures ("My God, it was cold! Too cold to go outside the hotel. You don't know how cold Peking is in winter!"). He also had been to Shanghai but had taken no pictures of my Broadway Mansions…which was all very well. The People's glorious revolution was not centered around any old buildings for which I had a memory-filled attachment.

Jai had come to dinner, but we were somehow not the gay conspirators we had been at the outset of the great assignment to Red China. Patently Americans and Indians have separate approaches to this vast, problematic country, but Jai had somehow been carried away, far beyond reasonable bounds and journalistic judgment.

Other Indian journalists, most notably Frank Moraes, had viewed China's progress as a Communist republic and had weighed it all out for value, merit and demerit. There was much to marvel at, and everyone who visited the country came back telling pretty much the same impressive story.

Jai's reaction to Red China was to devalue his own country's advances—to declare that however severe China's methods, her output was amazing. Glass in one hand, cigarette in the other, Jai put it succinctly:

"It's simply this—like it or not—more people have more in China."

We said nothing. Jai hesitated a moment as though he feared he had offended us as Americans.

"Do you think people are satisfied with 'more' at the price they pay?" John inquired mildly.

Jai looked impatient. "Oh, all this democracy and freedom! Freedom. What is freedom? Conditions in India today? Sometimes I think freedom is just another imported American luxury."

◆   ◆   ◆

John swung Johnny Pat up in the air one day and caught him—up and caught him. "Oh, Tito is coming, hooray, hooray! Oh, Tito is coming, hooray, hooray!" John sang to squealy JP. Turning to me, he said, "Tito next week. See all the official invitations and car passes on the desk? There'll be the usual *tamasha* (big "do") at Rashtrapathi Bhavan. We hear Tito's a tough boy who can really put away his liquor. Protocol is at great pains to bend its prohibition to accommodate Tito, at least in private."

Tito was no particular pet of mine, but I sifted through the crested and engraved press invitations with rising interest. "Tell me, now, what Great Ties of Friendship have Long United these two distant countries, India and Yugoslavia? Trade? Even acquaintanceship? Culture? Religion or lack of any? What 'mutual understanding' is there between India and Yugoslavia?"

"No, no, no. You're way off." John was testing JP's reflexes, standing him on his head in his crib. "No, the mutual admiration, dear, is Neutralism. Nehru's been wooing Tito for a long time now, and he's finally got him this far—to see India. Tito's not bringing his good-looking wife along, worse luck. Guess he had to leave her holding down the fort while his back was turned out here."

I got my first good look at Dictator Josip Broz Tito at the President's garden reception—along with a thousand and one other guests. At these formal receptions, the procedure is always the same. Immediately after the official guest has been led into the garden by his host, the venerable orthodox President of India, and all ranking government officials from Nehru on down have gathered to greet him, the national anthem of the visitor's country and India's Jai Hind are played.

It was during the anthems that I found myself frozen to attention on the lawn only an arm's length away from Tito. The contrast of nature, temperament, and politics among Tito and his Indian hosts in a truly free country was overwhelming. Someone whispered through his teeth at my elbow, *Time* man Alex Campbell: "My God, he's fat! Tito looks exactly like Hitler's Goering—same coloring, same expression, everything!"

He did indeed. My eye, however, kept contrasting Tito's face with the solemn row of expressions on the faces of India's hierarchy: gentle, sophisticated, polite but indifferent, dreamy, absent-minded. Nehru appeared watchful and solicitous.

Equally watchful and solicitous was his daughter Indira Gandhi, Tito's state hostess.

There was a spicy air of unreality, of strange bedfellows, as the anthems faded away and Tito stood in chatty company with President Prasad and scholarly, philosophical Vice President Radakrishnan. For things in common, these men had the weather to fall back on.

Milling around at close range were a mixed diplomatic crowd of neutrals and not-so-neutral, the Indian elite in their handsomest formal attire, which for the wives meant all the jewels they could possibly accommodate. For contrast, there was the conspicuous Reminder of the Masses, the People: here and there stood modest but pointedly invited Members of Parliament, representing many far-flung and distant towns and villages, and dressed characteristically in flowing shirts, dhotis and sandals, their foreheads occasionally adorned with some sort of religious or caste mark or a white gandhi cap.

Tito moved across the flowering lawns with heavy tread and probing blue eyes. He noted with obvious relish the bevy of Indian beauties draped in their most shapely saris and glittering dowry gems who flashed wide, white, warmer-than-neutral smiles at the Great Blond Bear. More and more, Tito paused and let male conversation go by his ear as he eyed the oomphy Indian girls with their silky skirts pulled formfit tight, their satin blouses clinging like bras and their golden midriffs bare and smooth above the waistband of their saris.

Speaking of ladies, Tito had brought one along as a gift for Nehru: a nude stone sculpture of a goosegirl in a pose best described as "modern." This huge ton-weight curio, some 8 feet high, had been lugged all the way from Yugoslavia and bestowed on Nehru's startled household as a personal gift that could not be refused or packed off hastily to a museum. Not that the goosegirl wasn't fetching, but she was so provocative and so naked that she drew strong reactions behind closed doors. What the devil to do with it? The goosegirl couldn't go in a basement or spare room; this might offend the Yugoslavs and muss up their neutrality. It was finally decided that as she was a strong, big-chested stone girl the great outdoors was the place for her, and there she was eventually lugged and placed in a section of the Prime Minister's garden where she was modestly hidden by tall, bushy shrubs.

We came upon the goosegirl one afternoon quite by accident. We had been invited to bring our nature girl, Mary, to see the teddy bear pandas Nehru kept in his garden. When we arrived, however, we found that the pandas had been sent to the hills for the summer. Strolling out of the garden, we suddenly saw Tito's token. Mary had the typical reaction of a child to modern art: "*Jeepers,* Mommy, 'spose something's wrong with her?"

"Not at all, dear," I murmured. "She has a lovely face, hasn't she?"

John, I observed, seemed quite fascinated with the goosegirl and was busy taking her picture from all angles. "You know," he said, "I like Tito's message. Nicest neutralism I've ever seen."

The Itch to Travel—The Chicken Pox Itch!

It was all my idea in the first place. I hadn't figured on the chicken pox. As always when I aim high and Think of Others, it backfires…on Others! And it always costs more than I figured, too.

But the real and final clapper on *this* project is that while we were wallowing in chicken pox John missed a big news break elsewhere, and the cable blast he got from London (Opposition Upcleaning Where Hell Hlavacek Query) did nothing to justify what was originally an educational, worthy idea: to take the twins with us, 500 miles and more, into the central heart of India to the princely state of Indore where the Prime Minister was to rally his well-besotted and too-cozy-in-office Congress Party before the national elections. The Nehru rally promised to be a colorful rustic fling (with cows) in a part of the country we had never seen before. Indore was putting on a big *meela* or country fair in honor of Nehru's visit.

Plans for Nehru's campaign were nothing to my own private little campaign, for I could see it would take far more than gentle persuasion to trap my Scribe into another trip with kids.

I would begin at breakfast as I crunched toast (how guileless can a scheming woman be with a mouthful of toast, curlers gone, and lipstick on).

"You know, darling," I got started, "sometimes I am amazed to think we have lived so long in this country and we hardly even know it. We need to get out more, get the feel of 'real' India…out in the villages, out where the real people are…away from the smug, tight little circle of New Delhi."

"Yeah—when you leaving? Anytime now?" John folded back his morning *Times,* crunched toast on which my butter *wasn't* melting. Why, I thought, he sounded positively churlish. My village line always annoyed him somehow. Then, too, my past record of good ideas—back to nature, out there behind the plough—was so bad it was just my sex appeal that got my husband to listen to me ever, *ever* again. And at that, this wasn't going to be any cinch, I could see. But they don't come any more determined than me, and I was dead-set on this Indore adventure, more so because I felt this time I had a few aces on my side:

First of all, it was winter, when the weather in India is the reverse of all other seasons, in heavenly extremes. It is peppy and cool by day, requiring sweaters and slacks for traveling. And love is not enough to keep you warm at night—you need a blanket, too.

In winter the dust isn't quite as bad as it is the rest of the year. The fields are all green or sulphur-gold with flowering mustard or lupin blue with pulse (a lentil called *dal*). Over all, the sun rides at half-mast and the sky is blue as Persian tiles.

Second, the children's school was closed through Christmas, New Year's, and on into late January. If I went along with the Sahib, as he wanted me to (he said), it would mean making elaborate arrangements to farm the children out to friends' houses or to have someone move in temporarily. Wouldn't it be easier just to take the two oldest along and drive down instead of flying? The children would learn something about the country, and this would be an Experience (oh, brother!) they would remember into their college days (what a prophet am I in everything but beard!).

And third, as a journeyman correspondent, like all newsmen, Daddy was away almost continually, coming home for clean shirts and more film for the cameras. Whenever possible, I felt, we should—we *must*—do more things together, especially in Indore with Nehru!

John read my mind as clearly as the *Times.* "Look, don't get all worked up to a big expedition. The rally in Indore is a story for maybe a day and a half, two days at the most. Not worth driving 500 miles just for that. I'll fly. And remember, we agreed long ago that we can't take kids along when we're working, right?"

I smiled sweetly and said no more. Who ever won anything at a breakfast table, anyway?

That night I fed the children early. Baths, teeth, potty, stories, and tuck-ins were all out of the way before John came home. I heated the baby's bottle early, too, so he would be content and *quiet.*

Then—ah, then—I mixed martinis and filled every bowl in the room with fresh, roasted-in-butter cashews of which the Sahib was inordinately fond. When he came home, made a string of phone calls, sent a cable, checked the late mail, showered and changed, and sank down on the sofa, I had all my traps ready.

"Look, darling, I might as well just come right out with it. I really want to make this trip to Indore in the worst way. Couldn't we leave a few days earlier than the rest of the press gang? Danji can help with the driving, and I can pack a picnic hamper. I can handle the kids when they get tired...but they'll be thrilled to go. It's only two nights on the road."

"Aw, cut it out," the Sahib rumbled. "You make me feel so mean and nasty. Traveling all that distance with kids! Look, it's almost to Bombay, a major haul. And *remember the last trip.*"

I did. It had been a nightmare, and even *I* had sworn Never Again. I remembered agonies of embarrassment when kind Indians, breaking every Hindu taboo, had taken us in for a meal and the two children, seeing and smelling what was coming, had cried out, "Oh, curry? We never eat *curry!* It burns our tongues!"

And those *hours* along the road, even on the fascinating Grand Trunk. Toilets? None. Drinking water? None. The thermos can only store so much, and on a trip it is always the first thing dropped and broken! Coloring books and crayons start off well but end too soon if the road gets bumpy and "the crayons go all jerky, Mommy!" Dolls, planes, modeling clay, *Mad* magazines...games: "I spy with my little eye something that begins with B—"

There was the time when the thing that began with B *was* a bee, and bloodcurdling screams went up just as John got caught in a country traffic jam behind the humpy backsides of a hundred water buffaloes. "Will you, for God's sake, see what's wrong with those kids?"

"A bee—*Owwwwww!*—No, it's a wasp—a *wasp!*—eeeeeh! It's a hornet...a yellowjacket!" Shriek, shriek!

"*Shut up!* How can I drive? Open the windows; it'll blow out!"

Hardly did we get past the water buffaloes and the bees than the fights began. Mike sat on Tiny Tears, or Ike "on purpose" threw a ball of Mike's modeling clay right out the window.

Having survived the sibling battles, we found that we were all hungry even though we had a hundred miles to go before arriving at the next Place. Awaiting our famishment: mashed Monaco biscuits, a package of Kraft cheese, and nothing to wash it all down.

I would then check reading matter to help us Endure: the little, fat, red classic Handbook with every battle, every Raj, and every date accounted for; old comics, old *Mad* magazines, old copies of the *Times,* an old history of India. Nothing very tasty, but as part of my plan is always to keep the children "learning," I reached for the history book.

"Children," I began, "suppose we read about the great kings who once rode their battle elephants down this very road. Do you know why it is called the Grand Trunk? Well, once upon a time..."

It gets to be 3 p.m. Endlessly in India the day gets that far and just seems to hang there, even in winter when one has been on the road since six (call it seven—I forgot my cosmetic kit and we had to go back). Three o'clock can be ghastly. The dust accumulation of the day becomes a powdered pollution of nostrils, eyelashes, hair, mouth, clothes. (When Nehru or State Visitors go out into the country, water boys run ahead for miles scattering straw and watering down the dust.) The children sag and go limp. Mighty emperors hold them, or me, no more. When the fireball of sun finally sinks down, the children are asleep. It becomes cooler rapidly, but we are all bone-beat and crab-tempered. Learning about "real" India deep in its rural fastness is an Endurance Test.

I remember, yes, indeed I do.

But Indore awaits.

I have on my lap the fat, little, tissue-paged red *Handbook of India, Pakistan, Burma and Ceylon* (a standard work you can no more do without than a telephone book). I freshen up John's martini, open the Handbook, and hand him a map. "See, if we start early…we go right down to Gwalior…right into John Masters' country…down to Jhansi where India's great woman warrior fought the British and met a cruel death, just like the French Joan (only she was not burned)…On, on down…" I traced the way to Sanchi, the famous Buddhist shrine where I was longing to see the great Stupa and especially the pillars and carved gateways that were truly, truly magnificent as scenes of busy, crowded everyday life in stone, perfect as French tapestries, with faces of ordinary people so *alive*, so real, one marveled at them with shivers running down the spine, considering their great age.

Either the map or the martinis or both were having their neutralizing effects on John. He reached for a scrap of paper and began to figure mileage and how long it all would take.

Now I played my trump card.

"Look, darling, if we leave a whole extra day early, we can do that Great and Good temple of love: Khajuraho!"

Really hooked now, John looked even more closely at the map. It was a long detour on the road to Indore, turning off to Banda, but neither of us had yet seen the "hottest" temple in India, although we had *heard* of it and we knew well it was a delight and sensation no American misses while in the country if he can possibly, or impossibly, help it!

Khajuraho is famous as a sex sideshow carved in stone. Nothing is left to the imagination. In fact, where most imaginations leave off, Khajuraho is only beginning, with a couple of extra girls worked into the Act. And I do mean Act! Khajuraho, unlike anything in the Western World, even the secret places in Pompeii, is equaled only by lewd Astonishments in temples in Nepal.

If the average American is twitted or shocked by all the stone *lingums* in India—when the average American first realizes what the devil lingums *are*—he will positively die at the display of Positions, one after the other, by the *hundreds*—carved on lingum-shaped towers at this wayside shrine to nakedest sex.

So talked about, so tantalizing, so unbelievable was Khajuraho made out to be, that everyone hearing of it had to "see" for himself! So popular were tours to Khajuraho that the manager of Pan American in Delhi used to set up one-day charter flights down and back. Reservations had to be made weeks ahead or one could never get a seat. Those who went before came back with *such tales* that a positive stampede was on to see the oldest girlie show on earth, where Position is *everything*.

Note: I make no apology for levity. If this is Hindu culture or "religion" and held up as such, it is more than leaning over backward in inviting reaction and comment. Hindus' cheeks flush angry scarlet at "ugly American" remarks about their culture, i.e., religion, which is so cheek by jowl by bosom with prostitution and three-girls-to-every-man. "Everything is symbolic," they cry, "the Western mind just doesn't understand!" Ask any boy over 16. I think he "understands" very well, but he does not confuse the soul and its "symbols"—purity, faith, the Star, the crucifixion—with the bawdy house or call its "symbols" a way of life the materialistic West must "learn" from.

Anyway, John's curiosity was as vigorous as the next boy's—once sold, he was sold in a big way. The map on the lap was an archway greater than the Moghuls—it was dotted with hundreds of names and places fanning up and out around Indore. "Why, on the way home—" John traced a route with a pencil, "there's Udairpur with its lakes and palaces…Chitor with its fort…Ajmer…Jaipur the jeweled city, and just outside, the Amber Palace that you visit by riding up the hill on an elephant…But hell, it all takes time," the Scribe groaned, "it's miles and miles of driving between each famous place. I can't be away so long. Delhi would be uncovered in my absence."

In the past, Standby Men, Standby Plans for telephones and telegrams to be forwarded, for John to make check-in calls at regular intervals, had just been so much chicken wire, telephones being what they are and telegrams arriving after the mails. But it was the only way, so another Cover and Standby Plan was set up with an assistant.

"We'll make the trip down to Indore all right," John shook his pencil at me, "but if anything develops in the news I will abandon you flat on the spot and fly off. Clearly understood?"

"Crystal clearly," I murmured and kissed his dear old bald head. Mentally I was already packed, geared, and gunned for the road.

The trip down went all too well. My anticipations, and especially John's, about the children proved to be mad exaggerations. Even the car held together—small wonder, for it had been sent first to the garage for an overhaul, and that was always risky before a long trip.

Did the twins "learn" about India? Possibly they learned more about Unca Donald, Huey, Dewey, and Louie, but they were quiet, privileged, brimming with good p's and q's! We found good government rest houses, met the friendly, responsive, touchingly generous and kind Indians one always finds far, far removed from capital cities. We did all the famous spots in 35-mm color (except Khajuraho—think of the children seeing *those* images accidentally flashed on a bedsheet tacked up on the wall for a screen!).

We even managed to roll into the hotel in Indore where all the press was staying only a few hours after the Delhi crowd (airborne) had checked in. Abe Rosenthal of *The New York Times,* Bob Elegant of *Newsweek,* Jim Greenfield of *Time,* Gene Levine of AP—oddly, no British press this time (had someone told them Nehru wasn't going to say anything?).

Gazing about the lobby, I recognized some Communist press and a sprinkling of thick-haired, woolly-looking cameramen from Eastern Europe. One young Czech correspondent was there with his pretty, ringlet-haired wife and two bouncy ringlet-haired kiddies.

Hlavacek and the Czech reporter greeted one another and had a friendly neutral chat as they always did when they met at receptions and weddings. But though I with my twins beamed at *her* (also an ex-newspaperwoman from Prague!) and she beamed back, kiddies in hand, we left it right there of mutual necessity.

Upstairs in the room with its heavy, plastic-upholstered furniture and glass-topped vanities and coffee tables (which would surely split in twain if any bearer put so much as a teapot upon them), Mary tiredly groaned and moaned: "Jiminee, I'm all itchy. I just itch, itch, *itch* all over!"

Preoccupied with hastily washing up for dinner, I paid scant heed to her first warning. John was so anxious to get downstairs to see what his cronies Knew in Advance that he didn't even wait for us. I sloshed a little soap and water around, combed hair, and we hurried downstairs too. The assembled Press had already dined on rubbery chicken, cold fried potatoes, and pasty glue pudding, but they came over to our table to wash everything down with Nescafé, there being no better stuff on hand. In wayside Indian hostels, I always say, you do far better on Indian chow that the cook knows all about, but those who won't go for curry have to take vaguely British-style victuals.

My point in describing the dinner table scene is not just to recall creation of the Best Laid Plans for the Congress Party rally the next morning, but to observe that we all sat squeezed in close together. Close to Mary, that is...

We left the boys comparing camera lenses and vital camera *prices* in Hong Kong (for some reason, correspondents are more likely to burst with pride about pictures that "get in" than any old columns of newsprint). I hurried the children upstairs to bed. My moment of truth awaited the strong light of morning.

Lighting in Indian hotels at night is a yellow blur from a one-watt bulb. I put Mary (scratching) to bed without noticing anything.

Thoughtfully I had made a point of ordering plenty of extra hot water for baths early the next morning. Before breakfast I started on the twins. Mike first, in and out, three shades celery-whiter with Mother India's road dirt washed off. Mary next—

When I got her into the bathroom, stripped, I muffled a small scream and called John.

"Just look—*look*—at all that!" I gasped, for Mary was as polka-dotted with red itches as if I'd seasoned her with paprika. Even the skin of her scalp under her hair was covered with red bumps!

"Good God!" John, who had to rush off early for Nehru's opening speech, was in a sweat. "What in hell's she *got?*"

"Does it hurt, Sweetie?" I patted Mary's poor spotty cheek. "Do you feel *anything?* Feverish? Sickish?"

"No," she replied calmly, "it just itches, *itches.* I just can't stop scratching, Mommy. Can't you make the itching go away?"

"Dear heaven," I prayed. "How *can* I make the itching go away?" Quick! It looked so catching, too. But first I had to find out what she had before anybody knew she had it.

John was thinking the same thing. "We must hide her. That's the *one* thing we must do. We'll make this room our isolation ward and not say a word to *anyone.*"

"What do you mean? We must get her to a doctor right away!"

John pulled me outside and whispered, "Don't you know what they do with contagious cases in India? They put you in an Infectious Diseases Hospital on the edge of town, like a leper! They won't take contagious quarantine cases in regular hospitals. Poor Ike—but damn it, I gotta move fast! But where?"

The telephone rang. John grabbed it. "Hlavacek. Yeah…umm…yeah, fine. But, look, you all go on ahead. I'll meet you over there. Thanks just the same. Yeah, sure, got lotsa plus X, but only a hundred feet for the Bolex."

Thinking of our cohorts gave me a new worry as I gazed at Mary. Last night, all of us were sitting so close together at dinner. Had she contaminated the whole American press with—with what? Red spots?

A bearer knocked at the door. John was quick-shaving in the bathroom. I put Mary in a closet. As a tray of breakfast came in, Mike, saronged in a towel, cried in an umpire's bellow: "Hey, Ma! Why're you putting Ike in the clothes closet?"

Shaved and dressed, John burst out of the bathroom.

"My God! I forgot about Mike. Any spots on him?"

"No…not yet."

Breakfasting with one hand and loading cameras with the other, John figured out the best way to "get a doctor" without "telling anyone" who would put her away with Infectious Diseases.

"Look, you and I will sneak outside somewhere and find a telephone away from the hotel. We'll call Piloo in Bombay and describe how Ike looks over the phone. The doctor can prescribe, and we'll just keep Ike in the room…maybe fly her back home."

Finding a telephone to make a "trunk" call away from the hotel was no snap in Indore, but we managed. Luckily we were early enough in placing our call to find Piloo still at home. I described Mary's condition, and Piloo diagnosed. "My dear, it's nothing to worry about. It sounds like just one possible thing: chicken pox. Yes, from what you say that must be exactly what she's got. Now, listen, you must get her away from the hotel. Let me see…Indore…who do I know in Indore to send you to? Perhaps Eddie can think of someone." A pause while Piloo consulted her husband. "He says there's a Canadian missionary hospital in Indore, an excellent place with a Canadian staff and a good doctor in charge. I forget the name, but you could take Mary there, I'm sure. Poor thing! Give her our love, and tell her not to scratch her face. Keep an eye on Mike; he will probably be spotted soon, too."

Not only was Dr. Piloo a lifesaver, she was so right besides. Mary did have chicken pox, a full-blown, galloping outbreak. Piloo was equally correct about the Canadian missionary hospital. Quickly we spirited Mary out of the hotel at a time when no one would observe her odd appearance, and even more quickly we checked her in with the Canadians. John left us there and rushed off to his job at the Congress Party session.

Hospital hospitality was amazing. The head of the mission-supported institution was a bustling lady doctor who greeted us like kinfolk on Thanksgiving Day. The "guest room" was the isolation wing, and we would be "quite comfortable" there if I would just do the nursing stint for Mary and keep her company, fetch her meals—"We are so short-staffed here, you understand. Now, Mary, we'll have your little itch under control in no time. Calamine lotion, dear, that will fix you right up. Try not to scratch your face. We don't want any scars on our face, do we now, dear?"

Days passed. John covered the Congress Party, and we covered Mary with calamine lotion. Mike, who was moved into Isolation too, became like a caged lion, but not a spot, nor a freckle, nor an itch appeared on him. The doctor finally agreed to let him out, and he was packed off to visit a Canadian family connected with the hospital school, who had children all safely past chicken pox.

Mary was literally "in the pink" in Isolation, a purely technical term, for that short staff at the hospital came in running droves to meet the Americans-connected-with-Nehru's-visit-who-have-the-chicken-pox! Magazines were brought, and children's prayer books and a Bible storybook or two. With plain, scrubbed faces, some touched here and there with the faintest, self-conscious smidge of lipstick or powder, these missionary sisters regarded us as visitors from another world—from newspapers, from New Delhi.

After Indore hotel cooking, the food in the hospital was possibly not Quebec gourmet, but simple food perfectly cooked has its own good taste and eye appeal. Hospital chicken was like something from home. We had only one meat-meal at midday, and two identical breakfasts, morning and night, of cooked cracked-wheat cereal. At first it seemed odd to sit down at 6 p.m. to a bowl of wheat porridge, but it was so delicious I used to save some of mine for John.

Mary improved rapidly and was soon so pampered and bug-cozy that John decided it was time I took French Leave from Isolation and spent a day outside. "Look, since Ike's okay and Mike's taken care of, why not plan to come with me on a trip? Nehru is taking off with his daughter and two grandsons tomorrow to a place called Mandu, some old ruins not far from here. The Congress show has fizzled out, the Fair is only so-so, but this Mandu junket might make a good picture story."

I made arrangements for Mary's care and was ready early the next morning.

Nehru had given strict orders that the trip to Mandu was to be a "breather"—a fairly quiet day of sightseeing. He especially did not want a big, ballyhooed turnout with mobs of police holding back mobs of people. His escort party from Mandu could include only five cars.

We were the only Press to show up, but we made ourselves inconspicuous on the tail end of the cars lined up at Nehru's tree-framed guest residence. On the stroke of the appointed hour, he appeared. A man of moods, he was clearly quick-tempered today, snapping fingers and having state ministers jumping faster than bearers. Even the famed rose in his buttonhole seemed to be bristling with thorns!

Pointing to each car with a small baton he often carried like a philharmonic maestro, Nehru inventoried the lot of us. He pointed to our car. John stepped outside and nodded a bright "Good morning, sir" to the Prime Minister. I, in my front seat, quickly beamed from ear to ear. We passed muster, and Nehru even managed a toast-crisp "good morning." Then I saw Indira, dressed in peacock-blue *khadi*, hurrying out of the house. She, too, looked carefully down the line of cars—and spied me. We were once again to be the only women in a touring party of men. She raised a hand in recognition, and I did the same. Then, without a wasted minute, we were all rolling at Nehru's pace down the driveway, pearled and sparkling with droplets of heavy dew and morning mist. The lead car, a sleek convertible in which Nehru was rapidly breaking the speed limit, had been loaned to him by the Maharani of Indore—a Californian, by the way, and how she happened to become the first lady of Indore is another tale.

At each village Nehru commanded his car to either stop or coast along slowly as he rose and greeted clusters of surprised, awed and gaping farmers and waysiders. Only at one or two points did he pause by hasty pre-appointment, accept garlands of flowers, and say a few words.

The Few Words were little, ad-lib pep talks: you must all work harder, we must all pull forward together, irrigate, build more schools, the future of our children depends on much hard work. Time and energy must not be wasted in petty local quarrels that pit Indian against Indian.

It was truly amazing to see so clearly the electric action and reaction—this business of *darshan* (holy magic derived from just being in the presence of the Great). Even more amazing was the reaction and visible effect the crowd's straining eagerness had on Nehru. He had begun the tour in a rather cross mood, tired, with circles making dark stains under his darker eyes. The Congress Party rally had been anything but inspiring; in fact, as a rededication and vote-getting yeast, the whole show had gone flat as a *chapati*. Yet here, within the hour, among ordinary countryside Indians—farmers X, Y, Zed, brown-skinned women in silver leg bracelets and red peasant skirts, small urchin village boys clad only in a wisp of old, torn shirt—all these upturned, trusting, worshipful faces restored this driving powerhouse of a prime minister who was past seventy. Exasperation, irritation, temper gave way, as we rolled from village to village, to a kind of new-battery energy, toughness, determination to pull or drag India bodily, if need be, onward and upward to a better life.

By the time we turned into the great-walled, sprawling, tumbled ruins of Mandu, Nehru was a new man. He sprang up the steps, hopped stone slabs, skirted crumbled cave-ins, joked and joshed good-humoredly with a Ruins Guide who appeared to be larding his guidance with colorful exaggerations.

I will spare the reader a Handbook's worth of legend on the Mandu ruins, although they were especially interesting because the boiling and blood-letting period from which they sprang was not only robustly Muslim but Afghani as well, and Mandu is a long, long way from the Khyber. What was more memorable than all the historic lore, however, was helping eat Nehru's robust lunch laid out on a long picnic table inside the old ruins. Local party *wallas* had really bestirred themselves and all the local cooks for miles around. The lunch was positive manna, entirely native, but luckily cutlery was provided.

Naturally, first to dine were Nehru, his daughter Indira Gandhi, and her two sons, who were clearly watching their p's and q's under Mama's quick eye and occasional whispered directives. But by the time we came slowly down the buffet line, Nehru had returned to the table for seconds. In good humor as well as good appetite, he deigned to play host, to serve oncoming plates with delicacies which might be skimmed over. As the Scribe and I approached, he heaped our plates: "Do you like fish? Oh, then try some of this, a local variety we do not get in Delhi, quite delicious, but watch the bones. And do have a bit of that—I don't know what they call it locally, but it is very tasty!" Nehru could have put live fish on our plates, bones and all, and we would have carried them away with tasty *darshan*.

After a full lunch of local specialties, Nehru withdrew to a private nook to have a short nap. The rest of us loitered about. I turned to a borrowed History of Mandu, an out-of-print edition so valued by the Canadians who loaned it to me that they had threatened to hold the twins hostage as a guarantee of the safe return of their only "living" copy.

Four prime ministers of India in a single photo: Nehru, Sanjay, Rajiv, and Indira.

"What have you got there? Books on Mandu are so hard to find, aren't they?" Startled, I looked up to find Indira Gandhi in her handspun *khadi* sari sitting down beside me. She had a book, too, and she handed it over to me in exchange for mine. She was very chatty and friendly.

"From what I've heard, Mandu has quite as romantic a history as the Taj," she observed, perusing my book. "It seems there were a pair of lovers who were violently opposed on all sides, but somehow they fared better than Romeo and Juliet. They triumphed over all, were finally married and lived on."

Indira, truly her father's daughter and possibly the most strong-minded and influential woman in India today, turned to me with a surprising remark:

"Love, even in storybooks, is not very dependable, is it? It comes like a storm and dies like a flower. From what I have read here and there of the Mandu legends, it seems that the lion-hearted Emperor who defied fire and brimstone for his lady love found marriage to her afterward to be so blissfully tame that he was soon bored and off seeking conquests elsewhere. Another pretty face…a bold dancing girl…another's wife…a maid in the fields…that was all it took, and the Emperor was in the saddle, away to the chase."

Indira sighed. "Romance is only romance, flimsy stuff. It cannot last forever. But it is a bit disappointing and rather sad, don't you think?"

I studied Indira. She looked very vulnerable, delicately confiding and wistful, and very young just then. How little romance, I wondered, had there ever been in her life? What had happened years ago to her own very young love, now that she lived apart from her husband, alone with Father and her two boys? Her marriage to a lawyer, Feroze Gandhi, had been a love match, not an arranged affair. Women who live without love often make consuming careers of their empty years. Suddenly I saw Indira with new understanding. She led an amazing life as a prime minister's daughter, confidante, official hostess, and unfailing travel companion, but at a price few women would want to pay.

Indira sighed and observed ruefully, "Could it be that surrender is the first step toward losing a man? When there's no more defiance, when the hurdles are down, when the conquest is won, Emperors look elsewhere. The story goes that the Mandu Queen was quite broken-hearted, for she truly loved her husband. She was quite a gifted musician and used to play a stringed instrument and sing about her lost love. Whether the Emperor ever came back to her, I don't know."

"Do you suppose," I asked, wondering about the dalliances of Emperors, "that Shah Jehan was *really* true to the Queen for whom he built the Taj?"

"Oh," Indira gave a mock shudder, "if we shatter the illusion of True Love about the Taj, we will have destroyed all its meaning! I'm afraid there may have been some palace ladies here and there, but at least Mumtaz was the favorite. She *must* have been."

"Fourteen children they had," I recalled. "That must have kept them pretty busy."

"Indira—"

We both looked up. Nehru had concluded his nap and was ready to resume the day's excursion. Indira rose at once, we exchanged books again, she smiled and was quickly gone. In her public performance for the remainder of the day she was a working partner of her father, in the role of a model social worker, lending personal encouragement and sympathy to the downtrodden. The day's outing had a business purpose in the end, and I understood then why Indira had chosen a *khadi* sari (inexpensive, thick, and bulky) instead of a silk one. The Prime Minister was to meet some nomadic Indian tribesmen called Bhils, upon historic grounds. In ages past the Bhils had been driven from "their" lands and had been rootless wanderers, migrants who survived as best they could. Now a move was being made to offer them a kind of reinstatement, to settle them peacefully upon reclaimed land.

It was an extraordinary reception, for although an enormous crowd of tough, tribal peasants turned out in striking native dress (running strongly to dyes of beet-juice red), the Bhils' attitude toward Panditji, while respectful, was also openly disenchanted, disbelieving. Free land? A new life? Fine words he speaks, fine promises he makes, but what does *he* know of our lot, of sweating food from a field of rocks without water? Never in India will *good* land be given away to Bhils. When the Leader goes back to Delhi, the very bosses of his own party will take away everything from us, and Panditji will never be told; he will never know.

I watched Indira Gandhi in her accustomed role. As Nehru spoke, she moved smiling toward the Bhil women who scowled in the sun. Stepping daintily among them, Indira carried an armload of flower garlands that had been given to Nehru. Murmuring pleasantries, she gracefully put one or two garlands around the necks of some of the Bhil women, who instantly removed them and tossed them indifferently to the ground. I had never before seen an Indian crowd so resistant to the Great Presence. The women had a fixed attitude for Indira: leave us alone! Still smiling, Indira moved quickly back to her father's side, taking her unwanted garlands with her. At the conclusion of Nehru's short talk, goodies and candy were flung down to the mob to lend a final, festive, goodwill note to the visit. There was a wild scramble—of children. Most of their elders, including the stern, red-skirted women, stood back and disdained to touch the free sugarplums showered down from the Mighty.

◆   ◆   ◆

We drove back to Delhi as soon as the Canadian lady doctor would release Mary. Along the long road home, Mike finally got his expected crop of red spots, handily at another mission hospital where we had stopped because John had known the head surgeon—another Canadian, bless him—years ago in China.

And with many hundred miles yet to drive, what to do about the second crop of pox?

The doctor more than reassured me. "For Pete's sake, lady, chicken pox are nothing. Look at that kid *eat*." (We had stopped for lunch.) "You don't have to worry about *him*. You've got small children at home—why rush the spots back to them? I'm not so sure about the theory of deliberate exposure in hopes of a mild case."

"But what about quarantine precautions? We had Mary in isolation in Indore. I don't want to put Mike on your hands; you have enough to do here—"

The homely, lined face of the missionary doctor was all mild reassurance: "Not necessary a'tall, not a'tall! Long as the kid feels okay, continue your drive home at a reasonable pace. There's not much you can do for him but slather him with the ol' calamine."

"Yes, but—heavens—won't he give a little contribution of chicken pox to every town and village along the way?"

The doctor was very patient in explaining to me that Mike would have to come into close, direct contact with the people in every passing village to give them anything so tame as chicken pox. "Be sensible. Just keep in mobile isolation. Don't let him go around shaking hands or coughing in people's faces and you'll have nothing to worry about. When you stop in hotels or government rest houses, don't take Mike into the dining room. Pour boiling water over his dishes and cutlery before and after he eats. He'll be past the worst by the time you get him home."

"If we stop to see something famous along the way, is it safe to let him out of the car?"

"Why not?" The doctor sliced himself a mango, and his prosaic calm finally convinced me that Mike would be "all right."

So on we went. At every stop I kept Mike in a room to himself, held strangers and bearers at bay. The climax of our ticklish problem was the visit to the Amber Palace outside Jaipur.

The palace itself isn't all that marvelous, but its location on the crown of a hill is a great enhancement—and even more so is the ride up the hill, which traditionally is done on the back of an elephant! Adorned for the glory road, and tourists, the elephant is draped in red hangings and baubles, his back chair is festooned, his trunk, brow, and flapping ears are all hand-painted with flowers!

When we arrived and climbed upon this girthsome beastie, a screeching orchestra inflicted itself upon us. Five little men sprang from nowhere, running along at the heels of our elephant playing old razors or bicycle parts on tin cans—the effect being a hideous rending, like bent fork tines on plates. Helplessly trapped aboard the Dumbo express on a slant of hill going to a palace, you do what all tourists are expected to do: you pay them—to go away—far away, which they do at once!

Mike, hanging onto his rolling elephant seat, tipped to 45-degree angle, was surely feeling no pain—and I assumed the flower-eared elephant was immune to chicken pox. We joggled under an elephant archway as a royal peacock took a flying leap and landed on the wall beside us. I became almost light-headed with such weird unreality: to think of taking a "sick" child with a contagious disease up a mountain on an elephant to an Amber Palace—on doctor's orders—

But that doctor's name sure wasn't Spock!

The last laugh was a ha-ha not funny at all:

There is a postscript to the Itch to Travel, a postscript as ironic as a rusty nail. In the persnickety circle of Americans in India, particularly in Embassy households, there is a great deal of anxiety about the Things Americans can pick up from servants. Worrying wives at great trouble and expense have their cooks, aihas, bearers regularly checked, tested, X-rayed—gone over with a geiger counter from spit to stool. Yet here was I, mother of four, and until Tai Bhai had gone abroad and had to be so intimately checked, I had never sent my home corps to our doctor unless they were ill, which was extremely rare. But this worried my friends, who tried awfully hard to worry me, too.

They might as well have saved their breaths, for in our case it was the *children* who gave the *servants* Things!

We had been home from Indore only a day when Danji came down with chicken pox. John sent him immediately to our family doctor—moon-faced, shy Dr. Chowla, who lived near the hotel gate. Dr. Chowla prescribed the identical treatment the twins had received—calamine lotion—and gave the identical warning: do not scratch the rash on the face. But alas for poor Danji and his dark good looks. He was one of the handsomest drivers in town, especially since John had bequeathed his war correspondent's uniform to him and a clever tailor had made it over to an enviable, dashing fit.

Danji had scratched his face, and weeks later to our dismay and his, noticeable pock marks appeared. He was acutely self-conscious about it and very upset. I did not realize the extent of his perturbation until a short time later when he came to me and mentioned that an auspicious (good luck and holiness combined) religious holy day was coming on the weekend.

"Memsahib," he pleaded, "I will be taking leave on Friday. Pana and I will go to the river. We go to Hardwar by train and I take a dip in the holy waters and pray God to take away the marks from my face."

I was touched, filled with remorse. Poor Danji. I reached in my purse and handed him money for his train fare and Pana's too. I feared even a stoic river dip (in mid-winter) would do little, but I was happy to let him go.

Monday morning he was back, buoyant and cured. The pits were gone—from his soul if not from his skin. He was happy, smiling, restored. The River had done its work well.

Grand Finale—At the Countdown of Five, A Roaring Boy, and While He Slept, I Hear a Song of India

The morning when one's fifth baby is born can be casual in the extreme. And so it was when James, the Fifth, arrived.

John was up before seven, coffee in hand, studying the morning papers. I reached for the *Times* myself and said with a sudden gasp:

"I think—something is happening—In fact—Dear God!—there—is—no—doubt!"

John glanced at me quickly as he picked up the phone, balanced the receiver on his shoulder, and began writing a cable. Parliament was in session, Nehru was to speak on foreign policy, the Opposition was disenchanted with the old line, and there was bound to be some strong, yeasty debate. A bad morning for birthing babies, obviously. For a newspaperwoman, my timing was unfortunate.

"You sure?" John's attention was divided. "I can drop you off at the hospital on my way to Parliament, but I'll be tied up all morning. Can you hang on until the afternoon?"

Sharing the birth of a first baby, or even a second, with Parliament would have had me in tears, but the fifth time around I was wondering whether I had put any toothpaste in my already packed suitcase, along with the package of birth announcement cards and the Pearl Buck book I was saving to read in the hospital.

Within the hour, I knew I would not be able to Hang On Until This Afternoon. I told John to hurry with his shaving, and I went to say goodbye to Suzy and Johnny Pat, absorbed in their breakfast. I kissed jelly-sticky cheeks as Tai Bhai seized my hand. "Ah, memsahib, God bless you, memsahib. You are feeling all right? Another *boy,* memsahib, a nice big boy baby for Tai Bhai?"

"Oh, no," I laughed, "this time it's 'Panch Sheila,' remember? Nehru has five principles, and we have five babies. This one's going to be a girl called Sheila…"

A great chatter of Hindi rose from the servants, none of whom were in favor of my idea of "Panch Sheila." (In Hindi, the number five is *panch.* When Nehru first laid down his grand brotherly love schemes in five golden rules for peaceful coexistence with Red China, but not necessarily Pakistan, the air was rosy with the new catch-phrase, roughly Anglicized to "panch sheila." As absolutely no girl's name goes well with "lava-check" except maybe Lily, John and I had decided, half in fun, to call our "fifth principle" Sheila!)

On the way to the hospital we were both so relaxed and casual that John asked me if he could stop and drop off a press pass to the Lok Sabha (the Indian name for Parliament) for a visiting newswoman from the *Wisconsin State Journal.* "Fine," I said, "but we can't linger long."

The Madison newslady came to the car as we arrived at her hotel. "How about lunch today after the morning session?"

"Sorry," I replied. "I've got a morning session of my own coming up. We're on our way to the hospital right now—"

"Why—why—one would never know. My dear, you look so casual…so relaxed."

"By the fifth time around, you're very relaxed, but we must get going—right—right—*now*—" I gasped, as for a moment I was twisted and knotted in a severe contraction.

John sped the car along the mall to Sita Sen's. "You're okay? Except for those twinges, you just don't look ready for anything."

At the hospital a nurse took charge of me, and she too remarked that perhaps I was a bit ahead of myself. "One would never believe you were really in labor," she said, shaking her head. Dr. Sen made the same remark when she arrived later on. John had rushed off to Parliament, and I was on my own.

My room was on the second floor. There was as yet no elevator in Sita Sen's new nursing home, but as Tenzing might say, I had only to relax, not talk, and breathe deeply and *climb* the steep, curved master stairway. It was mid-July. A small air-conditioned room awaited me. I was left alone to walk around until Sita Sen came to examine me.

If there was any reason for everyone protesting that I "didn't look like" I was ready for imminent birth, I can put it down to one thing only: diet. I had waited all this time, down to the fifth child, to get wise. Weight control in pregnancy—a careful science of selecting food for food value only, with no extra calories—pays absolutely golden dividends. Not only do you look wonderful (and every time people tell you that, you look even better!), but you go along with a light, springy step, you're peppy and doing things, you rise up from a chair with grace instead of a grunt, you sleep comfortably at night without the weight of a portable typewriter amidships, you can take long trips with your husband as I did to Ceylon (no doctor would approve), and best of all, delivery is just one big swoosh—by no means a breeze, or even painless, but without complications, neatly quick and done for.

Dieting is not a pastime I cherish. Give me griddle cakes in amber syrup for breakfast. For lunch, a tumbler of chilled blanco vino and a platter of lasagna oozing melted cheese that pulls out from your fork like strings of spaghetti. And for dinner, lobster newburg afloat in sauce, with apple pie for dessert. There is absolutely nothing to match the good things of life that come on warmed plates to your table and await the poised fork—no, nothing—not even the dry thrill of stepping on the bathroom scale and watching the black needle slow down after the 120 mark.

But still, I had made a fixed and determined effort to diet at the outset of this last pregnancy. I simply did not want anyone to know I was having yet *another* until the last possible months. I wore girdles, chose dresses with jackets, and avoided standing in profile. I was never so active, doing my full stint as den mother for Cub Scouts, and at the same time serving as a full-time Brownie mother for a troop of some fifteen jumping jellybeaner little girls with missing teeth like Halloween jack-o'-lanterns.

One is not necessarily "hungry for two" during pregnancy. The most effective method of checking waddle weight is one I worked out this way: If a light breakfast leaves you with hunger twinges by 10:00, get in the car and go somewhere, or take on a job that keeps your mind safely off snacks, or fill the gap with a cup of plain, unadulterated coffee or tea. To keep late-afternoon emptiness in line, I would sometimes just put a pleasant taste in my mouth by scrubbing my teeth with minty toothpaste or rinsing my mouth with a pink, well-flavored mouthwash. At night an extra cup of coffee well after dinner helped "put something" into the light emptiness that followed a meaty but otherwise skimpy meal.

There is a point in dieting where you can eventually coast along and lose weight without that painful effort, that rumbly-tummy denial, that uphill struggle to whittle away even a single pound. Habit sets in. You know better than to touch the cashews, potato chips, or brownies, and there is an automatic murmur of "No, thank you" ready on your lips when they come your way.

My severest test came at the eight-month mark. Diet-light or not, eight months is eight months! And in India's summer heat! But John had riots to cover, and he was off not only to Bombay but to my favorite emerald isle, Ceylon, as well. He eyed me with puckered mouth. "I know you are a sturdy, travelminded girl, old dear, but this time—can you really make it? How do you *feel?*"

Foolish question!

The streets of Bombay were running blood—some of the worst riots ever seen in that city were in full fury over what was ostensibly a language issue. This was, of course, not merely an emotional quibble over mother tongues (neither of them the "national language," Hindi), but in the clash of Gujaratis and Maharashtrians many other things were at stake: political predominance, jobs, rights, and privileges. For issues like these, Gandhi's "non-violent," morally superior Indians cut down men, women, and children in a savage orgy that brought out truckloads of steel-helmeted, heavily armed police. Even they were not always able to control the mad outbreak of passions that seem to lurk so close to the surface in masses of Indians and which flare up bloodily when the slightest spark is set off. Effigies of Nehru, and even Gandhi, were hung up on trees and set ablaze. Mobs broke into shops and smashed every statue of Gandhi in sight, snarling like a wolf pack that he was, after all, only a running-dog Gujarati.

Evangelist Billy Graham had just arrived in Bombay to conquer India with his amazing "Declare for Christ" campaign. Bewildered by the torrent raging around him, and forced to cancel all Bombay rallies at that time, Evangelist Billy had vainly tried to walk the streets and reach the Common Man: "God is love. Jesus saves. My name is Billy Graham. Why are you doing this?" Police finally demanded that he remain in his hotel or leave town, which he wisely did.

We also left town, flying away quickly to Colombo where more trouble brewed. The Indian Tamils were at riot-pitch and blood letting over a similar language-nationality issue.

Leaving the ten thousand and more angry men to settle their own arguments and to clear the blood from the city streets, we moved on to a more exciting story, this time in Ceylon.

We had heard for some time about a little snip of island called Delft (just like that expensive and lovely blue and off-white china from the Netherlands). Delft lies just off the coast from Jaffna in northern Ceylon. It could continue to lie there forever, undisturbed and forgotten, were it not for Delft's one fascinating feature: herds of wild horses.

Descendants of a stud farm maintained by the British Army hundreds of years ago, today the creatures run wild and are a rare sight to see. As news coverage of the Tamil riots would take us, together with a correspondent from the *London Daily Express,* as far as Jaffna, why not make the most of an irresistible opportunity to go across to see the wild horses on Delft? We learned that a little motor launch plied the waters from island to island—but this was monsoon season. If we were very lucky, the launch would be going on the only day we could spare for shooting a film of wild horses.

(Did I not declare that if you diet during pregnancy you are as peppy as all get out? Well, here was I at eight months with no more caution or good sense than you could crowd on top of a safety pin, venturing many odd miles—exceedingly "odd"—in an open boat to "help" my husband film wild horses!)

We set forth in a little, putt-putt open launch that cut daringly through the churning sea. The sun above us was frying hot. We had no shade, but we had brought bathing suits and towels for a possible dip in Delft. The towels proved merciful tents for sunshade.

We eventually reached Delft and found the wild horses, shrunk down to pony size. How beautiful they were—honey beige, wild-maned, long-tailed. What strangely moving phantoms of yesterday's history pausing only for a second to eye us with curiosity, then racing madly away in skitterish distrust of humans. As John moved in closer and closer with his Bolex movie camera, the largest herd, in one galloping leap, cleared the scrubby plains and plunged into the sea. They swam, thrashing about with much snorting and wheezing, watching anxiously for us to retreat so they might spring back again on dry land.

Forebears of these beautiful ponies had been bred under the sparkling bonnie-blue eyes of a dashing, mad Irishman named Lieutenant Nolan, who (legend relates) studded more than horses in his time. When the British called in their Nolan and abandoned their breeding farm, the horses were simply left to nature and the natives.

We had little time to explore the oddly fascinating island, as our boatman was eager to make the return trip to the mainland before any monsoon squalls appeared. Belatedly aware of My Condition, I too was eager to make haste to home shores before any Situations developed.

Safely back in Jaffna after a sickening, rocky ride home through the swelling seas, the Daily Express man remarked with more relief than admiration, "Your 'Sheila' will be a sturdy girl, quite! Must tell her someday about the wild horses on the godforsaken island of Delft, where she veddy likely might have been born."

Panch Sheila, who turned out to be Panch Jimmy, was born at noon during a sudden monsoon cloudburst that thundered down upon the skylights of the hospital delivery room. As in previous deliveries, I was given practically nothing: a whiff of something to inhale that smelled like the inside of a mildewed closet and had as much effect. But in seconds I could hear lusty boy-yells. Though I had no little brown sparrows on the overhead fan "for luck" this time, I relaxed on a cloud of bliss that it was all, all over...over completely for me, totally and absolutely, all this marvelous and mystifying and arduous business of having babies. Five was enough. I knew there would be no more.

John had not yet arrived at my bedside. I wondered vaguely, as from a great distance, if Nehru and the opposition were still at it in Parliament.

I fell asleep. When I awakened, there was John gripping my hand in wild excitement. What was he saying? Something…strange…nothing about a fine baby boy…something…about a *ship!* Then I came to with shock-suddenness. John shouted at me, "The *Andrea Doria*'s at the bottom of the Atlantic!"

Newswoman to the core, I shot right up in bed.

"What? *What?* We almost sailed on her. What happened?"

"La—la—la—ah-LAH—LAH—LAH" came from a smaller boat at anchor by my bed. Down amid Grandma Lyons' presents of rosebud-strewn diapers and baby shirts and pink ribbons, James was declaring his presence. No comic valentine like Johnny Pat, here was a bundle of howling good looks with a dimple in his chin and a tuft of blond hair. We forgot the *Andrea Doria.*

In the late afternoon John returned with all the children and a radiant Tai Bhai, who brought me a huge bouquet of auspicious red gladiolas she had either beguiled or bought from the hotel gardener. I thanked her warmly and remarked in a dry aside to Daddy that he had not honored manchild or Mama with so much as a daisy!

The next day an Indian sister brought to my bedside an enormous bundle, like a sheaf of wheat. All white-petaled flowers—

"What's this?" I rose up wondering.

Sister handed me a card on which were written two words:

"Daddy's Daisies."

◆   ◆   ◆

Mothers never know such peaceful luxury as those fleeting days when they lie back amid the hospital pillows writing out Announcement Cards or blue Airletters of Breathless Details to nearest and dearest…having visitors troop in with prettily bowed gift boxes…having afternoon tea served on a lovely tray in a quiet, quiet room, as you dawdle over the book you have "saved" to read during this precious interval. At night, babies were taken *out* so Mother could sleep as she would not, in all likelihood, be able to do at home for weeks to come.

I loved my silent, cool room, the orderly exactitude of my days when someone else did all my thinking and arranging and attending-to for me.

One rainy afternoon when there were no visitors, a pretty Anglo-Indian nurse came in, smiling, a complete study in hospital white: white starched cap, white starched uniform, white shoes, and in her hands a white enameled tray. I had missed my German sister, Gretchen, but this new senior nurse (whom I'll call

Nan) popped in smiling every day so that I felt I knew her better than all the others.

Most days, Nan hurried in and out with the strained manner of one who has too much to do and only one pair of hands. The sound of a buzzer ringing down the corridor exasperated her. She had a typical Anglo-Indian contempt for Indian city or village girls who were in training as sisters but who considered much of the hard work of nursing beneath them, as bordering on an aiha's job. "Those lazy, good-for-nothing Punjabis!" she burst out one day. "All they want to do is arrange the flowers, rock the babies, and pass out pills. They haven't the faintest desire to learn or to do their real job—they simply can't or won't be trained. There are only a few of us old hands around, and this is a big hospital. We can't be everywhere. It's only Christian girls who can be trained to be *real* nurses, but there aren't enough of us."

I always felt guilty for taking a single minute of her time and would wave her off with a hasty, "Fine, fine—I'm fine" whenever I could see that she was unduly harried.

Her visit to my room this rainy day was all the more unusual for I had not called her. She came in quietly, as if to pause and catch her breath. Gently she bent over Jimmy's crib, stroking his downy cheek. He was fast asleep and made no sound. Nan sighed.

"How lucky you are. Five of them…I don't suppose I shall ever marry and have even one little fellow like him. In this job, I just keep on and on, and the years slip by."

She confided she had loved someone "quite terribly" once, but to marry at that time would have meant giving up her job. After all the years she had put into training in India, Scotland, and England, she could not just "chuck it" to become a housewife. With more education perhaps she might even have qualified and become a doctor, for she truly "loved med'sin." It was not an easy life; you had to be born to it and love it, and give up a great deal for it. She gazed with soft wistfulness at my pink-swaddled Jimmy in his crib.

A boy came in just then with a tea tray, and I insisted Nan relax for a moment or two and have some with me. She shook her head, glanced at her watch and sighed, "I must dash off in a moment."

I asked her casually how it was that Jimmy had no identification marker on him—no name bracelet or tag of any sort. "How do you keep the babies from getting mixed up?"

"Oh, that's no problem," Nan smiled, "we have no need for markers here. So few babies are born in this hospital we do not need identifications. Once in a while there is a great rush, but just now there are only two other mothers and babies on your floor."

Somehow this news saddened me. I felt completely isolated from all the other births in India. Thousands of other mothers were elsewhere, in crowded quarters, in modest nursing homes or their own villages with their families and relatives and jillions of children all about—yet here was I alone and walled off with two other unknown mothers and two other babies in a kind of foreigners' air-conditioned palace.

I murmured something of this to Nan.

"Oh, no, my dear," she hastened to reassure me, "you're not so alone as all *that*. Upstairs in the ward we have lots of Indian patients and many mothers with their newborn babies. In fact, there is one mother—quite remarkable—She has quite a little story." Nan stood gazing out the window, in no rush to go about her legion of tasks. Her face had lost its firm authority, its "diagnosis" look.

"I did not know these people knew love as we know it," she began. "Love and marriage and—sex and intimacy—these things to Indians have an entirely different meaning than they do to us. I never thought any emotion entered into it at all, since absolutely everything for these people is dictated by religion or relatives. But I was wrong, and I did not know until this Indian girl in the charity ward came to us."

"She is very beautiful…most unusually so…for one so humble, so poor, and so painfully shy among strangers. She is—almost—like a brown velvet flower, if you understand what I mean."

"I assisted at her delivery, and that is how I got onto the case. It was very complicated, which is why Doctor sent for me to assist. There had been previous abdominal surgery and much scar tissue, but this timid little thing went through her ordeal with the courage of a lioness, so determined was she to give birth to her child. It must have been quite ghastly for her, but she fought it through like one obsessed and only collapsed when she knew her son had arrived, whole and strong and yelling. The face of that woman was unforgettable.

"We see this every day, you know, but this girl was quite different from the rest. We all remarked about her, and Doctor told us who she was. Actually the wife of our little *chokidar*, the man at the gate in the khaki uniform who stands on guard, fetches taxis, directs the cars to the parking area. He is such a modest fellow—somehow one has to look twice to see that he is even there.

"But when he came into the ward to see his wife and son—really—Why, I was quite moved to tears watching them and had to leave at once, although the mother is very weak and under constant check.

"Day after day, morning, afternoon, and night, the husband came to sit by his wife's bed and touch her hand to reassure her he was near. They did not speak much. It was enough they were together in the silent battle that she must pull through so that she might live.

"I became quite attached to these two, and as my duties kept me close by the girl I began making inquiries about them. Their story, sketchy and pieced together, explained in part their absolute devotion.

"It seems the little watchman was a poor fellow who supported an old mother and lived off somewhere in a tiny, miserable hovel. He was posted at the hospital gate on the main road out there in plain view of all passing traffic. You have seen the Rajasthani nomads called *Jats* who wander up and down the road between New Delhi and the old Fort?

"Well, it seems one night some of these rough Jat fellows approached the watchman at his post, drew him into conversation, learned he was not married but had a permanent job at the hospital. They made him a bold proposition: The most beautiful bride in the world could be his for a mere 300 rupees, say, cash in advance—a Jat bride, clever and smart and strong and all *his* for a pittance! It was true she could fetch no dowry—that is why her male kin had to secure her future so cheaply—but ummmm—*acha*—she was a beauty, fair as a Kashmiri, and a thousand times more delectable.

"The watchman sent them away in anger. Did they take him for a village fool? He was a decent man, a respected man who wore a smart uniform, who held a trusted position. Jats were gypsies, low-caste idlers, wanderers without homes, thieves and robbers full of cunning and tricks!

"The men taunted him with coarse jokes but went away, promising to return. Each day they passed by and called out to him, but the watchman sternly rebuked them, shaking his fist.

"Another night two fellows came back to talk again, to try harder to entice his imagination. A nice young woman to keep him warm, to look after him, to cook his food, to make him happy as one in Paradise…Again the *chokidar* refused and bid them be off before he called the police.

"The Jats were not easily discouraged or frightened, even of police. 'Very well, Stubborn Fellow, we will bring the bride to you. Then you shall see for yourself that we make no idle boasts! But now the price is *five hundred rupees!* Look at her just once—if you do not take her, then you are mad, and we will kill you on the spot!' They laughed, clapped the little watchman roughly on the back, and went off into the dark night.

"For a long time they did not return. In spite of himself, the watchman was filled with alarms and apprehensions. Every day he was on the alert, but the Jats did not come.

"Then one evening, just before dusk, a cart stopped by the hospital gate. It was an awkward time for the watchman, for late afternoon was the peak of the visiting hours and he was hopping busy with traffic, and taxis and cars almost bumper-to-bumper in the driveway. From the corner of his eye, however, the watchman saw the cart drawn up and waiting...quietly waiting for him. His heart began to pound, his forehead became wet with perspiration for he could see that there were several women in the cart.

"The watchman bolstered his courage by promising himself he would get rid of the lot of them once and for all this time! If they made trouble, he would whistle for the taxi *wallas* to come to his rescue. He could count on them—big, fierce Sikhs—for he put foreign lady patients into their taxis every day, and foreign ladies always tipped a good driver.

"At the first free moment, the guard rushed angrily up to the Jats' cart, roaring at them to push off at once and not to come back.

"One of the Jats seized his arm in a grip of iron.

"'Damn you, *shut up!* Stupid fellow! So much trouble you have caused us. What money we have paid out for the cart to fetch your Jewel of Heaven, which you do not deserve. Here she is, and by all the gods, you will see her!'

"The guard was lifted off his feet as another man grabbed his arm and held him as if in a vise as an older woman shoved a bent and cowering, delicate figure before his eyes. Bent over and shrouded in a saffron-yellow Jaipur scarf, the girl whimpered something pitifully but would not look up. With a vulgar oath the old woman ripped the veil from the girl's head, and the guard saw before him a face bathed in tears, but beautiful as a dream. That she was no willing partner in the bargain but was as trapped and driven as the guard moved his heart to her rescue at first sight. 'Do not be afraid,' he found himself trying to comfort her, 'I will not harm you. These ruffians are trying—to steal my life's savings—to make me marry you.'

"At the kindness in his voice, the girl raised stricken eyes to his face, and at that moment he loved her! He, a timid jackrabbit, suddenly strong as a Bengal tiger, knew somehow he had to save her and protect her if indeed it took every anna he possessed to free her from her cruel associates.

"After long argument and haggling over the price, the guard finally agreed to pay the staggering sum of 500 rupees cash for a hasty wedding before the next full moon. All wedding costs and a small meal were to be provided by the Jats, and the groom could bring some friends and they would be treated with all honors. Agreed…agreed…

"The groom-to-be turned back to the girl, who had stopped weeping and was listening apprehensively to every word.

"He could not bring himself to ask for *her* consent as well. He could barely find his voice to speak to her at all, but he managed to choke out shyly, 'It is arranged, then. You are my betrothed…until…our day…think of me and keep well.'

"At his words the girl covered her face with her hands and wept again. The Jats, murmuring among themselves, finally fixed on the exact date and place and hurried away in their rented, rattling cart.

"A wedding of sorts transpired. In spite of himself and his uneasy distrust of the rough Jat company, the groom was transported to new heights. A middleman friend was entrusted with the groom's precious hoard of money. He was not to pay it over until the groom and his bride, duly arrayed in auspicious bridal red and a tinsel-trimmed head scarf, were safely removed to the guard's modest living quarters for their bridal night. Every precaution was to be taken that the costly bargain should be foolproof.

"Finally the time came when the guard and his bride, who had not spoken a single word all evening, were alone together for the first time as man and wife. Trembling in spite of himself that this treasure was now all his, the groom spoke to his bride. He touched her hand. He had yet to see one smile upon that beautiful face, but he promised to woo her as though she were a dove.

"But for all the radiance of that starry wedding night, the groom was soon to discover a cruel tragedy which shattered all his dreams.

"His beautiful bride was at last revealed to him a dying woman, suffering a terrible advanced tumor that had been carefully hidden by her full garments.

"Falling at her husband's feet, the bride sobbed out her story. Her kinsmen had tried to find a cure for this thing that was slowly draining her life away, but there was none. Native remedies were attempted in vain, and city doctors were beyond consideration. In anguish quite beyond tears, the girl related, 'My brothers thought me young and beautiful and worth good money to them if they could find some poor fool and trick him before it was too late…What could I do? Where could I go? I—I—felt—soon I will be asleep and free—when it is all over—but you were so kind to me that day we met, and you did not know what you were saying when you bid me to keep well. I would have spared you this cruel trick, had I dared, had I known how. I beg your mercy. I am truly sorry. Forgive me, O good, kind Master, help me.'

"The husband who was never to know a single embrace—who had never loved a woman before in all his life—was overcome, torn between pity and anguish and livid fury that he had been tricked and fooled after all—and all his money gone! How could he ever find those villains, those desert rats, those sons of turtles! He could call the police, but what good was that? To keep quiet and save his face—yes, yes, that for the present he must do. No one at the hospital must know...nor his snooping relatives...nor his nagging old mother. If he could somehow hide this poor, sick creature, until he could think...

"A gentle hand touched his arm. His bride had managed to fix him a pot of tea. 'Let me—serve you, Master,' she begged in a whisper. 'At least I can do that.'

"And so the wedding night passed.

"In the days that followed, the Guard struggled to find some way out of his nightmare. One morning he held open the door for the Lady Doctor, Sita Sen, when she arrived at the hospital for her long, busy day. She smiled at him most kindly and thanked him as she always did even for the smallest courtesy.

"A sudden inspiration occurred to the little *chokidar:* that he might confess his experience without loss of dignity or respect to a *lady* doctor. Women understand many things which a man might scorn.

"He would watch for the right moment and ask to speak to her.

"Finally he did. The doctor asked that his bride be brought in at once for examination. It took some persuading to get the girl to consent, but she was assured she could slip in quietly when no one would see her, and that the lady doctor was not a white foreigner but an Indian and very, very kind and gentle.

"Examination confirmed the gravity of the girl's illness and that only surgery could save her. But so advanced was her condition that there was considerable risk involved, and the girl was very weak. Finally the operation was decided upon and quickly took place. Once it was made convincingly clear to the little bride that she had a fair chance to live a normal life if she would cooperate with the doctor—and her husband—she put up strong willpower to pull through. Although we gave her the best possible care, I observed that it was her husband at her side, day after day, gazing at her with love and encouragement, so proud of her slightest improvement, that helped most. Her recovery was their mutual triumph. The happiest day of her life was the morning she was able to leave the ward, moving slowly, step by step, holding her husband's arm."

Nan paused. A buzzer rang down the hall. "My dear—I did not mean to go on like this. But let me finish. We heard no more of the girl for quite a long time. Then one day she appeared again in great fear and alarm and pride—she was pregnant. But after her operation, with so much scarring, what did this mean?

Would she be all right? Doctor said she had a good chance if she took proper care of herself and came in regularly. The husband was a changed man—what strut and swagger! What a tough guy! How he barked orders to drivers and cabbies, how knowingly he held doors for expectant mothers. It was so amazing and touching. Finally his little wife was brought in to have her baby. For Hindus, of course, the birth of a child is always a tremendous event, but for these two it was a miracle.

"Now she has her son, has fulfilled a Hindu wife's obligation, and I suppose she feels at last she has repaid her husband for saving her life. Love and faith have done much. Funny how life rounds things out. We often think we are so sophisticated, have all the answers from science for all things…But these two Indians are my good luck—or good *faith*—charm, my proof of that flickering good candle in this naughty world."

◆   ◆   ◆

However much advance science makes in the field—or is it the clover meadow—of sex, pregnancy, and birth, my crown awaits him who can discover the way to a night's sleep once a perfectly healthy baby is brought home from a hospital!

I am one with Shakespeare's tortured kings. Crowned heads and new mothers never know the restored life of a night's repose. Oh, to sleep—to become a log from a petrified forest upon the pillows—from the 10:00 feeding until the 6 a.m. screams.

I know experienced, calm, sensible, book-read mothers who simply dig in and Endure those first weeks at home when everything goes by in a blur. A nightmare. With eyelids of peachfuzz, eyes red and sleep-fagged, heads hung in steam clouds over the sterilizer, they keep going on catnaps, cigarettes, and strong coffee. This can go on for *weeks*.

Experienced Daddies who *know* go on business trips far out of town and ease their conscience by sending a plane ticket to Grandma and begging her to come right away.

Now we have two non-sleepers. If there's a hired woman sleeping in temporarily as well, that makes *three* on the up and up night after night. Even if a weary mama worn to a bone is told to "just stay in bed" when the li'l nipper yells, sound waves penetrate. She is immediately wide awake and up, padding down the hall in her bare feet to see what's "wrong."

Nothing, absolutely nothing, is "wrong," of course. Maybe a burp went down instead of up…a rattle fell out of the crib onto the floor…a neighbor slammed a car door outside…I have even known hiccups to set in at 26 minutes past two.

Some babies, I hear from other mothers, sleep like set clocks ("baby" Bens?) from 6 p.m. to 6 a.m.! Such maddening exaggeration puts me all on edge. Babies I have known *well*, five to be exact, have much more pep than that, especially *between* the hours of 6 and 6!

There was a time when I even resented bitterly the Christmas carol "Silent Night." Surely Baby Jesus bellowed at least once or twice in His stable. He wasn't always *silent*.

By the time we got to the fifth baby, I thought I had really had more than my share of sleepless nights. Hollow-eyed and desperate, I phoned my new Indian pediatrician. She prescribed a safe sleeping sedative for both Jimmy *and* me, so that I would not even hear him cry if his dose wore off. The sedative did not work on Jimmy or me. Weeks later, I had Jimmy carefully checked over by two other doctors, our faithful family doctor and a nerve specialist. The consensus: we just had a howler on our hands. Not a damn thing was "wrong," and he would out-grow it in time. He did—when he was nearly a year old! John and I eventually worked out a system whereby Tai Bhai did night duty and slept in the daytime.

I was just emerging from the close-quarter baby world when I suddenly became involved in a shocking international scandal. It was the biggest news story in many a year—a love affair that had nothing whatever to do with love—Roberto Rossellini's!

An American housewife in New Delhi who moved in very arty, cultural circles, and who dressed in Indian handspun at all times, had heard Something in her own living room that rocked her to her flat Indian sandals! She and her husband had offered their cool, tiled living room as a gallery for a Sunday morning art show. The paintings on display were the work of one of India's most brilliant modern artists who had come up to Delhi from Bombay. As he and his American hosts were busily arranging the canvasses, the artist mentioned that he had another great admirer in Bombay: an Italian movie director, Roberto Rossellini, who came frequently to his studio. So enthused was the Italian husband of Ingrid Bergman that he had even offered to help organize a one-man show of the Bombay artist's work in Rome.

As housewives will, even highly cultural ones, this one skipped the art and pressed for more details about Rossellini and all the rumors that were going around. The simple artist told all he knew, which turned out to be a considerable amount, for he had also been asked to do a portrait in oils of Roberto's new "love," Sonali Das Gupta. He knew the lady well.

The excited housewife could scarcely wait to hear the last word before she ran next door, jumping the boxwood hedge, to find her Great and Good Neighbor, *Time* correspondent Jim Greenfield, who was even more Greatly Interested in what the artist reported.

The next morning, John happened to drop into the Time-Life office, and the correspondent, like the housewife, confided all in John with the understanding that two could work the story better than one, especially if one of them went quietly and quickly to Bombay. On second thought, it was decided, if either John or Jim suddenly appeared at the Taj Mahal Hotel in Bombay the story would be a dead giveaway to the competition. While investigation and double-checking was going on, they needed a third party to serve as an anonymous "cover."

It was finally decided that I would pass for just another housewife if I suddenly went to Bombay and checked into the Taj, taking a room across the hall from Roberto and Sonali. I knew Bombay well, had a number of friends in the social whirlwind who had eagerly and lavishly entertained a smooth, fascinating celebrity like Ingrid Bergman's husband. I should have no trouble quickly finding out the whole story, true or wildly exaggerated.

The story we heard then, but could scarcely believe, was that Rossellini had come to India on a shoestring. He had a flimsy comme-ci, comme-ça—maybe yes, maybe no—"arrangement" with the government to shoot a documentary film on India. Modern India. Nothing is as famous about Rossellini's technique as the fact that he works without a script, improvising scenes and dialogue as he goes along. Yet he had hardly arrived from Europe—leaving behind Ingrid and the three children—before he was looking for a "script girl." Right away! Even in India, where supposedly Hindu ladies keep close to home. Roberto found one readily enough in willowy, golden-skinned, well educated and intelligent Sonali Das Gupta, a Bengali beauty, married and the mother of two small boys, one of whom was just a tiny infant. Sonali's husband was an ambitious, fairly successful young Indian movie director. Das Gupta had effusively welcomed Rossellini, introduced him to his wife, invited him to his home, and even put one of his station wagons at Rossellini's disposal.

The meeting of Roberto and Sonali had been incendiary from the start. They wasted no time in getting down to the script. Torrid romance followed. Sonali apparently went full plunge, sandals over head, all caution gone, heedless of every restraining consideration. Her home, her children, family honor, her "good name," her religion—all became meaningless. She simply left her husband and moved into the Taj Mahal Hotel on the fifth floor, next door to Rossellini. There she remained in costly, air-conditioned luxury—room service daily for all three meals—for more than a month. Down the hall in another wing, in a small box of a hot room with only a fan for coolness, she had installed her newest-born infant son with an attending aiha. Her elder child she abandoned and never saw again. Relatives whisked him far away from the city, where there would be no reminders of "Mummy."

The plot quickly thickened in this little drama in which only the children were innocent, and word was out that—just like Ingrid's Stromboli—India and Italy were already joined in an as-yet-unborn child.

All that we heard then as ear-burning gossip has since come to pass as confirmed truth. A few years later in an Italian courtroom, Ingrid herself named Sonali's baby, a daughter born in Europe, as Rossellini's.

How weirdly estranged from the normal world of my own family I felt flying off to Bombay for a day or two to investigate the whole murky business. The story, of course, was not really Roberto and Sonali, but Ingrid's in faraway Paris where she was starring in a hit play, *Tea and Sympathy*. When a woman sacrifices All for Love—and pays the price that Ingrid paid, and will go on paying through her children, every woman in the world sits in fascinated judgment—some with tea and sympathy, perhaps, and pity, others shocked and satisfied that the grim laws of retribution have collected their full toll.

I had seen Ingrid Bergman only once. In my Washington newspaper days I had been at a Press Club dinner when she received the acting award of the year from the hands of President Truman. I had passed briefly through a receiving line and had shaken her strong, outdoorsy hand.

Dr. Piloo met me in Bombay with a warm embrace at the airport. But as we were driving into the city in her car, I told her quietly what I had come for, and her distaste was embarrassing. "Oh, Pegge, no, no! Of course, everyone in Bombay 'knows,' but oh dear, I hope you won't put out anything on that dreadful man and that foolish girl! Perfectly shocking—a disgrace to her family and her country! Think of the children—but then these women never do. Oh, I can't bear to talk about it. Tell me, how is Jimmy? Sleeping at last? Teething? How much does he weigh?"

Piloo drove me straight to the Taj, bid me goodbye and almost ran away. "I don't even want to know what you're up to! When it's all over, call me—"

I had no trouble engaging a room on the fifth floor, where I could watch Everything. Investigating Rossellini's wing, I discovered he had hired three or four guards who paced up and down the corridor, glowering at everyone who passed by. He had feared irate relatives might attempt violence.

The next morning I called on the Italian Consul, a light-hearted fellow with the title of Count and a diplomatic functionary position that did not overtax him. The Italian count was all oily, cologne-scented charm, kissing my unaccustomed hand as I entered and departed. Rossellini, yes, he knew him rather well. "Ah, yes. Maybe it would be possible for Madame to meet him for a little chat. Be so kind as to leave your card, Madame, and your telephone number."

Never did I expect the hotel telephone to ring that very evening and to hear that Rossellini—in dolce accents smooth as poured cream—would be "delighted" to see me.

Delighted? I knew only too well how he fought, loathed, and hated the Press. *Particularly*—salt, pepper, and Parmesan!—did he despise the *American* press!

I came directly to the point: "Mr. Rossellini, if I may just call on you for a very short interview—"

Purred Rossellini: "That will not be necessary, Mrs. Hlavacek. Where are you staying? I will come to you. Oh…" (long pause) "you are right here in the Taj—just down the corridor? Well, that is very—umm—convenient. When may I call on you, Madame?"

When he knocked softly on the door some ten minutes later I opened it to admit a quite amazing man. Of looks, he had none: he was bald, fattish, and fifty and looked every bit of it. He was casually dressed in sport clothes and sandals, but he was fastidiously groomed and, like his friend the count, faintly cologned.

He sank into an armchair, lit an American brand of cigarette, and studied me thoughtfully, without a word.

After some ten minutes of exploratory conversation about his Indian documentary, I thought I could "see" what it was he had that was so irresistibly charming to women of all ages: a gentle, kindly, convincing air of modesty, human warmth, innate sympathy, interest, and solicitous concern…all for *you!* Women could tell him they had a toothache or indigestion and he would make it all seem delicate and glamorous and quite within his great powers to soothe away. Perhaps with soft music, a view of Capri, and a good, chilled Chablis…

I worked my way discreetly around to Ingrid and matters on the domestic front, and how were all the three kiddies?

He responded with utmost candor. Although theirs was a "happy" marriage where the children were concerned, professionally two careers created a great strain. "So it is," he sighed, but the soft eyes looked suddenly sharp and cold, "that we have agreed not to work together any more."

I asked if he had seen *Anastasia,* then playing to packed houses in Bombay. In fact, all over the city were enormous billboard portraits of a soulful Ingrid with streaming blonde hair in her starring role. There was even a large plywood cutout figure of Ingrid in her Anastasia costume by the porter's desk in the hotel lobby, where Roberto checked his key and picked up his mail and messages every day.

Roberto exhaled a nostril trail of cigarette smoke. Some of that gentle softness wafted away as he spoke. "Yes, I have seen Anastasia. It was terrible! Awful! Her worst picture! Absolutely the worst acting she has ever done." (Italian shrug, palms to ceiling) "Forgive me—you asked me, and I must be honest. I am sorry, but it is so."

"Well, then," I inquired, "have you seen your wife's current play, *Tea and Sympathy?*"

A mood of anger settled in. More heavy drags on his cigarette. Then, "*Tea and Sympathy?* Why, yes. Ingrid's great triumph? That was largely *my* doing! I had been asked to consider the script. If I liked it, I might direct and get Ingrid to star. I agreed to look it over and a script was sent around the house, but in English. English is not my best language. I speak it—you see for yourself, not well—but I read it even worse! I sent for an Italian translation, but one was not immediately available. Time passed. I was busy. I forgot about the script lying around the house. But Ingrid picked it up. She read it and was quite mad about it! Right away—oh, she must do it! It was perfect for her—just her dish—a misunderstood woman who helps a misunderstood student! I know my wife. Even before I had read the thing, I knew Ingrid had made up her mind. I also knew it was not my play—I did not even like it—but I told Ingrid to go ahead. Of course, she had not waited for me to say 'yes.' She was already studying with a tutor to perfect her French accent for the part. She is a perfectionist in the smallest detail. When she works, she works—like one who moves mountains!"

The play, which eventually opened in Paris, marked the turning point in Ingrid's career. After years of failure in cooperative ventures with her husband, here she was making a sensational comeback, acclaimed not only on the continent but in America (with *Anastasia*). As her play settled down for a long run, Ingrid moved her children back to Paris. Roberto had said goodbye to them there in early December and had flown to India, in a perhaps desperate attempt to match Ingrid's triumph with one of his own, to recapture his own lost laurels and prestige.

Mention of the children in Paris prompted me to make some remark about his missing Christmas with them. Italian shrug, no comment.

"Tell me about your twins," I persisted. "I am very interested, being the mother of twins myself."

So we talked *twins!* This mutual fascination with the extreme differences in fraternal twins brought the only genuine spark out of him where children were concerned. The Rossellini-Bergman girls, although the same sex, were really fraternal, he insisted, not identical, in their personalities and development. One was a complete tomboy, daring, adventurous, mischievous, full of boundless energy. The other was the extreme opposite: a shy, sensitive introvert.

What gifts had he sent the children from India?

Nothing.

What had he sent Ingrid?

He laughed dryly, "Oh, a picture of me riding on an elephant!"

"What, no saris? Ingrid would look enchanting in a silk and gold sari. Some of the best shops in India are right downstairs in the lobby."

Roberto flashed me a wicked look. "I am a very busy man, a working man. I have no time for shopping. But then, our wedding anniversary is this Friday. Maybe…I should send something. Anyway, I will be telephoning Ingrid in Paris. You must put that in your article. Most people forget we are just an old married couple."

"Which anniversary will it be on Friday?" I asked. "How many years has it been now?"

"Why—why, this will be our seventh," he replied in a rather flat voice.

(As John observed when I told him: "Aha! The seventh year is always the most fatal. It's the itchiest. The Broadway play with Marilyn Monroe proved that. Watch your step, my girl!")

"I do hope," I went on as casually as a hungry dog who smells his bone is not far off, "there is nothing to the stories going around. It would come as a disillusioning blow to the women of the world if—if anything happened to your marriage after all you and Ingrid have been through."

Laughing smoke screen. "Ha, ha! Tell the women of the world they have nothing to worry about! Our marriage is quite safe, I assure you. I will not disillusion them—or my wife. But will you—please, Madame—remember that I did not kidnap Ingrid. She came all the way from America after me, begging to star in one of my films. She is—a wonderful person. I know how she has suffered, better than anyone else. But I also know she is a very strong woman, *in many ways stronger than I…*"

Silence fell. Then abruptly he turned on the light bonhomie again.

"Tell me—what else is it the women of the world want to know?"

I dared to joke: "Frankly, what it is you've 'got.' What do so many women 'see' in you?"

He roared with laughter. "I don't know what they 'see' myself. Look at me—a simple fellow—not good-looking—much too fat, but I am on a diet! No, I think perhaps there might be something exciting about my work. India is for me a very alive, brilliant, exciting country. I have long been a great admirer of Mahatma Gandhi."

Keep Gandhi out of this, I thought.

"Now, tell me—if you can," I played my last ace, "what is all this about Sonali? Let's be perfectly honest—if possible."

Rossellini flushed with sudden embarrassment. "There is absolutely no truth whatever to stories you may have heard. She is working for me. I pay her a salary. She earns every penny, I assure you, and she has been a very great help to me."

He rose to depart. "Madame—charming—a great pleasure. I have stayed much too long. Tomorrow I must be up early. If the weather clears" (it was monsoon season) "we shoot before seven." He bowed slightly, all smiles which did not reach his long, narrow, dark-brown eyes.

I smiled and said lightly, "Don't forget—at least *one* sari for Ingrid for her seventh wedding anniversary!"

"Okay, okay," he joked in return, "maybe I should send *seven*—one for each year, eh?"

He laughed again and was gone. It had been a superb performance. Although his denials about Sonali were of course untrue—he had urgent and pressing reasons for trying to gloss over everything until he could get her quietly out of India—I am certain there was much truth in what he said about Ingrid. When our stories hit *Time* magazine and the *New York Daily News* they were vehemently denied by her, but we knew, and she did, too, how appallingly true and sad and disgraceful it all was.

This scandalous episode and the excitement that it created in India and the world press at the time is a perfect example of what the Public wants to read…and talk about…down to the last tasty, worked-over crumb. Not only were news stories humming on the wires, but Sunday supplements appeared, Ingrid's whole controversial past was revived in pages of pictures, slick magazines jumped in too with the "story no one knows" about Ingrid (and was there really anyone who didn't "know" everything by this time?). Books appeared in which Ingrid revealed "hidden" reasons why a woman's Greatest Gamble had been lost. Apparently so long as she sobbed and "suffered" and "paid" to the last moan of audible anguish, Women of the World were prepared to relent, to go back to seeing her movies, to pay to read more articles about her, to even favorably consider this "new one," this fellow named Lars. Poor Ingrid, I felt, did indeed deserve a home for her children at long, long last

For the first time to Photoplay,

Rossellini discusses his marriage to Ingrid. This

is the story the newspapers didn't get

EXCLUSIVE:

ROSSELLINI TALKS

Rossellini maintains his and Ingrid's troubles didn't start in India, although they reached headline proportions as a result of his relationship with young Indian beauty, Sonali Das Gupta, while producing a documentary there. Ingrid, he says, never shared his enthusiasm for the movie project

The balding, fifty-one-year-old movie director looked as though he needed a bath. He had showered and shaved less than half an hour before but—drenched in the heat that hangs like a shroud over Bombay at dusk—he was already rumpled again, and his clean white shirt stuck wetly to his chest.

"My wife. . . ?"

Roberto Rossellini lit a cigarette and began talk about his wife, Ingrid Bergman, due Sonali Das Gupta, and the scandal that was erupting in bazaars, fetid back streets, chic d parties and air-conditioned government offices all over India.

The Bombay newspapers had called him a "villain" and a "seducer" and demanded that he be booted out of India on his plump posterior. Prime Minister Nehru had labeled him a "rascal" and allegedly suggested that Sonali's husband have him beaten up by hoodlums. He seemed oblivious to all of this. He had been persuaded to give this one exclusive interview by Count V. Lavison, Italian Consul-General in Bombay and—after the first wary moments—he hunched forward in his chair and spoke unguardedly.

"My wife. . . ? Ingrid is a very independent woman. A strong woman. In many ways much stronger than I. I will be quite honest. (Continued on page 99)

by PEGGE PARKER

I was so happy to leave all this Bombay melodrama and to hurry home to *my* children. Jimmy had cut a tooth. Everyone was fine but under a strain of confinement. Rumors of Asian flu of unprecedented proportions were sweeping over the country, closing schools, restaurants, theaters, and in the gasping summer heat, even the swimming pool outside our hotel suite.

Things with the office—United Press—had come to a total impasse for us in India. Of necessity, there would have to be a change. But after so many years—nearly twelve for John—enough was enough! John felt it was all for the best.

Suddenly one day a cable was delivered to our room as I sat spooning Pablum into Jimmy in his highchair. John was still working in Bombay.

The cable was a message of congratulations for John, who had just been granted a one-year study fellowship by the Council on Foreign Relations! This meant that John was free to study subjects of his choice at Yale, Princeton, or Columbia University. The fellowship began with the fall semester, and this was now July.

Jimmy got no more Pablum that morning. I telephoned John immediately and read the cable to him. He was delirious. "Oh, no—no? My God! Columbia for a year—think of it! Read it all again, slowly. Lemme write it down. Oh, Sweetheart, *we'll all be going home!* The kids will go wild—a year in the States! I'll be home on the night plane."

We had a bottle of champagne to celebrate when John arrived that evening. All the children had "tiny tastes"—and all loved it, especially Jimmy, who yelled for the biggest "tiny taste" of all!

Oh, to announce to a ring of upturned faces that we were going home on a big, big boat to America—to *live*—was like setting off firecrackers! They went screaming around the room throwing pillows, magazines, newspapers, the telephone book, anything handy, up in the air! Wheeeee! Then there was a debate over which was better: top bunks on boats or sitting next to the window on airplanes.

"And will we live in *a whole house* in 'Merica, Mommy?"

"An' kin we see *Gunsmoke*...an' Disneyland...*an' snow*...An' kin we take Lulu?" (our beautiful blue-eyed and pregnant Siamese kittycat!)

Over our champagne glasses John and I were in complete and automatic agreement that Tai Bhai of course "must" go, too. She could no more be left behind than the baby. She was not young, she had no husband, no family to look after her. She already had a passport and all those precious papers. There was a bit more champagne left in the bottle. I passed a glass to Tai Bhai and poured it out for her.

"We are going home to America, Tai Bhai—and we hope you will come with us, as always," I said gently. "You are part of our family, too."

She burst into tears, but she never spilled a drop of her champagne.

It was a great moment.

John took a look at himself in the mirror. "Man—get a load of the new college kid!" He ran a hand over his bald head. "Crew cut to the skull bone, but hell, all of us intellectuals have 'high foreheads.' Wonder what it'll be like on a college campus with a lot of kids in their twenties. How many years has it been—don't tell me! I don't know how I can be so lucky. Guess I'd better get a letter off to Columbia, or to the Council people telling them I want to be enrolled immediately at the Russian Institute."

As I turned out the last lamp light that night, my hand paused in midair. My quiet queen, my beloved stone lady, had surely been watching the delirious Hlavaceks, for she wore a new smiling look.

I put my hand gently on her regal head with its coiled Grecian headdress. "Goodbye, India…goodbye…How much you have given us: the best years of our lives here, from my wedding day to the birth of three children. We shall never forget you. And now, Sweet Queen, goodnight."

Mike and Mary hold the Langhammer portraits described by Pegge in
Diapers on a Dateline.

TRAVEL THE WORLD
WITH TITLES FROM HLUCKY BOOKS

Slow Boat to China
THE PERSONAL DIARIES AND LETTERS OF PEGGE PARKER, 1962-1981

PEGGE PARKER
EDITED BY JOHN HLAVACEK

Slow Boat to Pakistan
THE PERSONAL DIARIES AND LETTERS OF PEGGE PARKER, 1951-1952

PEGGE PARKER
EDITED BY JOHN HLAVACEK

alias Pegge Parker

PEGGE PARKER HLAVACEK

DIAPERS ON A DATELINE
THE ADVENTURES OF A UNITED PRESS FAMILY IN INDIA DURING THE 1950s

PEGGE PARKER HLAVACEK

letters home
AN AMERICAN IN CHINA: 1939-1944

John Hlavacek

UNITED PRESS INVADES INDIA
MEMOIRS OF A FOREIGN CORRESPONDENT 1944-1952

JOHN HLAVACEK

'Teen Topics
By Pegge Parker

The Greatest Generation
Reflected in Vintage Advice Columns

FREELANCING IN PARADISE
The Story of Two American Reporters Who Supported Their Family by Covering Turbulent Times in the Caribbean, 1958-1963

JOHN AND PEGGE HLAVACEK

Hlucky Books

www.HluckyBooks.com
www.HluckyBooks.com

www.ingramcontent.com/pod-product-compliance
Lightning Source LLC
Chambersburg PA
CBHW031248090426
42742CB00007B/366